W 5066940 0

AF745924

WESTHILL COLLEGE LIBRARY

Weoley Park Road
Birmingham B29 6LL
Tel: 021-472 7245

A fine will be charged if this book is returned after the last date stamped below.

24 APR 1990
30 JUN 2000
26 FEB 2004
-6 JAN 2005
21 MAR 2005

BOOK NO. 76841
Author GRANT Charles.
Title An Economics primer.
Class 330 GRA

An Economics Primer

CHARLES GRANT

An Economics Primer

Basil Blackwell

© Charles Grant, 1985

First published 1985

Basil Blackwell Ltd
108 Cowley Road, Oxford OX4 1JF, UK

Basil Blackwell Inc.
432 Park Avenue South, Suite 1505,
New York, NY 10016, USA

All rights reserved. Except for the quotation of short passages for the purposes of criticism and review, no part of this publication may be reproduced, stored in a retrieval system, or transmitted, in any form or by any means, electronic, mechanical, photocopying, recording or otherwise, without the prior permission of the publisher.

Except in the United States of America, this book is sold subject to the condition that it shall not, by way of trade or otherwise, be lent, re-sold, hired out, or otherwise circulated without the publisher's prior consent in any form of binding or cover other than that in which it is published and without a similar condition including this condition being imposed on the subsequent purchaser.

British Library Cataloguing in Publication Data
Grant, Charles
An economics primer.
1. Economics
I. Title
330 HB171

ISBN 0-631-14091-3
ISBN 0-631-14092-1 Pbk

Library of Congress Cataloging in Publication Data
Grant, Charles (Charles R.)
An economics primer.
Includes index.
1. Economics. I. Title
HB171.5.G778 1985 330 85-7364
ISBN 0-631-14091-3
ISBN 0-631-14092-1 (pbk.)

Typeset by Photo·Graphics, Honiton, Devon
Printed in Great Britain by Billing and Sons Ltd, Worcester

WESTHILL COLLEGE LIBRARY
76841
27.5.86.
D06076 £22.50
330 GRA

Contents

Preface

In teaching Economics at a foundational level – which has included a wide range of courses at different types of institutions in several countries – a frequent question that I have been asked is to recommend a book that summarizes the main principles and models of analysis. Apparently, there is a wide gap between the short 'guides' to Economics and the voluminous textbooks which are currently available. The former are usually focused on the definition and brief explanation of economic terms, which is useful but does not constitute an adequate conceptual development of the principles of analysis. This of course is precisely the purpose of the latter, but here the complaint has been that their extensive treatments may actually tend to be counterproductive. This is especially true for the majority of students taking Economics as part of another degree/diploma or professional course, who lack the time for more intensive study; but, on more than one occasion, I have felt that even more advanced students of Economics have had difficulty 'seeing the forest for the trees'.

This comparatively slim volume is my response to this problem, with the emphasis on succinctness and clarity in the development of topics. This does not always mean that it is *easy* to read. By its very nature the book's exposition tends to be logically tight and condensed, requiring careful reading. In several areas – for example, the introduction to macroeconomics *via* a simple model of neo-classical general equilibrium with both a consumption-goods section and a capital-goods sector – the material does in fact go beyond the standard introductory textbook limits. Wherever this occurs it reflects my belief that the gaining of perspective – the realization that there is a *corpus* of theory, although it may justifiably be the target of criticism – is of paramount importance. Moreover, in order to apply the theory sensibly to real-world events – a key criterion for many professional courses at least – a slightly more advanced approach is necessary. To take up the preceding example, it helps to understand the apparent problem of Britain's 'de-industrialization', and the concomitant growth of the service sector, if students have some familiarity with the notion of relative sectoral capital-intensivities. Similarly, Keynes' theory of unemployment equilibrium – which is often presented as *the* basic model of macroeconomics – can be much better appreciated as a critique of these neo-classical adjustment processes.

At the same time, as its title indicates, this book is not intended as a *substitute* for existing textbooks, nor for the series of lectures and tutorials which are central to most courses of study. In fact, I suggest to my own students that they skim the relevant chapter, then read one of the many available textbooks (I have no strong preferences) on the same subject, then attend the lecture. *Afterwards* they usually find that a more careful reading is highly beneficial, and especially so in revising for examinations!

Finally, the student or teacher considering this as a learning aid might ask about the absence of problems or case studies. All I can say, apart from the desire to keep down the length of the book, is that in my own teaching I select such material as suits the course. For numerate undergraduate students I might formulate a problem mathematically; for professional students (e.g. MBA's) this could be equally *in*appropriate, and instead I might take up a current case in marketing and examine it from the economist's point of view; for senior managers on short in-house training programmes I might well draw material from the week's business/financial press, etc. These applications are undoubtedly the most rewarding part of the teaching function, but also the least universal. What they do all depend on is a clear understanding of the nature of the problem under discussion and the economist's method(s) of approach. This book is intended to transmit the basic principles of economic analysis as efficiently as possible, and thus to provide not only a convenient reference, but also an overall perspective for all students of the subject.

CHARLES R. GRANT
Arundel, Sussex

Introduction

This book presents Economics as the study of production and consumption activities within a market context: specifically, how the interaction of individual choices determines the quantities of goods and services produced, the way in which they are produced; and as a closely-related question, how they are distributed. These same questions are equally relevant for all societies, but in other forms of economic organization individuals' freedom of action is more strictly proscribed. This is especially true of so-called 'command' economies – which would include our own wartime experiences of government-controlled production and household rationing – but would also apply to so-called 'traditional' economies in which these activities conform to custom. Where we draw the line is a matter of judgement, since it is obvious that even in our own economy individual choices are in fact molded by social norms; and indeed, many 'radical' economists would argue that what we call free market activity is very much a manifestation of the social – e.g. 'class' – structure.

Be that as it may, the orthodox approach adopted here takes both the technology available to producers ('firms') and the tastes, or preferences of consumers ('households') as given elements in their respective decision processes, along with whatever resources they might possess at the point where our analysis begins. They are then free to do as they wish, and our purpose is to discover what that will be. In this sense, Economics has rightly been described as 'the science of rational choice'.

Chapter 1 begins with the theory of the household, describing choices concerning demand for goods and services, saving and labour supply, in an abstract manner characteristic of pure economic analysis. The point is not to say how any particular household will behave with respect to these items, but to identify some key elements that serve to determine its behaviour. 'Applied' economic analysis concentrates on estimating the magnitudes of these influences, and is therefore concerned with prediction.

The next three chapters deal with the theory of the firm. Chapter 2 examines its revenue structure, which depends on the nature of the demand for its product(s). This in turn depends crucially on the degree of competition that the firm faces, ranging from pure monopoly to 'perfect' competition. However, oligopoly – 'competition among the few' – is a situation in which the firm's demand conditions are almost necessarily unknown, and in order to discuss this market form simple game theory is introduced. Chapter 3 examines the firm's cost structure, distinguishing between short- and long-run contexts. In order to do this it is necessary first to examine production conditions, and here it is assumed that inputs (of 'labour' and 'capital') are at least partially substitutable. Chapter 4 then combines cost and revenue structures in deriving the conditions for profit maximization, including some interesting extensions. The possibility of competition is then reconsidered to show that profit would tend to be eliminated in the long run. In the special case of 'perfect' competition this leads to the very important analysis of the mechanics of 'supply and demand'. The pursuit of alternatives to profit maximization is briefly discussed; and in conclusion, the ability of collusive firms to prevent competition – e.g. as with 'limit pricing' – is also considered.

An essential feature of the market economy that emerges from this analysis is that individual producers and consumers typically face constraints on their activities which are neither governmentally nor socially imposed. Instead, they face impersonal 'market conditions', generally in the form of price-quantity relationships; and in the case of 'perfect' competition, in the form of given prices alone. These prices are themselves the outcome of the interactions between buyers and sellers – households and firms acting in both product and input markets – and thus, a competitive market economy can be seen as an enormously complex feedback mechanism. The analysis of markets is clearly important for all of the individual agents; in fact, every action by every firm and household presupposes something about expected market conditions, even if it is only implicit in the same way that we rely on the force of gravity to continue each time we take a step. Moreover, it is apparent that market conditions may be rather more volatile than the laws of nature, so in this sense the study of the principles of economic analysis can be particularly useful.

However, the point of studying Economics is not only to construct a (highly stylized) description of the market mechanism, but also to ask whether it is efficient, in the sense of not being able to get more out of our initial resource endowments. Chapter 5 thus shifts the focus of attention from so-called 'positive' to 'normative' economic analysis, by first defining the concept of Pareto-efficiency and then examining conditions under which market economies will or will not achieve it. Means by which governments may intervene to attempt to correct misallocations of resources are then considered. Conversely, the effects of government intervention in order to redistribute goods and services – typically at some cost in terms of lost efficiency – are investigated.

Part II continues to be concerned with the question of market efficiency, not so much in the sense that resources might be allocated inefficiently by the processes of supply and demand (making the assumption of perfect competition), but in the sense that the market feedback mechanism itself might be unstable. In such cases some resources – such as human labour – might not be allocated to any uses at all! Chapter 6 therefore begins by presenting the so-called 'Classical' case for the stability of the market mechanism. A very simple economy in which there are five markets – labour, consumption-goods, capital-goods, bonds and money – all characterized by supply and demand conditions – is constructed in order to illustrate the nature of general or 'circular-flow' equilibrium. An assumed change in aggregate household saving behaviour is examined to show how the set of equilibrium prices should alter so as to maintain general market equilibrium at the new levels of activity. In Chapter 7 the basic model is extended to include both a foreign sector with flows of goods and bonds ('trade' and 'capital' flows), and a government sector which engages in 'fiscal policy' (i.e. taxing and spending). This extended model is used to demonstrate the effects of these sectors on the set of equilibrium prices, hence levels of activity.

The remaining three chapters centre on the debate surrounding this view. Chapter 8 begins by outlining a version of the Keynesian critique of Classical economics, in which it is not the failure of the wage rate to adjust, but instead the failure of the interest-rate mechanism that causes unemployment. However, by re-introducing the assumption of fixed wages it is much easier to construct a Keynesian model of income determination and to explain the associated concept of the 'multiplier'. Chapter 9 puts the controversy initially in the format of the IS-LM diagram, but then takes up the Classical ('Monetarist') contention that this focuses on the substitutability of money and bonds and ignores the substitutability of money and goods: i.e. the 'real balance' effect on spending. This is followed by a discussion of the 'New' Classical concepts of permanent income, velocity and 'rational' expectations. In Chapter 10 these alternative theories are applied to the experiences of the Depression of the 1930's and the 'stagflation' of the 1970's. The neo-Keynesian Phillips curve approach is developed and contrasted with the expectations approach. Also, the elements of the system of monetary control are briefly and critically examined. The chapter concludes with a discussion of the problem of the 1980's – so-called 'structural' unemployment – and its corollary Classical ('supply-side') *vs* Keynesian ('planning') alternative solutions.

It will be apparent that we are dealing with quantitative – i.e. measurable – phenomena, particularly prices and quantities. This has great advantages when it comes to applications, and in maintaining a rigorous logical consistency in the exposition of its theoretical models, but has inevitably led to increasingly mathematical approaches far beyond the level of most introductory students. At the same time there is no escaping the essentially mathematical – logical – nature of the subject even at this initial level. The compromise has been to adopt a predominantly diagrammatic approach, with little further mathematics. However, it is therefore essential for any serious student to familiarize him/herself with the meaning of economic diagrams – to 'read' a curve – prior to attempting to use them for analytical purposes.

Finally, let me say that once you have acquired the skill to study Economics it ought to become a subject of progressively greater understanding, precisely because it is a matter of logic. Many of the well-known controversies, particularly in macroeconomics, are based on the failure to resolve issues empirically, thus allowing competing theories to survive intact. This also serves to explain why it is that economists have seemingly attempted to apply their models to every facet of human activity: quite simply, everything we do can be depicted as the outcome of rational choice! If you reach the stage of proficiency in Economics where you begin to appreciate that it is literally whatever economists do, then you will be well on the way to becoming an economist yourself.

Part I Microeconomics

1 Theory of Household Behaviour

Outline

Synopsis

The purpose of this chapter is to examine the determinants of household behaviour concerning the demand for final goods and services and the supply of labour and capital inputs. As mentioned, in all instances the 'household' is a single entity regardless of the actual number of persons involved in these decisions.

I begin with the decision regarding the allocation of a given level of expenditure between two or more products, which depends on their prices. I define aggregate demand and cross-demand curves, and with respect to the latter, the notions of complementarity and substitutability. The diagrammatic interpretation of the *ceteris paribus* assumption and its violation as shifts in the respective curves is discussed, and the effects of changes in the level of consumption expenditure itself is examined. I also introduce the unit-free concept of *elasticity*.

The discussion is then broadened to consider the allocation of a given income between consumption expenditure and saving, introducing the distinction between income and substitution effects, which may have opposite effects. The same is true of the work–leisure decision, discussed briefly at the end.

Introduction

Conceptually, the sequence of household decisions might be something like this: given the household's initial *endowments* of human capital (labour efficiency or simply 'inherent ability') and physical capital (through *inheritance*, typically in the indirect form of financial claims on physical assets), it decides how much labour to supply. This decision is taken over its whole lifetime horizon, and includes the kind of work as well as sub-decisions about further investment in human capital in order to augment its endowment (e.g. an MBA). With this lifetime occupational and earnings profile in mind, the household then decides on its lifetime consumption – and simultaneously, saving – profile. For example, many households own little or no initial physical capital, so have to rely on their labour earnings. Typically, these households *borrow* early on – e.g. to buy a house – becoming net savers (i.e. suppliers of capital) in later working years, and eventually using up their net accumulated savings ('dissaving') in retirement. Finally, the specific goods and services it buys are decided with regard to this 'budget' and with regard to the *prices* of these goods and services.

In reality, all these decisions are taken together, not sequentially; nor are they made once-and-for-all. The whole set of decisions may change continuously over time, largely because of unplanned occurrences.

Nonetheless, we will assume that there is no uncertainty about the outcome of decisions; and proceed to examine these decisions in reverse order, as though the other aspects of the household's behaviour could be completely separated and determined beforehand.

In practical terms this means that we begin with the household's decision about which consumer goods it buys, under the assumption that it has already decided how much to spend on consumption in total.

1.1 Product demand decisions

1.1.1 Household reactions to price changes

Consider a representative household: how does it allocate its given consumption budget to different goods and services? One obvious answer is that the pattern of its expenditure reflects its tastes or preferences. This is undoubtedly the most important factor, but it is not the only one. I prefer champagne to beer, so why do I consume so much of the latter and little of the former? Simply, I am being guided in my choice by their prices. To be specific, if the price of champagne were to fall, as it did so I might well increase my champagne consumption – and probably decrease my beer consumption. The same effects – more champagne and less beer – are also likely to ensue from a rise in the price of beer. On the other hand, a fall in the price of beer and/or a rise in the price of champagne would be likely to result in my increased consumption of beer and decreased consumption of champagne.

In summary, it is likely that consumption of champagne will vary directly with the relative price of beer-to-champagne: e.g. a rise in this latter price ratio leads to a rise in champagne consumption, and vice-versa for beer consumption.

However, beer and champagne are *substitutes* from my point of view. In fact, the preceding statement is another way of expressing this notion. Suppose we took instead the opposite example of bread and butter. These are likely to be *complements* in the sense that as the price of bread rises relative to the price of butter the consumption of both commodities moves in the same direction. If bread is more expensive with butter the same price, I may consume less of both (not less bread and more butter as in the case of substitutes); whereas if butter has become cheaper with bread prices unchanged I may consume more of both (not less butter and more bread as in the case of substitutes).

Aggregation: demand and cross-demand curves

Of course, different households have different preferences which manifest themselves not only as different consumption patterns at prevailing prices, but also as differing responsiveness to changes in prices. One household's increase in champagne consumption might be quite rapid for even small decreases in its price, whilst another's consumption could be virtually unaffected. It is even possible that households differ in their views of goods as substitutes or complements. For example, the American habit of combining peanut butter and jelly appals most Britons, who see the two as entirely alternative sandwich spreads. Therefore, when we come to the *aggregate* demand – for product '*x*' – we are adding up a wide variety of consumption decisions.

Nonetheless, we assume that the aggregate *demand curve* (Fig. 1.1a) showing the quantity (*Q*) – of product '*x*' – related to its own price (*P*) has some validity. Specifically, household's *tastes* are assumed to be unchanged as *P* varies (my strength of preference for champagne over beer is unaffected by their prices); and in addition, all other prices are also assumed to be unchanged. In other words, we are looking at the *sole* effect of the price of '*x*' itself on the aggregate (i.e. total) demand for '*x*'. The assumption that all other prices are being held fixed is known as the *ceteris paribus* ('all other things equal') assumption. From a diagrammatic point of view it is a necessary assumption in order to draw a single curve in a two-dimensional plane.

This demand curve is assumed to be continuously downward-sloping (the possibility of upward-sloping segments is discussed in Appendix 1B). However, there will be *cross*-demand curves for '*x*' with respect to every other identifiable product ('*y*', '*z*', etc.). Two of these are shown: one (Fig. 1.1b: 'the cross-demand curve of "*x*" with respect to "*y*"') is *up*ward-sloping while the other (Fig. 1.1c: 'the cross-demand curve of "*x*" with respect to "*z*"') is itself *down*ward-sloping. This shows '*x*' to be an (aggregate) *substitute* for '*y*' and to be an (aggregate) *complement to* '*z*'. Symbolically, we define:

Substitutes:
(e.g. *y* and *x*) $$\frac{\Delta Q_x}{\Delta P_y} > 0$$

and

Figure 1.1a Own-demand curves for '*x*'

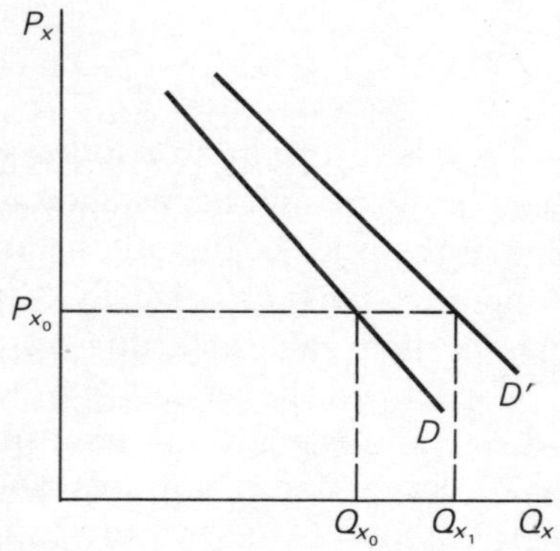

Figure 1.1b Cross-demand curve for '*x*' with respect to '*y*'

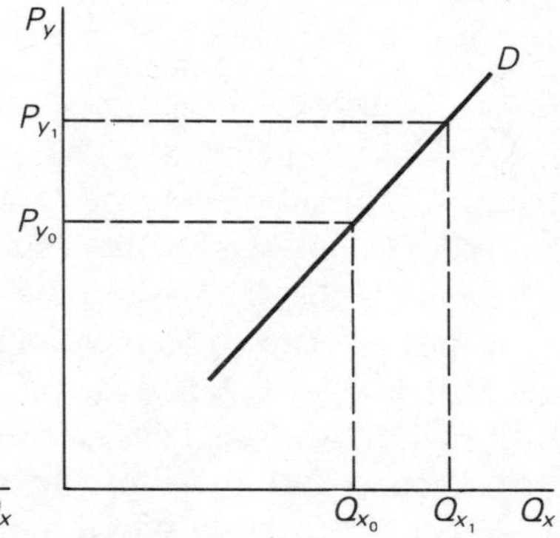

Figure 1.1c Cross-demand curves for '*x*' with respect to '*z*'

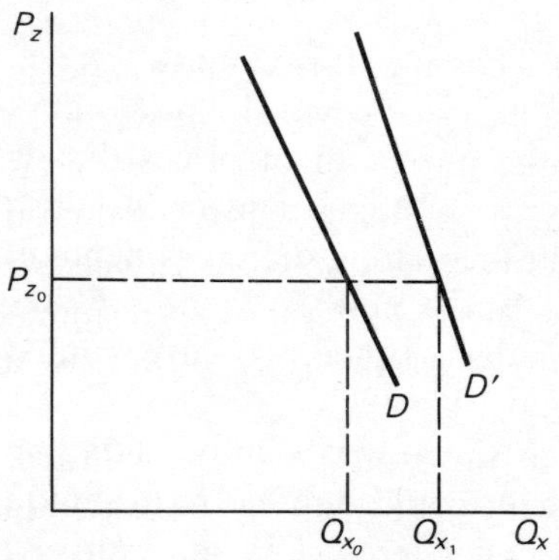

Figure 1.1d Expenditure curves for '*x*'

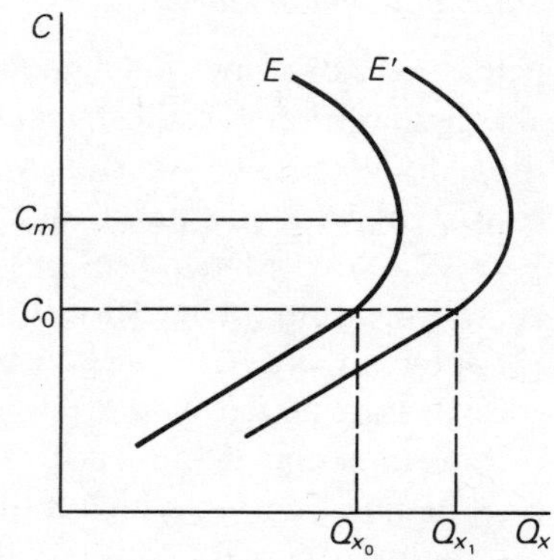

The initial quantity of '*x*' is Q_{x_0}, which is consistent with the initial prices P_0 of all three goods, as well as the *given* level of consumption expenditure (C_0). A rise in the price of '*y*' (to P_{y_1} in Fig. 1.1b) moves us *along* this cross-demand curve to a new '*x*'-consumption level of Q_{x_1}. Note that '*x*' is shown as a substitute for '*y*'. With prices of '*x*' and '*z*', as well as total consumption expenditure unchanged, the new quantity, Q_{x_1}, must occur along the new, shifted curves shown in Figs. 1.1a, c, d. That is, the *ceteris paribus* assumption – in this case the constancy of P_y – upon which these original curves were drawn is violated. Note also that '*x*' is a complement to '*z*', and that above expenditure level C_m, '*x*' becomes an inferior good.

Complements:
(e.g. z and x) $$\frac{\Delta Q_x}{\Delta P_z} < 0$$

The symbol 'Δ' means 'the change in' whatever variable follows. Therefore, for substitutes the change in the quantity consumed of one has the same sign as the change in the price of the other. For complements the changes are of opposite signs. Graphically, the ΔQ values are shown as increments in their values starting from initial levels (Q_0 to Q_1 and P_0 to P_1 respectively; hence $\Delta Q = Q_1 - Q_0$, $\Delta P = P_1 - P_0$). Thus, a positive ratio (definition of substitutes) means that the cross-demand curve slopes upwards and vice-versa as originally stated. (If $\Delta Q_x/\Delta P_z = 0$ the two products are independent: the cross-demand curve is a vertical line.)

Shifts in demand curves

If the price of some other good does change, this violates the *cet. par.* assumption. To illustrate what happens when the price of 'y' rises, for example, we start with the initial set of prices that is consistent with the initial quantity of 'x' being consumed (Figs. 1.1a–d). Now P_y increases and we move along the cross-demand curve, showing an increase in Q_x. But if neither P_z nor P_x has changed, in order to be consistent these other two curves must shift to the right.

Alternatively, if the price of 'x' rose we would move along its own-demand curve, which adjustment could only be represented by (leftward) shifts in the other two curves. (As an exercise, consider how the cross-demand curves for 'y' and 'z' with respect to 'x' would shift as P_x rose.)

Hence, what we have shown is that with given preferences the composition of consumer demand is determined by prices. The quantity demanded of any one product depends on every product's price, and if only one product price changes it causes changes in consumption of every product: less of itself and complementary products, and more of substitute products. The magnitudes of all these changes depend on the magnitude of the price change itself and on the slopes of the respective schedules. These effects are shown diagrammatically as movements *along* those curves relating quantities to the particular price which has changed, and simultaneously and equivalently as shifts in all the other curves.

1.1.2 Changes in expenditure

Now we broaden our scope slightly to consider the effects of a change in the total (household) consumption budget. In fact, the way this comes about could be either a switch out of savings into consumption with unchanged income, or a change in income affecting both saving and consumption. In practical terms suppose I have 'more money to spend': how does this affect my demand for (hence purchases of, hence consumption of) champagne and beer? Certainly, if my preference is strong I will buy more champagne. This could be considered the normal reaction for most goods, but it may not hold for all of them. For example, it is certainly conceivable that even though my total spending has increased, and although I am generally consuming more of most items, I very well might have reduced my consumption of beer. In a sense, you could say that now I can 'afford' better things, so tend to stop purchasing items I bought when I was worse-off. These discarded items are called *inferior*.

Aggregation

When we attempt to examine how the total ('aggregate') consumption of 'x' by all households varies with change in total consumption expenditure on *all* goods, we run into conceptual problems. This is because there is an infinite number of ways that any change in total expenditure could be distributed amongst households, each of whom has possibly a different propensity to spend on product 'x'. For example if aggregate consumer expenditure in a year rose by £100M, there would be quite substantial differential effects on consumption of champagne and beer if: (1) it meant an extra £10,000 per annum for the richest 10,000 households; or (2) it meant an extra £10 p.a. for the 10M lowest-income households.

Nonetheless, we assume that the aggregate expenditure curve for any particular good 'x' has some validity. Diagrammatically (Fig. 1.1d) an upward-sloping curve, i.e. for which:

$$\frac{\Delta Q_x}{\Delta C} > 0$$

shows 'x' to be a *normal* good (the change in quantity demanded is in the same direction as the change in total consumption expenditure, C). Conversely, if

$$\frac{\Delta Q_x}{\Delta C} < 0$$

the curve has a downward slope and in this case ‘x’ is said to be an *inferior* good.

It is important to realize that a normal good can become an inferior good beyond a certain level of expenditure. This also applies to substitutes and complements: at a certain price of ‘x’, ‘y’ may become a complement, having been a substitute at lower prices of ‘x’, or vice-versa. Indeed, in order for a good to *be* inferior it *must have been* normal at low expenditure levels (verify the sense of this).

1.2 Elasticity measures

It is usual to measure responsiveness, not in terms of *slopes*, but in terms of *elasticities*, defined as the ratio of *percentage* changes. For example, the *elasticity* of the demand curve for ‘x’ (‘the own-price elasticity of demand’) (η_{xx}) is:

$$\eta_{xx} = \frac{\Delta Q_x / Q_x}{\Delta P_x / P_x}$$

The *cross*-elasticity of demand (for ‘x’ with respect to ‘y’) is therefore:

$$\eta_{xy} = \frac{\Delta Q_x / Q_x}{\Delta P_y / P_y}$$

And for ‘x’ with respect to ‘z’:

$$\eta_{xz} = \frac{\Delta Q_x / Q_x}{\Delta P_z / P_z}$$

Why do we introduce this change? Because elasticities are *unit-free*. If I tell you that the demand curve for beer in Japan has a reciprocal *slope* of (minus) 2M litres *per* 1000 yen (¥1000) and the American demand has reciprocal slope of (minus) 8.8M US gallons *per* \$1 would you grasp immediately which had the more price-sensitive demand? Not likely. But if I tell you instead that currently beer demand in Japan declines by 5% for a 20% rise in price (elasticity = (−)¼) and that in the US it declines by 10% for a 5% rise in price (elasticity = (−)2), the comparison is rather easier. Mathematically, the price and quantity units are eradicated because, for example:

$$\frac{\Delta Q_x/Q_x}{\Delta P_x/P_x} = \frac{\Delta Q_x}{\Delta P_x} \cdot \frac{P_x}{Q_x}$$

That is, elasticity equals one-over-slope (the 'reciprocal slope') times price-over-quantity.

The steepness of the slopes of the *expenditure* curves can also be misleading, so we typically refer to the 'expenditure elasticity of "x"' (e_x) as:

$$e_x = \frac{\Delta Q_x/Q}{\Delta C/C}$$

$$= \frac{\Delta Q_x}{\Delta C} \cdot \frac{C}{Q_x}$$

i.e. as the ratio of the percentage change in the quantity of 'x' demanded to the percentage change in total consumption expenditure. If this measure is greater than one (elastic) 'x' is sometimes called a 'luxury' good; if less than one (inelastic) 'x' is a 'necessity'.

The change in total consumer spending and its accompanying change in the quantity of 'x' demanded is shown as a movement along the expenditure curve for 'x'. As you should expect, this change causes shifts in the demand curve of 'x' as well as all the cross-demand curves relating the quantity of 'x' demanded to all other prices. These curves will all shift to the right – more 'x' at any given levels of prices – for a rise in expenditure if 'x' is normal, and vice-versa.

As you can see, the elasticity measure has the same sign as the slope of the respective curve: i.e. it is negative for the own-demand curve and for complementary cross-demand curves, but positive for substitute cross-demand curves. If we ignore sign – i.e., look at the absolute value of the general elasticity measure $|\eta|$ – we can categorize elasticities as follows:

$$\begin{aligned} |\eta| &= 0 &&= \text{'perfectly \textit{in}elastic'} \\ 1 > |\eta| &> 0 &&= \text{'inelastic'} \\ &= 1 &&= \text{'unit-elastic'} \\ \infty > |\eta| &> 1 &&= \text{'elastic'} \\ |\eta| &= \infty &&= \text{'perfectly elastic'} \end{aligned}$$

You should be able to verify the sense of these for demand and cross-demand curves.

In many instances we assume that the aggregate demand curve for a product ('x') is linear: i.e. it is a (downward-sloping) straight line with constant (negative) slope. From the definition of own-price elasticity of demand, we can see that elasticity will vary. This is because, with slope = $\Delta P_x/\Delta Q_x$

$$\eta_{xx} = \frac{1}{\text{slope}} \times \frac{P_x}{Q_x}$$

as we established above. So, when P_x is high enough to wipe out demand ($Q_x = 0$) elasticity is infinite. But when $P_x = 0$ ('x' is a 'free good') elasticity is zero. As a matter of fact, it runs from infinity to zero along its whole length, and is unit-elastic at its midpoint as shown.

On the other hand, a demand curve with *constant elasticity* has a variable slope. Diagrammatically it is represented as a rectangular hyperbola. This is because when P_x is large and Q_x is small, for elasticity to be a given constant $\Delta P_x/\Delta Q_x$ – the curve's slope – must be large (the reciprocal slope, $\Delta Q_x/\Delta P_x$, is therefore small). Likewise, when P_x is small and Q_x large, the same elasticity is maintained if the slope is small (reciprocal slope large).

For upward-sloping curves (e.g. a cross-demand curve for complements) slope and elasticity are more closely related. A linear curve (straight line) which intersects the vertical axis has elasticity greater than one (but diminishing), whereas if the line intersects the horizontal axis it has elasticity less than one (but increasing). A straight line emanating from the origin (a 'ray' from the origin) has constant unit-elasticity.

1.3 Savings decisions

The next step is to consider how a given total income is divided between consumption expenditure and saving. Saving may take many forms, but for present purposes we think of it as the acquisition of interest-bearing financial assets (bonds, or equivalently, shares) which are issued by borrowers (business firms) to finance 'real' physical capital formation. In other words the supply of financial capital (savings) by households is converted into physically productive plant and equipment. Later on, we will consider borrowing by government to finance current expenditure.

The rate of return on savings is thus the rate of interest paid by borrowers, and it is this that chiefly influences the saving–consumption decisions of households. Consider the initial situation where I have a given money income, and faced with a particular rate of interest I decide to save so much. The rest I spend on current consumption, in accordance with the pattern of product prices, as previously described. Now let the rate of interest rise: how does this affect my saving behaviour?

Intuitively, you might expect this to increase my saving and hence decrease my current consumption. The reason you probably have implicitly in mind is that the opportunity cost of current consumption is now higher. Whereas before, £1's worth of current expenditure maybe meant forgoing £1.02's worth of expenditure next year (or, at 2%, £1.78's worth in 30 years when I retire) it now means forgoing, say, £1.04's worth next year (or, at 4%, £3.12's worth on retirement). Since I now will get more to spend later for every £1 saved now, there is a decided tendency to save more. We call this the *substitution effect* of the price change (i.e. the change in the rate of interest).

However, there is another effect at work. The rise in the rate of interest applies not just to an extra £1 of savings, but to all I save. So, if I am intending to save £100 this year (with luck) this will now give me a lump sum to spend in 30 years of £312 as opposed to the £178 I would have had at a 2% rate of interest. An extra £1 of saving now merely increases my future payment to £315.12, as opposed to £179.78 as before.

The crucial point to note is this: with a much larger future payment to come anyway, the subjective value of another £3.12 to me may not be worth sacrificing £1's worth of current consumption. If my future lump-sum had remained at £178 so the 4% only applied to additional saving, the extra at that point would have been worth it. Now it may not be. In fact it is possible that I would rather trade the opposite way: an additional £3.12 subtracted from an initial £312's worth of future payment may be worth less than an additional £1's worth of current consumption.

If this looks like having cake and eating it too, you are right. The rise in the rate of interest is a windfall for me. The substitution effect encourages me to save more but the income effect just described might tend either way. In fact, if the income effect is negative I might end up consuming more and saving less, even though my future pension could still be greater than before the interest-rate rise. On the other hand, the income effect might not be sufficiently negative to outweigh the substitution effect.

To summarize, it is possible that household savings will continually rise as interest rates rise, or that at some point savings will actually start to *fall*. The net effect depends on the strength of income and substitution effects. The same theoretical ambiguity affects the aggregate savings curve, showing total saving as a function of the interest rate: it may be upward-sloping, backward-bending, or even completely interest-insensitive (inelastic).

1.4 **Work–leisure decisions**

Finally, we consider the decision about the level of income, on the slightly unrealistic assumption that the amount of labour the household supplies is a matter of complete choice. Ignoring income from capital – either inherited or as an accumulation of past savings – income is simply wage income: the quantity of labour supplied (of a particular kind) times the wage rate per unit. Thus, at a particular initial wage rate (or if you prefer, 'salary') the household works so many hours per week, yielding so much income. Some of this is saved (depending primarily on the rate of interest) and the rest consumed (in accordance with the pattern of product prices).

Now let my wage rate rise. This encourages me to work more (i.e. longer hours) since every hour I used to spend idly – 'at leisure' – now has a higher opportunity cost in the form of forgone present (and future) consumption. For example, at £5/hour I don't want to work more than 40 hours/week (128 hours/week of 'leisure' including sleep). This must be because the £5 I get from a 41st hour of work does not yield as much subjective satisfaction as the 128th hour of leisure. That is, that 128th leisure-hour is worth more to me than £5 even when I am free to spend/save the £5 however I choose. (But the 129th hour of leisure must be worth less in subjective terms than £5: why?)

Now my wage is raised to £10/hour, which is likely to be of greater value to me than the 128th and maybe even the 127th, 126th, . . . hours of leisure. However, this incentive to increase my work effort is a reflection of the substitution effect. The income effect, which is always present in a price change as well, arises as follows. The extra £10 for working a 41st hour is worth more than a 128th hour of leisure on the basis that my income from 40 hours' work is £200. But since the wage rise applies to all my work, I would in fact be earning £400/week. At this level of income it is not certain that even an extra £10 is worth giving up another hour of leisure. In fact, it might be that £10 on top of £400 is worth less than an hour's additional leisure, so I might work fewer hours. It is quite possible, for instance, that I would end up working 30 hours/week for an income of £300 – a gain of £100 – but with 138 hours of leisure; that is, I have converted the windfall rise partly into more income (to spend and/or save) and partly into more leisure. Although the marginal 10 hours of leisure probably yield successively less additional satisfaction (how much time can I spend in the garden?), so too does each additional £1 of income yield less satisfaction than the one before (do I really want the third case of champagne?) I settle at the point where the extra satisfaction lost from one activity (leisure) just balances the extra satisfaction gained from the other (income).

In my example the income effect is negative and outweighs the substitution effect, but this is not a theoretical necessity. Some people might work more under the same conditions, depending on their underlying preferences. When we aggregate the labour-supply behaviour of all these diverse households we obtain an ambiguous aggregate labour supply curve. As 'the' wage rate rises, it may slope upwards, bend backwards, or be completely wage-inelastic (thus raising an interesting question about the effect of income-tax cuts on work effort).

Summary

Going back, the key to understanding the economic theory of household behaviour is to see that they react to prices in accordance with their given – and possibly diverse – preferences. In a simplified context, the wage rate (the price per unit of labour, measured in 'standard' units) determines the supply of labour and hence income. The *rate of interest* (the price of financial capital) determines the supply of financial capital, to be embodied in physical capital. Simultaneously, with income determined, consumption expenditure is also thereby determined. And finally, product prices determine the composition of consumption expenditure. To repeat a word of caution: in a rigorous theory of household behaviour all these decisions would be simultaneous. For example, accumulated savings would affect income because of interest payments, on top of wage earnings.

A change in any price will affect the initial position. This is shown graphically as a movement along curves which relate various quantities to that particular price, and to be consistent, as simultaneous shifts in the other curves.

The magnitude of these changes obviously depends on the magnitude of the price change, and crucially upon the various elasticities. This is necessarily an empirical matter – that is, we have to look at actual economies to determine these elasticities – since in theory there is no reason to expect any particular direction of change, let alone its magnitude. For instance, a rise in the wage rate might mean more or less labour supplied; a rise in the interest rate might mean more or less capital (savings) supplied; a rise in the price of '*x*' might mean more or less '*y*' purchased; etc. Hence, the usefulness of the theory is in identifying the important relationships, leaving the task of measurement to the 'applied economist'. As a final note on this point, however, it ought to be mentioned that perhaps at least as important (for firms) as discovering the current and/or historical patterns of demand for their products is the attempt to change them. In practice, this means operating on household's preferences (e.g. through advertising) and product development.

Appendix 1A 'Expenditure' and 'income' elasticities

As we have explained it, the household allocates a given expenditure ('budget') in accordance with prevailing prices. When the budget changes we observe changes in consumption of different commodities according to their expenditure elasticities, defined for 'x' as:

$$e_x = \frac{\Delta Q_x/Q_x}{\Delta C/C}$$

where C is the amount spent on consumption. If Y stands for income (no taxes) and S for saving, we have:

$$C = Y - S$$

In the literature it is common to speak of 'income elasticity':

$$\epsilon_x = \frac{\Delta Q_x/Q_x}{\Delta Y/Y}$$

but the reference is often to what we have defined more precisely as 'expenditure' elasticity above.

In fact, the two measures will be equal if C is a constant fraction of Y, since we know that for a ray from the origin (strict proportionality),

$$\frac{\Delta C/C}{\Delta Y/Y} = 1$$

i.e. the elasticity of consumption with respect to income is one.

However, many economists question this relationship, proposing instead that, at low levels of income, C would be greater than Y by virtue of negative saving. The fact that we never observe an economy at such a low level of income is irrelevant, since its significance as we know is that

$$\frac{\Delta C/C}{\Delta Y/Y} < 1$$

i.e. along the lower 'consumption function' consumption expenditure changes proportionately less than income (see Fig. 8.5b). In terms of our present discussion this means that the income elasticity of demand is less than the expenditure elasticity:

$$\frac{\Delta Q_x/Q_x}{\Delta Y/Y} = \frac{\Delta Q_x/Q_x}{\Delta C/C} \times \frac{\Delta C/C}{\Delta Y/Y}$$

Appendix 1B The Giffen effect

We have seen that the operation of the (negative) income effect may overwhelm the positive substitution effect of a change in the rate of interest, or in the wage rate. Hence both the supply of financial capital and the supply of labour may be backward-bending.

The question we ask here is whether this counter-intuitive result could apply to the demand for a product ('*x*') as its own price changes. In other words is the demand curve always downward-sloping? The answer to this latter question is 'no', but actual cases of upward-sloping demand are likely to be very rare.

The cause of this phenomenon – known as a 'Giffen effect' after the nineteenth-century economist who first gave it an explanation – is the same dominance of income over substitution effects. But in the case of product demand, the product must be inferior.

Consider a fall in the price of '*x*'. It thus becomes relatively cheaper than other goods, so consumers would tend to buy more. But recall that a decline in prices is equivalent to a rise in total money expenditure with prices unchanged. If all prices fell in the same proportion the correspondence would be exact, but even if only one product price declines there is still some (perhaps small) equivalent effect in terms of total money expenditure. It is perhaps easier to imagine this in terms of cost-of-living index. A fall in one price will lower this index, meaning that households have in aggregate increased their 'real' incomes. For a normal good, this rise in real income – literally, if the price of '*x*' has fallen the household can initially buy exactly the same amounts of all goods and have money left over – will induce some additional spending on '*x*'. That is, not only do we buy more '*x*' at the expense of other products (the substitution effect arising from a change in relative prices), but also since we have effectively more to spend, we spend a bit more on '*x*' as well as other (normal) goods, (a positive income effect).

If the product is inferior there will be a negative income effect. The extra money – a manifestation of a rise in real income – makes us feel – rightly – better off, so we buy less '*x*' on this account. However, this has to overcome the substitution effect in order to increase demand for '*x*' in total. Therefore, it is likely that not only must '*x*' be inferior, but also constitute a significant proportion of total spending (so a change in its price significantly affects real income through the cost-of-living index). Although such examples are rare, this nonetheless demonstrates the possibility that even the demand curve can have an upward slope: there is not a simple price–quantity relationship in household behaviour that we can *a priori* say is upward- or downward-sloping.

Appendix 1C Indifference curve analysis

A general diagrammatic representation of household choices is given by the 'indifference curves' of Fig. 1C.1, drawn for the particular case of a consumption-allocation decision between two products ('*x*' and '*y*').

Taking any one of these curves, say U_0, every point along that curve – each point representing a different combination of the two goods – yields equal satisfaction or 'utility' to the consumer. The typical curve is convex to the origin, showing for instance that if the household is initially consuming much of '*y*' but little of '*x*' (point Q_A), then it would be willing to give up quite a lot of '*y*' for a bit more '*x*'. However, as more and more '*y*' is traded for '*x*' this 'marginal rate of substitution' (m.r.s.) diminishes, until at point Q_B the household would require a large increase in '*x*' to compensate for a small decrease in '*y*'. (Consider the psychological interpretation if these curves were straight lines, or even concave to the origin.)

Indifference curves lying to the north-east of U_0 show combinations which are preferred to U_0; i.e. yielding a higher level of utility because they allow consumption of more of both '*x*' and '*y*' as shown (although more of both would not necessarily be chosen); and vice-versa.

The actual point chosen depends, as we have seen, on prices (P_x,P_y) and the (predetermined) level of expenditure (C_0). This constraint is shown diagrammatically as a 'budget line'. Algebraically, this corresponds to:

$$C_0 = P_x \times Q_x + P_y \times Q_y$$

that is, the budgeted amount (C_0) is spent on '*x*' or '*y*'. If no purchases of '*x*' are made ($Q_x = 0$) then the *maximum* amount of '*y*' that can be consumed is:

$$\max Q_y = C_0/P_y$$

Figure 1C.1 Indifference curve representation of optimum choice

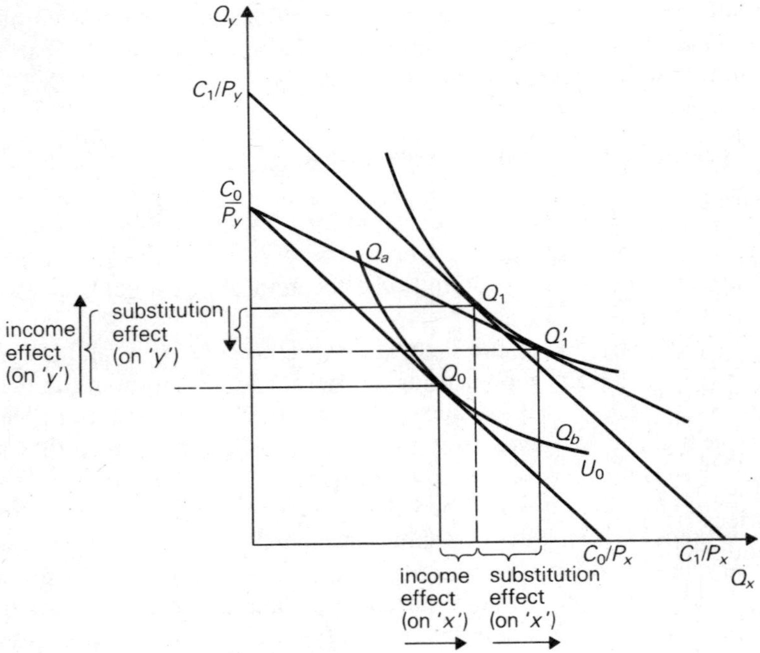

Initially, the representive individual consumes amounts indicated at Q_0. A change (in this case a fall) in the price of 'x' pivots the budget line from its 'anchor-point' where $Q_y = C_0/P_y$ (outwards) and leads to the new chosen point Q'_1. Alternatively a change (increase) in budgeted expenditure (from C_0 to C_1) shifts the entire constraint-line parallel to its original position – that is, the relative prices of 'x' and 'y' are now the same as before – and leads to point Q_1. Note that the former price change can therefore be thought of as consisting of an income effect – as if expenditure had increased – and a substitution effect: a further movement along the indifference curve (from Q_1 to Q'_1).

which is shown on the vertical axis. Likewise, if $Q_y = 0$, then:

$$\max Q_x = C_0/P_x$$

as shown.

The consumer can attain any point (combination) along the budget line connecting these two extremes. As shown, the chosen point (Q_0) is where it is just tangent to an indifference curve. Why? Because any *preferred* – or for that matter, equivalent – point is unattainable with the given spending limit; whereas any other attainable point is inferior to Q_0.

Now what happens when the budget changes; e.g. increases from C_0 to C_1? As shown, the budget line shifts outwards, in a parallel fashion, and leads to an increased consumption of both 'x' and 'y'. However, if for example 'x' were *inferior*, the new point (Q_1) would be above and to the *left* of Q_0.

Alternatively, when expenditure remains fixed but one of the *prices* change (say, a fall in P_x), the budget line pivots as shown. We expect this to lead to a rise in Q_x (corresponding to a downward-sloping demand curve) but note that it is possible to draw the indifference 'map' so that Q_x might fall.

As noted, a price change has two effects: (1) a substitution effect (the movement along the initial indifference curve as *relative* prices change); and (2) an income effect (the shift in the notional budget line reflecting increased real purchasing power from the price reduction). If 'x' were sufficiently inferior, the latter could overwhelm the former and produce a 'Giffen effect'.

Finally, it is important to see that the other decisions facing the household are amenable to the same treatment. In the case of allocating a given income in one period between consumption in two periods (work and retirement), the relevant price variable determining the slope of the budget constraint is the rate of interest. In the case of allocating a given amount of time between leisure and income (resulting from work), it is the wage rate. In fact, as we shall observe again, it is possible to formulate almost any decision problem as the search for a tangency between indifference curves (objective or criterion functions) and budget lines (constraints).

2 Demand, Competition and Market Structure

Outline

Synopsis

This chapter first looks at market structure, which is manifested as the relationship between the aggregate demand curves constructed in Chapter 1, and the demand, or *average revenue* curve actually faced by a particular firm.

Beginning with pure monopoly, two further types of market structure – monopolistic and 'perfect' competition – are classified according to the nature and extent of product substitutability.

Then, dividing firms into more general perfectly or imperfectly competitive categories on the basis of their ability to affect market price, I derive the relationships between *linear* average revenue, or firm specific demand curves, *total* revenue curves, and the very important *marginal* revenue curves. The relationship between price, or average revenue and marginal revenue is neatly expressed in terms of the own-price elasticity measure.

Following a brief caution on the difficulties of actually estimating the relevant elasticities, I then look at a fourth type of market structure for which the firm's own-demand curve is unforecastable, even in principle. *Oligopoly* presents a situation of interdependent markets requiring a so-called 'game-theoretic' approach. The chapter outlines some very elementary games, summarizing in the form of a kinked demand curve, but is led to conclude that firms in this situation would be likely to collude as monopolists.

Introduction

On the initial assumption that all output is sold at a *uniform* price (the so-called 'law of one price'; but as we shall see later on, firms may be able to *discriminate* between purchasers by charging different prices for the same product), a firm's total revenue (TR) is obviously just the product of price times quantity, i.e.:

$$TR = P \times Q$$

We want to relate TR to Q (the 'revenue schedule' or 'TR curve'). In order to do this, we clearly need to relate P to Q; but in fact, we have already established this relationship between price and quantity, embodied in the downward-sloping demand curve reflecting consumer behaviour. However, this was an aggregate demand curve (for product '*x*') and may or may not be directly relevant to any single firm producing '*x*'. The firm's demand curve, relating its own price for '*x*' to its own sales, will usually differ from the aggregate relationship in a way that depends on the competitive structure of the industry. Given the possibilities for confusion, we try to use the term 'demand curve' for the aggregate price–volume relationship, and refer to this relationship – as perceived by the individual firm – as its *average revenue* curve.

2.1 Market structure: orthodox types

In general, competition from other suppliers of '*x*' will affect both a firm's market share and the price-sensitivity of its sales. The former relates to the position of the firm's average revenue (*AR*) curve, and the latter to its slope or elasticity. Normally, as competition increases (e.g. through entry of new firms) we expect each firm's share of the market to shrink (leftward movement of the *AR* curve) and its scope for price variations to diminish (a flattening of the *AR* curve). However, it is useful to distinguish at least three "stages" in the analysis of competition: monopoly, monopolistic competition, and 'perfect' competition.

2.1.1 **Monopoly**

This is the simplest of all to explain, since by definition the single firm is the sole supplier of product '*x*'. Hence, its *AR* curve is identical to the aggregate demand curve (Fig. 2.1a). Of course, this does not mean that it is impervious to external occurrences. For example, if income falls the monopolist producing a normal good would experience lower sales at the existing price, whatever that might be. Likewise, if the price of a substitute good '*y*' were to fall, or the price of a complementary good '*z*' to rise, the monopolist's *AR* curve would shift leftwards also.

2.1.2 **Monopolistic competition**

You may have noticed that the ability of the producer of a substitute product ('*y*') to affect the monopolist's *AR* curve means that even monopolies can face competition, in the sense described. Our definition of a so-called 'pure' monopoly is one for which the cross-elasticities of demand are zero, thus insulating the monopolist from this type of competitive pressure. It does not mean that the own-demand elasticity is zero (a vertical *AR* curve). That is, either existing producers of substitutes can alter their prices or, in a dynamic economy, new or existing firms can introduce new substitute products. This acknowledges the fact that firms can make both 'price' and 'non-price' decisions. Most of our focus is on the former, but the latter is an important subject, underlying, for example, our present discussion of product differentiation. At the same time this view rather begs the question of how we ought to meaningfully *define* a product '*x*'. For example, suppose Adams (*A*) and Bloggs (*B*) have identical apple orchards, but the crates in which their apples are sold at grocers have different labels – perhaps one plain and the other elaborate – or maybe the apples

Figures 2.1a, b and c Three types of (product) market structure

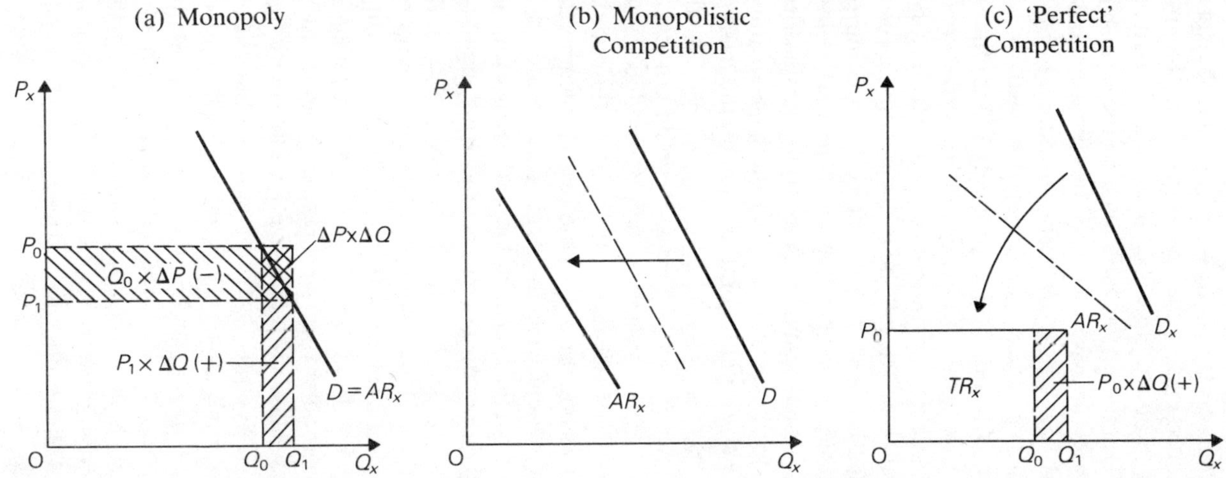

(**a**) Monopoly: a single seller (producer), therefore facing aggregate demand for '*x*'. A fall in price from P_0 to P_1 decreases revenue by the shaded area: $Q_0 \times \Delta P$, and increases it by the area: $P_1 \times \Delta Q$. The sum of these two components is equal to $P_0 \times \Delta Q + Q_0 \times \Delta P$ *less* the cross-hatched rectangular area: $\Delta P \times \Delta Q$. (**b**) Monopolistic competition: producers of (differentiated) substitutes shrink the market for '*x*', but the firm retains influence over price (a degree of monopoly). Therefore, a firm in this situation will also need to reduce price in order to sell more, as in the 'pure' monopoly case. (**c**) Perfect competition: substitutes are undifferentiated (infinite cross-elasticity of demand); the firm becomes a price-taker. Unlike either of the previous imperfectly competitive structures, the firm in this situation does not need to alter price. The change in total revenue is simply $P_0 \times \Delta Q$.

are wrapped in different-coloured paper. A strict application of our definition would indicate that both *A* and *B* are 'monopolists', albeit with extremely high cross-elasticities of demand between each others' products, since each is the sole producer of his own specially differentiated product. In fact, it is this notion of qualitative product differentiation, as embodied in the quantitative measure of cross-price-elasticity, that provides the usual basis for defining 'products', or more precisely, 'product-groups'. Namely, specific (branded) products with *high* cross-elasticities of demand thereby reveal little qualitative product differentiation and should be treated as a single 'product', whereas low cross-elasticities reveal considerable differentiation and therefore become dividing lines between products. The exact magnitudes used to divide product groups are a matter of choice, depending on purpose and, perhaps more realistically, on data availability. Note, however, that the usual Standard Industrial Classification (SIC) scheme typically aggregates products on the basis of jointness or high production substitutability rather than on the basis of demand substitutability as argued here.

Returning to our apple growers, *A* and *B* would for every conceivable purpose be treated simply as 'apple' producers, an industry which is likely to have at least hundreds, if not thousands, of suppliers. If Adams (*A*) bought out all the rest to become the sole apple supplier, he would at that stage be considered a monopolist with respect to the product 'apples'. However, he would not have achieved monopoly power over the 'fruit' industry, and would face potential competition from producers of oranges and bananas, for example. Upon acquiring all fruit producers, Adams would then be a monopolist with respect to the product 'fruit', but not with regard to 'food', etc. In short, we can define '*x*' as narrowly or broadly as suits our purposes, to include firms' products with 'high' cross-elasticities (relatively undifferentiated) and exclude those with 'low' cross-elasticities (differentiated products). Having done this, if all the products in the '*x*' grouping or industry are supplied by a single firm it is a monopoly. However, the existence of other products with cross-elasticities too low to justify inclusion in '*x*' but high enough to significantly affect the '*x*'-monopolist's *AR* curve implies the potential for *monopolistic competition*, especially if these other industries ('*y*', '*z*', etc.) are also highly concentrated.

Imagine now that a monopoly supplier of 'x' (apples) does in fact experience monopolistic competition; e.g. the Orange Growers' Association cuts orange prices, or some new kind of tropical fruit starts being marketed in the domestic economy: what happens to the 'x'-monopolist's AR curve (Fig. 2.1b)? Obviously, one effect is that it shifts to the left: the 'x' market shrinks as apples lose market share to other fruits. On the other hand, since apples remain a reasonably differentiated product, we should not expect much of a change in the own-price elasticity of the AR curve. That is, although his market has shrunk, the monopolistically competitive producer of 'x' still has a considerable degree of price-making ability, in the sense that variations in his price have a limited impact on sales volume. In fact, if E = the own-price elasticity of the firm's AR curve (at a particular point on the AR curve), $1/E$ is often called the 'degree of monopoly' exercised by the firm. In diagrammatic terms, this is shown by the fact that the shifted AR curve still has a significant downward slope.

2.1.3 'Perfect' competition

In contrast with this monopolistically competitive outcome, suppose instead that Adams suffers the entry of new apple suppliers into the existing fruit market. In this case it is clear not only that his market share will decrease, but also that his own-price elasticity of demand (the elasticity of the AR curve) will increase (Fig. 2.1c). This latter effect is due to the close similarity of the competitors' to the existing product in qualitative terms; or what is the same thing, a reflection of high cross-elasticity of demand. In diagrammatic terms this weakening of Adam's monopoly power is shown by the flattening of the AR curve (note that as this happens, the 'degree of monopoly' diminishes). In the limit competing products become qualitatively identical ('homogeneous') and the single firm has no pricing flexibility, having become a price-taker facing a perfectly elastic AR curve. This appears to show not only that a rise in any firm's price would wipe out its sales, but also that a fall in its price would restore a monopoly position by capturing the whole market. As we shall see, this latter strategy is not viable on cost grounds. This limiting case is known as *perfect* competition, indicating a situation in which several suppliers sell virtually identical products, with no freedom in pricing as a consequence.

Many textbooks specify as additional requirements that: (1) there is a large number of firms, (2) there is freedom of entry and exit, and (3) there is perfect information about product prices and qualitative characteristics. At an introductory level we always assume the last condition in all contexts. The first two conditions are presumably sufficient to produce a mutual price-taking market structure, but they are not necessary for this result. Also, as a matter of definition any structure other than perfect competition (p.c.) is known simply as 'imperfect' competition (i.c.) whether competition actually exists or not. (Contrasted to monopolistic industries, whether competitive or not, in which products are differentiated and the firm has some flexibility in pricing.) Thus, even though the aggregate demand curve for 'x' (apples) may remain unaltered, the individual, perfectly competitive apple grower nonetheless might perceive his effective AR curve as perfectly elastic.

2.2 Marginal and total revenue relationships

The distinction between a price-taking perfectly competitive firm and a price-making monopolistic firm is crucial to the form of the total revenue (TR) curve faced by each. Specifically, having established that (total) revenue is the product of average revenue times quantity sold, we can see that in the former case TR at any given output Q is diagrammatically interpretable (e.g. Fig. 2.1c) as the whole *area* under the AR curve measured at the given output, e.g. Q_0.

For the latter case of a monopolistic firm, the graphical interpretation (e.g. Fig. 2.1a) of TR is as the rectangular area under the AR curve measured at any given Q and corresponding P. The remainder of the area under the AR curve (roughly, a triangle), whilst representing amounts that some consumers would have been willing to pay, is not actually obtained by the firm. In fact, as we can see, if the monopolistic firm wants to increase its sales (equals output, recall) it must lower price. But this means that although its revenue increases by the additional amount sold at the new price, some revenue would be lost, as shown by the fact that consumers who would have paid the original higher price can obtain the product at the lower price. Thus, the increment in total revenue (ΔTR) is the sum of the positive vertical slice (approximately $P_0 \times \Delta Q$) and the negative horizontal slice (approximately $Q_0 \times \Delta P$).

Whether the net outcome of these two effects is positive (a rise in *TR* for a fall in *P*) or negative (a fall in *TR* for a fall in *P*) is not immediately obvious from the simple diagram. First, we must define a very important concept known as *marginal* revenue (*MR*), as follows:

> *MR* is the *net* change in total revenue *per* unit change in output (sales). Symbolically,
>
> $$MR = \Delta TR/\Delta Q$$

i.e. it is the ratio of the increments in *TR* and *Q*. Strictly, a marginal value refers to infinitesimal increments, written with a '*d*' rather than 'Δ' symbol. Thus, $MR = dTR/dQ$; but for our purposes the 'finite' form will do.

We already know that ΔTR is composed of two effects:

$$\Delta TR \approx P\Delta Q + Q\Delta P\ .$$

corresponding to the area slices on the diagram. If ΔP is negative (a fall in price), then ΔQ is positive (sales increase) and vice-versa. We want to know if, for an assumed fall in *P*, $P\Delta Q$ outweighs $Q\Delta P$ or not.

Divide the preceding expression by ΔQ:

$$MR = \frac{\Delta TR}{\Delta Q} \simeq P + Q\,\frac{\Delta P}{\Delta Q}$$

That is, the firm's marginal revenue is equal to the price it charges less the amount of revenue 'given up' on the quantity it could have sold at a slightly higher price. For a positive ΔQ which we have assumed, the sign of *MR* (positive or negative) will be the same as the sign of ΔTR; i.e. if *TR* is rising then *MR* will be positive, and if *TR* is falling *MR* will be negative.

The second step is to divide the right-hand side of the last equation by *P*, so as to re-write the expression for *MR*:

$$MR = \frac{\Delta TR}{\Delta Q} \simeq P\left(1 + \frac{Q}{P} \times \frac{\Delta P}{\Delta Q}\right)$$

At first, this looks worse than before. But look closely at the last term, which is:

$$\frac{Q}{P} \times \frac{\Delta P}{\Delta Q} = \frac{\Delta P/P}{\Delta Q/Q}$$

You should recognize this as the ratio of two *percentage changes*; i.e. it is an elasticity measure. But of what? In fact, it makes more sense to look at the reciprocal = $(\Delta Q/Q)/(\Delta P/P)$, which gives it exactly the same form as the earlier own-price elasticity of demand. However, it does not refer here to the aggregate demand curve, but to the firm's perceived demand curve, which in order to distinguish, we have called the firm's *AR* curve. In abbreviated form, we finally obtain:·

$$MR = P(1 + 1/E)$$

Where E is the symbol used to represent the own-price elasticity of the particular firm's average revenue curve.

So, since P is always positive, it should be apparent that *MR* is positive (hence, *TR* rises as P falls and Q rises) if E is less than -1 (e.g. -2, -3, etc.). As before, you may prefer to state this alternatively as the absolute value of E being greater than 1, on the understanding that the sign of E is negative. Conversely, *MR* is negative (hence *TR* falls as P falls and Q rises) if E is greater than -1 (e.g. $-3/4$, $-1/2$, etc.). In other words, *TR* rises for a cut in price if demand (*AR*) is price-elastic and falls if demand is price-inelastic.

As we have established previously, if a downward-sloping curve is *linear* – a straight line – it has variable elasticity ranging from infinite at its vertical axis intercept to zero at its horizontal axis intercept, being equal to one at its midpoint. Applying this to the case of a (monopolistic) firm with a linear *AR* curve (Fig. 2.2a), we find that its *MR* curve is much steeper (twice as steep in fact) and cuts the horizontal axis at the level of sales at which $E = -1$ (verify that $MR = 0$ at this point). Beyond that, *MR* is negative. The steepness of the *MR* curve is a reflection of the fact that although the *AR* curve shows the price at which different quantities can be sold, *MR* is price less the amount given up by lowering price in order to sell another unit of output. Corresponding to this (Fig. 2.2b), total revenue (*TR*) must initially be rising as *AR* is elastic

Figures 2.2a and b *AR*, *MR* and *TR* curves for a monopolistic firm

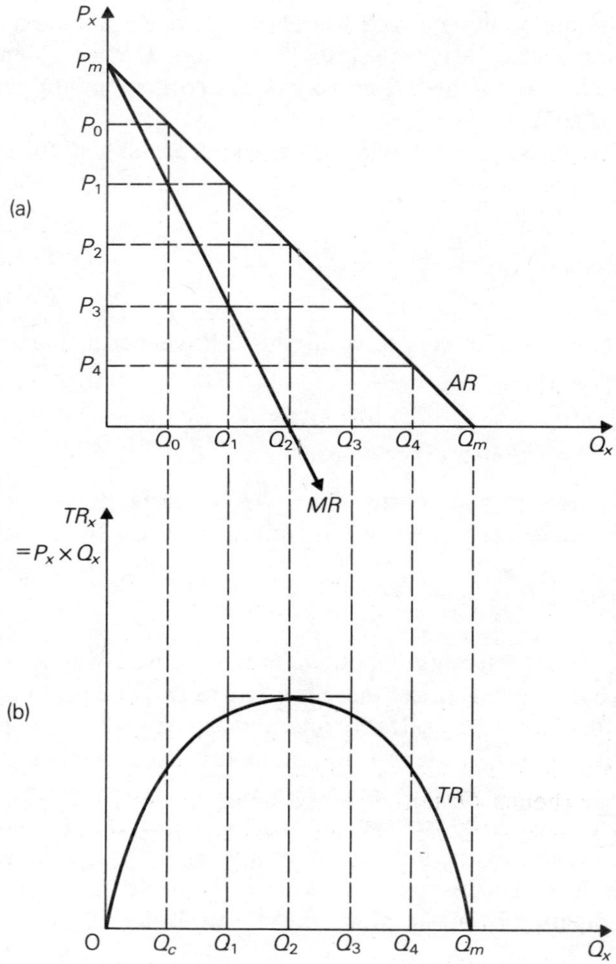

Marginal revenue (*MR*) is equal to the slope of the *TR* curve at each level of Q_x. It is positive but declining until at Q_2 it is zero. This occurs at the midpoint of the *AR* curve (where it is unit-elastic; i.e. $|E| = 1$), indicating that the increased revenue from a small increase in volume (just beyond Q_2) is exactly balanced by decreased revenue which arises because previous units are being sold for less. As *Q* increases – i.e. as *P* falls – *MR* becomes increasingly negative as the latter effect increasingly predominates (the *TR* curve is becoming more steeply negative).

and ultimately falling as AR is inelastic. It reaches a maximum at the point where AR is unit-elastic; i.e. where $MR = 0$. Hence, for linear AR curves, the TR curve has the corresponding parabolic shape as shown.

Notice finally that MR is graphically interpretable as the slope of the TR curve, which is:

$$\text{slope of } TR = \frac{\Delta TR}{\Delta Q} = MR$$

This should make it easy to verify that TR reaches its maximum at $MR = 0$.

Perfect competition: a special case

For a perfectly competitive firm, AR is perfectly elastic ($E = (-)\infty$). Therefore, applying our formula, it must be true that:

$$MR = P$$

That is, for a perfectly competitive firm marginal revenue is simply equal to the (given) price: there is no extra revenue given up when such a firm increases sales by one unit, since it does not need to lower its price in order to do so. In turn, this implies that TR always rises as Q (sales) increases, as is indeed shown to be the case (Fig. 2.3b). Moreover, since MR is constant (equal to P, which is taken by the firm as a constant selling price) the slope of the TR curve is constant: i.e. TR is an (upward-sloping) straight line emanating from the origin (a 'ray' from the origin).

2.2.1 **Forecasting revenues**

In terms of practical decision-making, the perfectly competitive firm would be most interested in forecasts of future prevailing market prices, but would not need to undertake any additional analysis of its 'own' market since this would be indistinguishable from every other firm's market. On the other hand, a monopolistic firm would need to consider its own market position in addition to the aggregate market forecasts. (Of course, being a monopoly without competition would mean that these were identical concepts.) In particular, a firm with some degree of monopoly power –

Figures 2.3a and b *AR, MR* and *TR* curves for a perfectly competitive firm

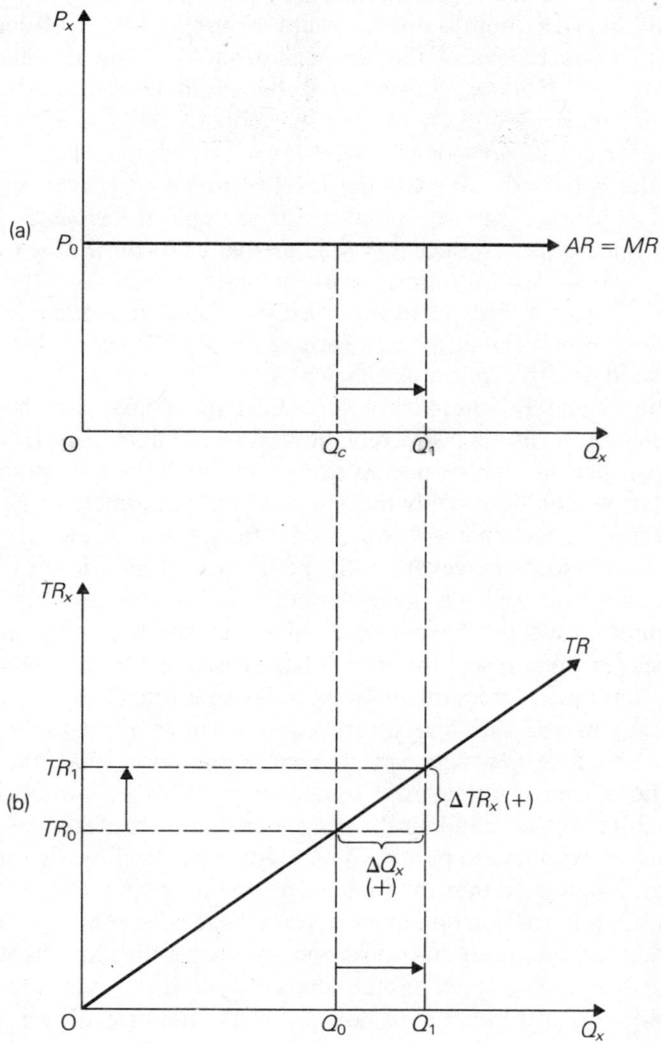

For perfectly competitive firms, *MR* is constant and equal to price (P_0): that is, the slope of the *TR* curve is constant.

i.e. some control over price – would want to estimate its own-price elasticity of demand (*E*). In addition, cross-elasticities of demand would likely be important, as would income elasticity of demand for its product. That is, the firm would want to know the shape of its *AR* curve, and how any external changes in other product prices and incomes were likely to shift it. Knowing the elasticity of the *AR* over a range of possible sales levels would enable us to trace out the *TR* curve, showing the level of revenues related to each level of sales. Likewise, knowing for example the cross-elasticity with some other product '*y*' would enable us to show how the *TR* curve was shifted for (alternative) forecasts of changes in the price of '*y*'. Forecast changes in the price of '*z*' and in average income could also be related to their impact on the *TR* curve through a knowledge of the relevant elasticities.

Unfortunately, the ability of a firm to estimate its demand elasticities is usually severely limited. If it had experienced a longish period of time during which, say, only its own price had varied, we could probably make a good direct estimate of *E*; or, if only income had changed, we could estimate income elasticity. As will be obvious, however, both these, as well as prices of other products, will typically have varied. That is, the *ceteris paribus* assumption will not have held. Under such conditions the market forecaster must resort to more sophisticated statistical techniques (e.g. multiple regression analysis) to try to estimate these elasticities. Even so, the forecaster requires sufficient data for this exercise, together with an implicit assumption that the true elasticities have not altered significantly. In other words, if the structure of demand, reflecting consumer preferences, has changed, attempts to pin down elasticity values will be doomed to failure. Note also that the longer the period of time over which a firm has information on incomes, prices and sales volumes – which is good from a purely statistical point of view – the more likely it is that structural change in the market will have occurred; e.g. through the introduction of new products, and/or evolving tastes.

2.3 **Oligopoly: interdependent market structure**

Nonetheless, it is in principle possible to identify a firm's AR curve and the effects upon it of changes in other prices and incomes. Indeed, many firms employ economists for just such a function.

However, we have assumed so far that there is an objectively identifiable *AR* curve, whether the firm is monopolistic or perfectly competitive. Although in some cases this may be true, for an uncomfortably large number of cases it may not be true, in which case there is really no such thing as a *TR* curve. The reason for this can be clearly illustrated in the case of monopolistic competition: the actions of competitors are assumed never to anticipate each others' behaviour; instead, every firm always reacts to perceived conditions. Thus, '*x*'-firm's competitors independently decide to introduce new products or vary their prices on existing ones. The '*x*'-firm then finds its revenues affected and presumably adjusts its own price and output. The other firms then adjust their prices and outputs, *ad infinitum*. The ultimate outcome of such a process was investigated for *duopoly* (two firms) by Cournot as early as 1838. At each stage of this competitive adjustment process each firm has a known *AR* curve that shifts in a known or at least forecastable way. But suppose that there really were interdependences in the sense that, for example, a change in the price of '*x*' at any stage had a completely unknown impact on sales, because it depended entirely on the unknowable reactions of competitors – who in turn would be uncertain about each others' actions as well as the '*x*'-firm's? The same element of uncertain demand pertains not only to the monopolistically competitive model in which a number of firms typically produce differentiated products, but also to those industries in which, although the products are virtually identical, there are only a few large firms. This is called (undifferentiated) oligopoly (with monopolistic competition in which there are only a few (large) firms often called differentiated oligopoly, reserving the term 'monopolistic competition' for a situation where there are many, small firms).

The problem arises because although no firm is in a pure monopoly situation, able to effectively ignore the actions of other firms, neither is any firm so small as to be a price-taker: changes in its output clearly will affect other firms, and vice-versa. This situation of interdependence, combined with the uncertainty of rival oligopolistic firms' behaviour, is characteristic of a game such as chess or poker, and in fact economists have utilized so-called 'game theory' to tackle the problems of analysing oligopoly. The basic approach is to realize that the firm no longer has an objective 'pay-off' (revenue) from its actions, but instead has a range of potential pay-offs depending upon its own combined with its rivals' actions.

As a first approach to understanding games, we take a very simple problem arising from the earliest applications of game theory (during World War II) by postulating an initial situation in which the naval commander of a superior fleet (*A*) is in pursuit of the inferior fleet of the enemy (*B*). However, with the fleets at anchor on opposite sides of an island, each commander can only hope to anticipate the action of the other. To simplify the problem we will allow each commander to sail his fleet north (*N*) or south (*S*), but not east or west (the island itself and mainland nearby on either side of it prevent this). Nor can they sit still, since they are running out of food.

Suppose *A* sails north and *B* sails north. In this case, let us assume that *A* sinks 2 of *B*'s ships. On the other hand if *B* sails south, although the prevailing currents would allow *A* to turn around swiftly, the damage to *B* would be only 1 ship lost.

If *A* sails south, however, while *B* does likewise, *A* inflicts a loss of 3 ships on *B*; but if *B* had sailed north, *A* would be unable to catch up at all.

We can now write the *pay-off matrix* for the "game":

		B: *N*	*B*: *S*
A	*N*	2	1
	S	0	3

The numbers in the cells are as explained. There is only a single number in each cell because *A*'s gain is *B*'s loss. This makes it a two-person (*A* and *B*) *zero-sum* game: what one loses the other gains. *N* and *S* are the players' *strategies*.

A would of course like the outcome 3, whilst *B* would like the outcome 0, but neither can ensure these consequences by his action; i.e. there is no objective pay-off. Instead, suppose that *A* is risk-averse and focuses his attention on the worst outcome of each of his strategies. If *A* chooses *N* (sails north) the worst that can happen is 1 ship sunk (the best is 2); whereas by choosing *S* the worst is 0 ships sunk (the best is 3). Therefore, we might expect *A* to sail north, because this is the best of the worst cases.

A has adopted a so-called '*maximin*' strategy. At the same time *B* looks at strategy *N* and finds his worst outcome to be 2 ships lost (the best is 0); whereas strategy *S* yields a worst outcome of 3 (the best is 1). Hence, if he too is averse to risk, he will sail north, thereby adopting a '*minimax*' strategy (minimizing the worst outcome). Therefore, we can predict that both sail north.

Alternatively, notice that if *A* and *B* were risk-lovers they might adopt 'maxi*max*' and 'mini*min*' (best of the best) strategies. Therefore *B* would gain sail north, but *A* would sail south (verify this).

A classic example of a *non*-zero-sum game is 'Prisoners' Dilemma', which starts with two suspects charged with a crime. Their strategies are either to confess (*C*) or not confess (*NC*). Such a game might have the pay-off matrix shown below. The pair of numbers in each cell shows the sentence – say in years – for *A* and *B* respectively.

		B: *C*	*B*: *NC*
A	*C*	10,10	1,20
	NC	20,1	0,0

Thus, if *A* and *B* both confess: they each receive 10-year sentences; whereas if neither confesses they go free. However, if one confesses and the other does not, the confessor gets a minimal sentence and the other fellow carries the burden almost alone (20 years). You should be able to verify that if *A* and *B* are risk-averse and try to minimize their maximum possible sentences, they will both confess! On the other hand, if they were risk-lovers (trying to get the absolutely best deal) they would go free. It is rather interesting to speculate that law-abiding people are probably more risk-averse than habitual law-breakers, who may be willing to take the risk of non-cooperation with authority. If so, it seems to imply that the prisons are full of innocent people whilst the guilty go free.

This type of mutually disadvantageous outcome can equally well result from oligopolistic rivalry. In the next matrix each firm (*A* and *B*) can either raise prices ($P\uparrow$) or maintain them ($\bar{P}$).

	(*B*) $\bar{P}$	(*B*) $P\uparrow$
$\bar{P}$	0,0	15,−5
$P\uparrow$	−5,15	10,10

The results in terms of revenues are shown for each pair of strategies: e.g. if both raise prices each will increase revenue by £10,000. But if only one raises its price, the other will gain to the first firm's detriment. Again, you should ascertain that risk-averse firms will not upset the *status quo*, although both would prefer the outcome generated by raising prices simultaneously.

This *impasse* can be depicted diagrammatically (Fig. 2.4a) by the so-called 'kinked' demand curve as shown. Here we have considered not only a *rise* but also a fall in price as well. The consequence of the former move is perceived – by the oligopolist – to result in drastically reduced sales, since other firms are expected not to follow (*B* would be better off still once *A* had raised its price). Conversely, if *A* cuts its price, the perception is that other firms will follow, so the effect on increased sales is limited. In sum, the firm is facing an elastic *AR* curve for a price rise and an inelastic *AR* for a price fall; hence, it is at the peak of a *TR* curve as shown. The associated *MR* curve has a vertical discontinuity at this point, as shown. In effect the first segment corresponds to the flat *AR* curve, and the second to the steep *AR* as indicated by the dashed extensions. However, note that this is not a true revenue schedule as was the case before. It gives the same picture wherever the initial price and quantity happen to be, which is to say that we cannot independently measure the firms revenue-sales volume relationship because it depends on the actions of other firms.

One result of this theoretical embarrassment is a tendency to sweep the mess under the carpet. Specifically, it is fairly clear that cooperation among interested parties (*collusion* as it is usually called) would benefit all of them. So, since the real world is (thankfully) not like a police cell, it is both natural and easy for firms to collude, either explicitly (e.g. IATA, the International Air Transport Association) or implicitly (e.g. any manufacturers' or trades conference). Therefore, although retaining an oligopolistic form, industries can behave effectively as monopolies. They may then share in the collective TR curve, each according to its share of output, as though they were branch plants of a single central office. Indeed, we do observe a number of such industries in which 'price leadership' is the *modus operandi*. If this is the case, it implies that to speak of a single firm's *TR* curve is meaningless, since in effect it has abandoned independent price and output decisions.

Figures 2.4a and b *AR*, *MR* and *TR* curves for an oligopolistic firm

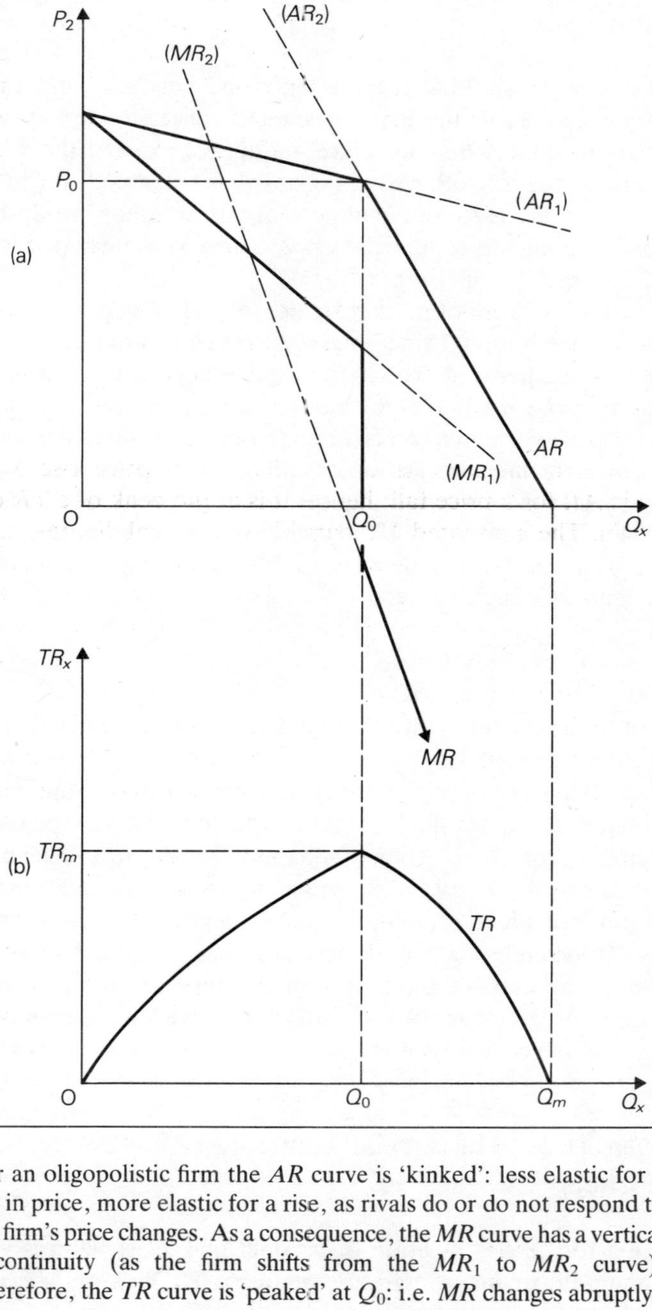

For an oligopolistic firm the *AR* curve is 'kinked': less elastic for a fall in price, more elastic for a rise, as rivals do or do not respond to the firm's price changes. As a consequence, the *MR* curve has a vertical discontinuity (as the firm shifts from the MR_1 to MR_2 curve). Therefore, the *TR* curve is 'peaked' at Q_0: i.e. *MR* changes abruptly.

Summary

'Monopoly' means that there is only one producer of a product ('*x*'), hence it faces the market demand curve (for '*x*') as its own average revenue schedule. 'Pure' monopoly exists if there are no substitutes for '*x*'; otherwise there will be competition to some extent. In the extreme, competition from other producers of virtually identical products leaves the firm as a mere price-taker; i.e. a 'perfect' competitor.

For this last form of market structure, total revenue rises in line with volume (output) since marginal revenue – the increment in total revenue per unit change in output – is positive, constant and equal to price (average revenue). For imperfectly competitive firms it is necessary to lower price in order to raise sales volume: hence, marginal revenue is less than average revenue (price) because there is some revenue lost on units that could have been sold at a higher price, which must be subtracted from the revenue gained on the increased sales. The relationship between price (AR) and MR is given by:

$$MR = P(1 + 1/E)$$

where E is the elasticity of the firm's AR (or if you prefer, own-demand) schedule.

Identifying own-price as well as relevant cross- and income-elasticities for a product '*x*' is a difficult task, but possible in principle. This is not true of oligopolistic market structures in which there are a few large producers whose demand conditions are interdependent. Here there are no underlying 'true' elasticities to be objectively estimated: the situation is more like a game. Although we can see the nature of this type of problem, general solutions are lacking. As an alternative we observe that firms might collude so as to benefit all (e.g. through price 'leadership').

Appendix 2 The parallel structure of factor markets

Parallel to the classification of product market structures we can define input, or *factor* market structures. To illustrate we use the labour market as our example, but everything in this case can also be applied to capital markets.

As we already know, the aggregate labour supply curve for the whole economy may slope upwards, bend backwards, or even be perfectly inelastic with respect to the wage rate. Even in these latter instances, the labour supply to a particular industry (making and selling '*x*') is likely to be upward-sloping since it is that industry's going wage rate that is assumed to be rising, on the *ceteris paribus* assumption that wages in other industries are constant.

Now if there is only one buyer (a *monopsony*) of labour in this industry, that firm faces the entire industry's labour supply curve by definition. On the assumption that this is upward-sloping the firm therefore has some ability to control the wage rate – i.e. some 'degree of monopsony'. Analogously to monopoly (a single *seller*), pure monopsony exists when there are no (close) substitute occupations for the labour employed in the '*x*' industry (a single firm): it is a 'captive' labour force for all intents and purposes.

However, suppose other alternative occupations become available. As wages in these industries rise and/or as the number of alternatives increases the monopsony's labour supply curve shifts to the left.

'Monopsonistic competition' describes this process, but refers to a situation in which each firm employs differentiated labour. New industries have siphoned off the producer's labour force, but the firm still has some degree of monopsony.

As you probably expect, the limiting case is where there is not only competition from other industries shrinking the '*x*'-producer's labour market, but their demand is for exactly the same kind of labour (if you prefer, 'skills') that '*x*' utilizes. This means that the labour supply curve becomes flatter and ultimately, infinitely elastic: the case of perfect competition in the labour market.

It is interesting to note that although the competitive processes in product and factor markets are completely analogous – in the former, structure depends on the substitutability of goods in the eyes of consumers; in the latter it depends on the substitutability of inputs in the eyes of producers – the individual firms may be competing with different groups of firms in respect of each. For example, manufacturers of wood and plastic furniture compete in that product market, but not in the labour market. For the latter industry, chemical manufacturing would be far more important with respect to labour supply conditions.

3 Production and Cost Analysis

Outline

Synopsis

This chapter presents a straightforward analysis of production and cost functions. I begin by assuming that only the input of labour is variable ('short-run' analysis) and derive the total, average and marginal product curves, including a definition of short-run output elasticity relating the latter two measures.

Variable (labour) costs as a function of output are the mirror-image of the total product curve, and I immediately derive the associated average and marginal cost curves, including a measure of short-run cost elasticity. The symmetry with production relationships is apparent.

Introducing fixed, or invariant capital costs I need to introduce several curves: the total cost curve, being the sum of the variable and fixed cost curves; and the average total cost curve, being the sum of the respective average variable and average fixed-cost ('unit overhead') curves. Fortunately, marginal costs are unaffected.

In the long run I assume that the representative firm faces increasing, followed by decreasing, returns to scale or size. I first portray this with a small number of plant sizes, but by allowing capital to be infinitely divisible I construct smooth, U-shaped average and marginal long-run cost curves.

I conclude by examining changes in relative labour and capital costs, drawing inferences regarding the structural composition of output for the economy as a whole (relevant to Macroeconomics).

Introduction

The economic view of the firm is as a *producer* of goods (and services). The production process consists of utilizing *inputs* – which may be owned as in the case of plant and equipment or hired as in the case of labour – to yield a final *output*, which is presumably demanded by ultimate consumers as described previously. The discussion of the firm's production activities will always deal with the 'integrated' firm using primary inputs to produce final output for consumption. It is normally the task of the firm's management to judge not only market demand, but also to operate production as efficiently as possible, in the following sense: *viz.* so as to obtain a given output at the least cost; or equivalently, to obtain the most output for a given cost. As we shall see, this involves two types of 'efficiency': (1) in the technical sense of getting maximum physical output from given input(s); and (2) in an economic sense of finding the least expensive combination of inputs for any given output.

The purpose of this chapter is to examine how this can be done. In particular, there are two kinds of external, or environmental, constraints under which the firm operates. One is the available technology – perhaps one, several or many ways to combine inputs (so-called 'techniques of production') to obtain a given output. The second is the prices of the inputs which are used, and over which the firm may or may not have any influence.

In order to simplify the analysis, I conveniently ignore the many different inputs into the actual production process, and concentrate on just two: (1) labour, which is assumed to be measured in terms of efficiency units (e.g. one hour of professional service equals two hours of semi-skilled labour equals three hours of unskilled labour); and (2) capital, which is physically the plant, machinery and equipment with which labour works. In order to measure this quantity we will assume that it is exactly reflected by its money value. In our tranquil world historic cost, current replacement cost and the market value of the equipment are all equal. If there were divergences, then for present purposes the current cost of replacing physical assets would be the most appropriate money measure. That is, a £20M plant embodies twice the physical capital of a £10m plant, etc.

3.1 The short run

The initial focus will be on the short-run situation, by which we mean that the capital stock is fixed and the quantity of labour is variable (or generally, a period of time during which at least one input cannot be varied).

3.1.1 Production

If the variation in the amount of labour were such that an increase resulted in no change in output, while a decrease resulted in a complete cessation of production, then it is clear that there is absolutely no alternative to the specific technique being used: a certain amount of output requires so much capital and so much labour; more of either does nothing but waste resources, and with less there is no output at all (a so-called 'fixed coefficient' technology).

However, we normally assume – a very important assumption – that over at least some significant range of output the amount of labour can be varied even though the other inputs (capital) are fixed ('variable-coefficient' technology). This can be illustrated (Fig. 3.1a) with the total product (*TP*) curve, where as shown, we

Figures 3.1a and b *TP*, *APL* and *MPL* curves

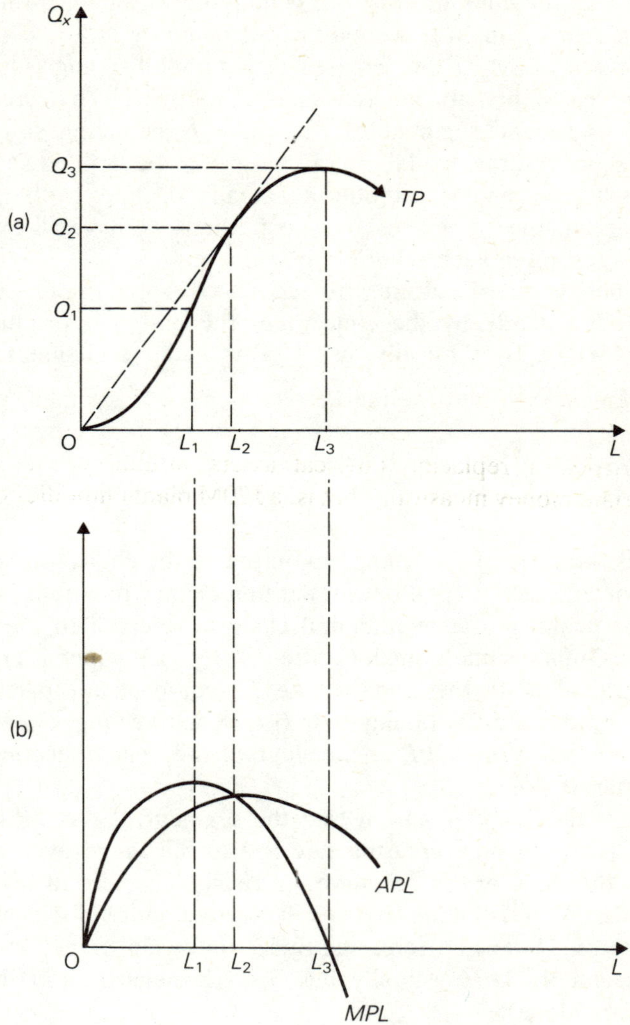

The marginal product of labour (*MPL*) in '*x*' is equal to the value of the slope of the *TP* curve: it is rising from zero to L_1, and falling thereafter. However, average product (*APL*) rises until L_2, at which level the ray from the origin (Fig. 3.1a) is tangent to the *TP* curve: i.e. $APL = MPL$. Beyond L_3 *MPL* is negative (*TP* is actually falling).

assume that the amount of labour is infinitely variable, from zero to any potential quantity we may wish to employ.

The shape of the *TP* curve shows output initially rising as labour input increases, first at an increasing rate, followed by a decreasing rate. This second segment of the curve is depicting so-called 'diminishing returns' (to labour) in a sense to be defined shortly. Eventually, we show that output actually declines with larger labour input: the employees are – as perhaps we have all experienced – getting in each other's way.

The behaviour of output with respect of labour input can be summarized neatly by the concept of the *marginal* product of labour (*MPL*). Symbolically, using 'Δ' to mean 'a change in' we define:

$$MPL = \frac{\Delta Q}{\Delta L}$$

i.e. it is the ratio of the change in output to the change in labour input, or 'the incremental output per unit change in labour input'. Strictly speaking, the incremental changes referred to are conceived as infinitesimally small (written as dQ/dL), which is graphically equivalent to the slope of the *TP* curve at any particular *point*, as indicated. By taking finite (i.e. visible) changes in Q and L we are measuring *MPL* as the slope of the line connecting the two separate points.

Now it should be apparent that the segment of the *TP* curve where it rises at an increasing rate is also the range over which *MPL* – the slope of the *TP* curve – is rising. The second segment shows that *MPL* is falling (but is still positive: more labour means more output, but at a decreasing rate), and when we get into the third segment, *MPL* actually has become negative (*TP* has a downward slope).

Graphically (Fig. 3.1b) *MPL* itself rises and then falls as output increases through the addition of labour.Then it must reach some maximum value, which as shown, coincides with the point where *TP* reaches its steepest slope (a 'point of inflection').

However, the average product of labour (*APL*) – i.e. simply output per labour unit:

$$APL = \frac{Q}{L}$$

behaves slightly differently. Graphically, *APL* is the slope of a line ('ray') from the origin to any particular point on the *TP* curve, as shown.

It can be seen that this slope rises and then falls, but its turning point is different from that of the *MPL* curve: *APL* reaches a maximum at an output level greater than the maximum of *MPL*. The reason is this: although *MPL* is falling beyond its maximum, it is still above *APL*, which by definition averages-in earlier low *MPL* values. Therefore, *APL* is being pulled up because it is averaging-in an *MPL* still greater than the average of all the preceding *MPL* values.

Furthermore, as long as *MPL* exceeds *APL* it must be pulling *APL* up. Conversely, when *MPL* falls below *APL* – it is necessarily declining more rapidly – it must be pulling *APL* down. Therefore, the *MPL* curve must pass through the maximum of the *APL* curve as shown. This is also shown by the fact that at the maximum of *APL*, when the ray from the origin is at its steepest, this ray is just tangent to the *TP* curve. But we already have established that the slope at a point on the *TP* curve is the MPL at that point; so at that point, $MPL = APL$. (You should be able to verify that prior to this $APL < MPL$ and beyond, $APL > MPL$.)

We can define the (short-run) elasticity of output with respect to labour input (ϵ_L) as:

$$\epsilon_L = \frac{\Delta Q/Q}{\Delta L/L}$$

$$= \frac{\Delta Q}{\Delta L} \times \frac{L}{Q}$$

$$= MPL/APL$$

That is, the ratio of the percentage change in output to the percentage change in labour input is simply the ratio of *MPL* to *APL* at any point. From the preceding discussion we can see immediately that: $\epsilon_L > 1$ as *APL* rises, $\epsilon_L = 1$ at *APL*'s maximum, and $\epsilon_L < 1$ as *APL* falls; or, in other words, output with respect to labour input is elastic as long as output-per-labour unit ('average labour productivity') is increasing, unit-elastic at the point of maximum (average) labour productivity, and inelastic when (average) labour productivity is falling.

3.1.2 **Costs**

Variable costs

In the short run, regardless of the level of output, the firm's capital costs are just as fixed as the physical equipment they are paying for. However, the firm's wage bill is a variable cost which does depend on the level of output. What we want to do now is to look at this relationship.

The simplest way to see this is to turn the *TP* curve around, showing the amount of labour input required at each level of output rather than output at each level of labour input. This raises the possibility that firms might use more labour than minimally required for given output, or derive less output than can be maximally obtained from a given labour input. This is the problem of achieving technical efficiency, and we always assume that firms are technically efficient by considering them to be on the *TP* curve rather than below it.

Labour, or variable cost (*VC*), is then nothing more than the required amount of labour (in standard units) times the given wage rate (per standard unit). Symbolically:

$$VC = w \times L$$

where w is the wage rate. If this is taken as a set price by the firm, which presumably is likely to be the case in an economy where labour is mobile and can easily move from low to higher wage sectors (for the contrasting case see the Appendix), the *VC* curve (Fig. 3.2a) will have exactly the same shape as the reflected/rotated *TP* curve. The only difference is that the vertical axis scale is in money units rather than in physical labour units.

Symmetrically with the *TP* curve, the *VC* curve rises, first at a decreasing rate and then at an increasing rate as output rises. Ultimately we show that, although output may decrease, *VC* still continues to rise. As you might expect, these segments correspond to segments of the *TP* curve: the point of inflection on the latter curve, at which MPL reaches its maximum, corresponds precisely to the point on the VC curve where its (point-)slope is at a minimum; and where TP turns down (MPL negative) the *VC* curve bends backwards.

Figures 3.2a and b Short-run cost curves

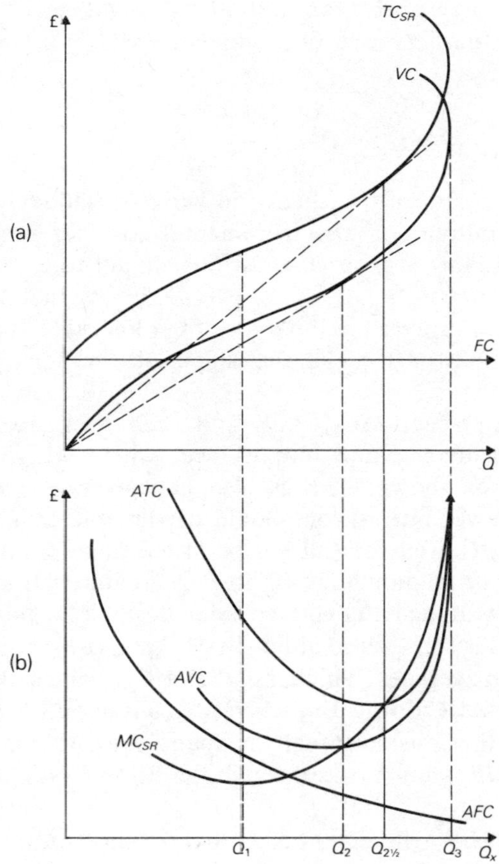

The variable cost (*VC*) curve is an image of the short-run total product (*TP*) curve. The short-run total cost (TC_{SR}) curve is the sum of the variable and fixed cost (*FC*) curves. The average fixed cost (*AFC*) curve is a rectangular hyperbola, showing the progressive spreading of overheads. The average variable cost (*AVC*) curve is U-shaped due to the assumed reverse-S shape of the *VC* curve, and the average total cost (*ATC*) curve is the vertical sum of the *AVC* and *AFC* curves. The short-run marginal cost (MC_{SR}) curve graphs the value of the slope of the *TC* curve, and passes through the minimum of both the *AVC* and *ATC* curves. This is also shown by the tangency of the rays from the origin in Fig. 3.2b to the *VC* and TC_{SR} curves, respectively.

In order to give precision to this correspondence, we define the (short-run) marginal cost of production (MC_{SR}) as:

$$MC_{SR} = \frac{\Delta VC}{\Delta Q}$$

i.e. it is the ratio of the change in variable (labour) costs to the change in output, or 'the incremental cost per unit change in output'. (Again, in a strict sense this should refer to tiny increments in Q and VC – i.e. $MC_{SR} = dVC/dQ$ – so that MC_{SR} can be graphically interpreted as the slope of the VC curve at a point. Our definition takes MC_{SR} as the slope of the line joining two separated points.)

As we can see, MC_{SR} falls and then rises, reaching some minimum value, at the output level where MPL reaches its maximum, as shown. This is also how average variable costs (AVC) behave, but as you should expect, the minimum of the AVC and MC_{SR} curves will not be at the same point. In fact, as illustrated the minimum AVC is at a greater output level than min MC_{SR} with the latter curve passing through the min AVC from below. This is so because although MC_{SR} is rising it is still below AVC, which averages-in higher earlier MC_{SR} values; therefore it is still pulling AVC down. But when MC_{SR} is above AVC – since it rises faster this must eventually happen – AVC is being pulled up; therefore MC_{SR} must pass through the turning point of the AVC curve.

Our final short-run definition is that of (short-run) variable cost elasticity; *viz*:

$$\begin{aligned} \nu_{SR} &= \frac{\Delta VC/VC}{\Delta Q/Q} \\ &= \frac{\Delta VC}{\Delta Q} \times \frac{\Delta Q}{VC} \\ &= MC_{SR}/AVC \end{aligned}$$

That is, the ratio of the percentage change in variable costs to the percentage change in output (in the short run) is equal to the ratio of short-run marginal cost to average variable costs. Hence, you should be able to verify that short-run costs are inelastic as average variable costs are falling, unit-elastic at the minimum of AVC, and elastic as AVC rises (and conversely for the elasticity of output with respect to short-run costs). Note that:

$$AVC = \frac{VC}{Q} = \frac{w \times L}{Q} = w/APL$$

Thus, when AVC is at its minimum, for a given w, APL is at its maximum. In other words, not only do min MC_{SR} and max MPL occur at the same output; min AVC and max APL also coincide, but at a higher level of output. There is a complete symmetry of short-run production and cost structure.

Fixed and total costs

Recall that in the short run there are capital costs to be met regardless of the level of output, hence they are treated as fixed costs. In reality, a portion of these costs would correspond to physical depreciation of the capital stock ('plant'), but we will ignore this and treat capital goods as though they never wear out. However, quite apart from depreciation the investment in physical plant (in principle valued at replacement cost) represents a use of funds (i.e. financial capital) that could have been invested in other activities. Indeed, if the firm hires capital, by means of borrowing funds, this foregoing of alternative investments is explicitly embodied in the contractual obligation to pay interest. 'The' rate of interest – we ignore the spread due to risk factors, etc. – is the going rate of return that those funds could have earned elsewhere; hence it is necessary to pay (at least) that much to obtain capital services. This is completely analogous to the situation with respect to labour services, where again the firm needs to meet the going wage rate in order to hire labour.

The conclusion that the cost of capital is in each production period the rate of interest times the cost of the capital stock (equals the value of the investment in money terms) is valid even when the firm owns the capital. That is, it makes no difference whether the firm raises funds from borrowing or from the issue of shares. Although there is no contractual obligation to pay dividends to shareholders such that the 'yield' on shares is equal to the rate of interest, unless the foregone or *opportunity cost* of those funds is explicitly recognized the cost picture is distorted. The simple idea is that those capital resources could have earned the going rate of interest elsewhere, and it is that rate – in the absence of a specific contract – that should be used as a charge against the firm. Much the same argument applies to owner–managers. Although labour is directly provided by owners, so there is no contractual obligation concerning their payment, in order to assess the cost of those resources to the firm it should charge the going wage rate: the opportunity cost of labour (per unit).

Having taken into account all cost factors, the short-run total cost curve (TC_{SR}) is simply the vertical sum of the *VC* and *FC* (fixed cost) curves as shown (Fig. 3.2a). Note that the slope of the TC_{SR} curve at any level of output is the same as the slope of the *VC* curve, since the slope of the *FC* curve is zero. This means that when we refer to marginal cost (MC_{SR}) it makes no difference whether we are referring in the strictly correct sense to the slope of the TC_{SR} curve or to the slope of the VC curve, since:

$$MC_{SR} = \frac{\Delta TC_{SR}}{\Delta Q} = \frac{\Delta VC}{\Delta Q}$$

However, we can distinguish different average cost curves. We have already looked at AVC (average variable costs). The behaviour of average fixed costs is shown by the AFC curve (Fig. 3.2b). This curve is a rectangular hyperbola, indicating that for small output levels the fixed cost per unit ('unit overheads') is very high, whereas for large outputs the average fixed cost is approaching zero. The shape of the curve is such that the area under it corresponding to any combination of output (Q) and *AFC* levels is constant – i.e.:

$$\begin{aligned} FC &= Q \times AFC \\ &= Q \times \frac{FC}{Q} \end{aligned}$$

Average total costs (*ATC*) are defined as:

$$\begin{aligned} ATC &= AVC + AFC \\ \frac{TC_{SR}}{Q} &= \frac{VC}{Q} + \frac{FC}{Q} \end{aligned}$$

Graphically, the ATC curve is the vertical sum of the AVC and AFC curves. In the lower ranges of output its behaviour is dominated by the behaviour of average fixed costs, and ATC therefore declines rapidly as output increases. But eventually, as AFC becomes relatively small, ATC begins to reflect the behaviour of the AVC curve. In fact, as shown the ATC curve becomes *asymptotic* to the AVC curve (meaning that it approaches it as a boundary but only reaches it infinitely far out; e.g. the AFC curve is asymptotic to the horizontal axis). Thus, we have the typical U-shaped AVC, ATC and MC_{SR} curves as shown. Note that MC_{SR} passes through the minima of both AVC and ATC curves. This latter intersection occurs because although MC_{SR} is rising – and is already pulling AVC up – it is still below ATC, hence is pulling ATC down. When MC_{SR} is above ATC it will be pulling ATC up, so must pass through its minimum.

3.2 The long run

In the long run (all inputs variable), the firm faces the more complex decision of how to combine labour and capital in order to achieve the least cost for any given level of output. For the short-run case this problem of economic efficiency clearly did not arise; instead, the firm had 'only' to achieve technical efficiency by getting as much out of its labour input as was physically possible (i.e. it should be using up-to-date 'best-practice' methods of operation). Now the problem is widened: management has to choose between alternative 'best-practice' techniques embodying different combinations of inputs; and these decisions depend crucially on relative input prices, as we shall see.

3.2.1 Production and costs

First, consider the production possibilities when the capital stock is also allowed to vary. As illustrated (Fig. 3.3a), a larger 'quantity of capital' (i.e. worth more in terms of money cost) yields a higher level of output at every level of labour input – an upward shift of the TP curve. Alternatively, we can look at this as showing that any given level of output can be obtained using less labour with more capital. This is an illustration of the principle of substitutability between inputs. Although we only show four sizes of capital stock or 'plant', we can imagine that if capital were infinitely divisible – like labour is assumed to be – there would be an infinite number of *TP* curves, each just fractionally above its predecessor. In such a case, there would be an *infinite* number of combinations of capital and labour which might be chosen. Our question is: 'how does the firm choose which combination to use?'

Obviously the firm chooses the cheapest technique to produce any given output, which is a problem of 'economic efficiency'. Consider the effect of the increased capital stock – an upward shift of the *TP* curve – on the *VC* curve (Fig. 3.3b). You should be able to verify that the latter curve shifts downwards by the same proportion that TP shifts upwards. So variable – or as we shall now call them explicitly – labour costs decrease. But the larger capital stock is more costly, hence increases fixed – or as we now call it explicitly – capital costs. Thus, in terms of the short-run cost curves, the VC curve shifts downwards whilst the *FC* curve shifts upwards. What is the net effect on *TC* as we increase the quantity of capital?

As we have shown it (Fig. 3.4a) for low levels of output, the smallest plant has the lowest total costs, but is overtaken – at the first 'switch-point' – by a larger plant. This plant has lowest costs over the middle range of output levels, but is eventually overtaken – at the second switch-point – by a still larger plant, etc. Equivalently, we can say that average total costs are lowest for the three plants over their respective output ranges. But are the *ATC* curves successively higher or lower or at the same level? This is in reality an empirical matter, but we typically assume that initially, the minimum point of the *ATC* curve occurs not only at a higher output level for larger plants, but also at a lower cost level, as shown (Fig. 3.4b). However, eventually these economies of scale (size) are exhausted and the firm encounters diseconomies of scale, illustrated by the fact that the minimum level of successive *ATC* curves is rising. To repeat the point, there is no *a priori* reason why min *ATC* could not continuously rise; what we have assumed here corresponds to the case of a U-shaped short-run *AVC* curve. Falling *AVC* corresponds to a short-run output elasticity greater than one, or 'increasing returns to labour', and vice-versa for rising *AVC*. In the long-run case we make the same kind of assumption with respect to returns to plant size.

The long-run average cost curve (simply '*AC*') is the lower boundary of the *ATC* curves. This shows the cheapest way to produce any given level of output. With four specific plant sizes

Figures 3.3a and b Effects of variations in capital on output and costs

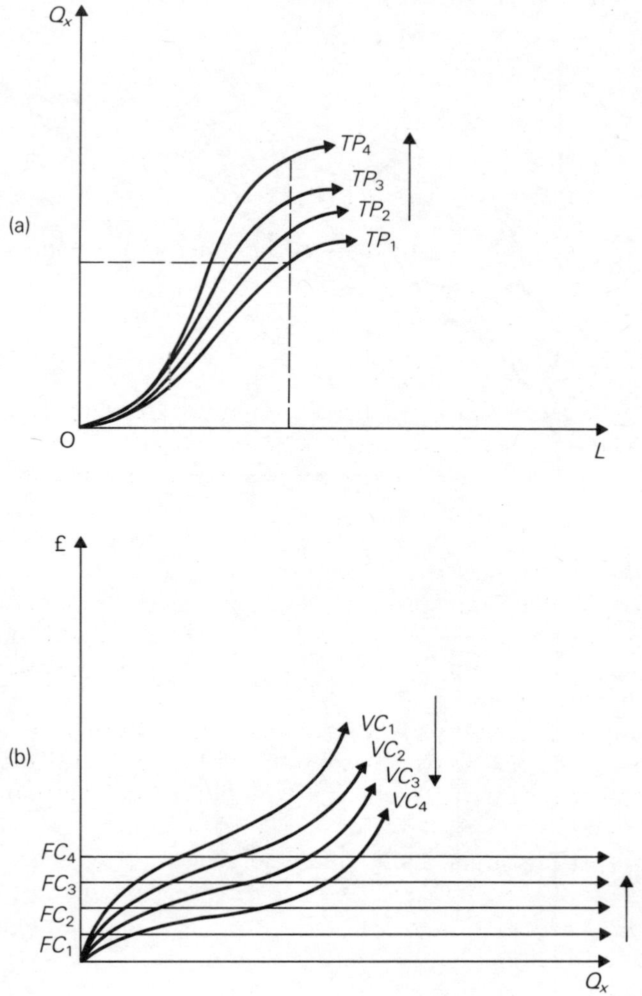

As the capital stock (size of plant) increases (from K=1 to 4), the *TP* curves shift upwards: (a) more output for any given labour input; or equivalently, (b) less labour input for any given output. As *TP* shifts up, *VC* shifts down: lower labour costs for any given output (as per (b) above); but as *K* increases, fixed (capital) cost increases.

Figures 3.4a and b Long-run total and average cost curves

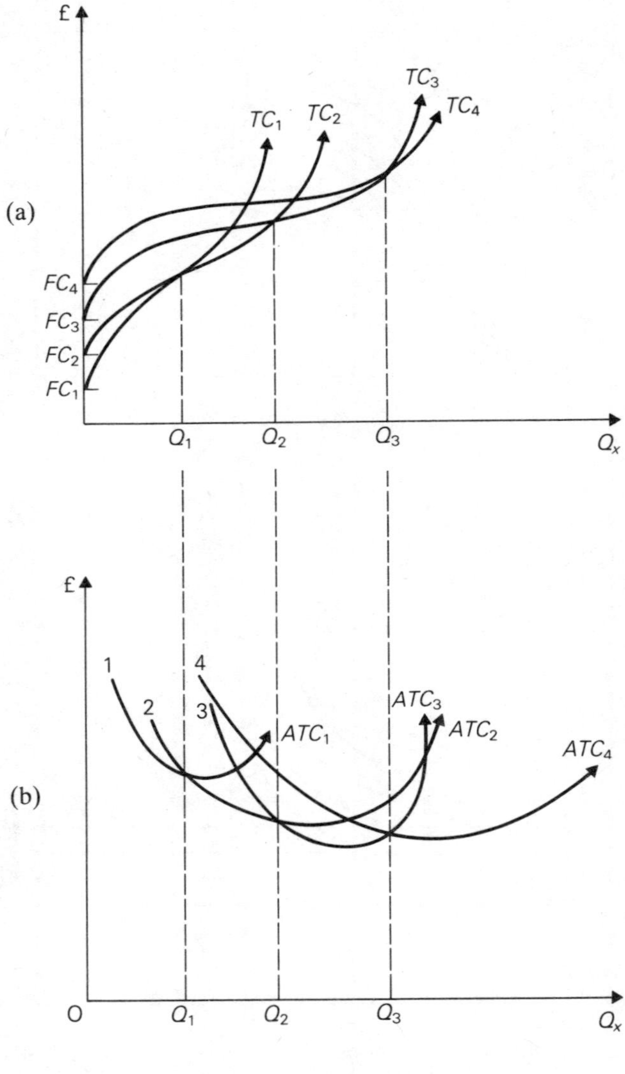

The long-run (economically efficient, or least-cost) total cost curve is the lower boundary of the 'spliced' short-run *TC* curves. Hence, plant size '1' has lowest costs up to Q_1, plant '2' from Q_1 to Q_2, etc.

there are four ways to produce any of these given output levels, as shown, ranging from the technique with relatively little capital and relatively more labour (the most labour-intensive technique) to that with relatively little labour and relatively large capital input (the most capital-intensive – or least labour-intensive – technique). At the given output level the average costs of production are represented by the respective *ATC* values. The lowest *ATC* is the chosen technique, since all others have higher costs.

The long-run marginal cost (simply '*MC*') curve is more peculiar. Over the range in which the smallest plant would be chosen the MC_{SR} curve associated with that plant applies. At the switch-point where the next largest plant would be used, the relevant curve is its MC_{SR}, etc. But these short-run MC_{SR} curves represent the marginal labour cost: that is, at any given output, the applicable MC_{SR} curve shows the incremental cost of another unit of output when only labour input is increased. Apparently, any incremental capital cost is being neglected, but how do we deal with this?

One answer is to add, at the switch-point, the whole of the extra capital investment cost. For instance, the marginal cost of the very first unit of output is the MC_{SR} at its beginning plus the amount of the investment – the cost of building the plant. The marginal cost of the second unit, however, is simply the MC_{SR} at that point. When the firm switches to the next-sized plant the marginal cost of the first unit after the switch is the $\mathrm{MC_{SR}}$ of the second plant at this point plus the additional investment cost of building the second plant; i.e. its cost less the cost of building the first plant. However, the marginal cost of the second unit produced by the second plant is just the MC_{SR} appropriate to that plant.

Fortunately this problem disappears with the extension to infinite capital divisibility. Imagine now that the *ATC* curves are extremely close (Fig. 3.5). For one thing, the *AC* boundary (or as it is usually called the 'envelope') curve becomes a smooth, elongated U-shaped curve as shown. For another, the marginal capital cost involved in moving from one level of output to the next (i.e. producing one more unit) is now itself infinitesimal and can be neglected. Therefore, the long-run *MC* curve corresponding to this limiting case is also a smooth, U-shaped curve passing through the minimum of the long-run *AC* curve for the same reason as previously discussed. (Notice the similarity with the short-run MC_{SR} and *AVC* curves.)

Figure 3.5 Long-run *AC* and *MC* curves

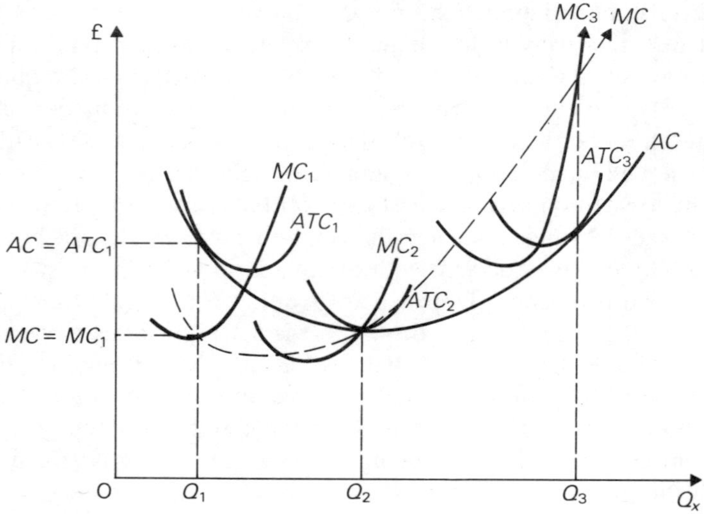

To produce Q_1 the firm uses plant '1', even though this is *not* the lowest unit-cost level obtainable with that plant; but it is the cheapest way to produce Q_1. For Q_2 and Q_3 plants '2' and '3' are the best choices (remember: plant size is now infinitely divisible). The long-run *MC* curve is the locus of the short-run *MC* levels (e.g. MC_1) taken at each level of output.

In this limiting case of infinite capital divisibility there is an infinite number of ways of producing any given output, each associated with a different size of plant ('quantity of capital'); and correspondingly, a different quantity of labour. Each technique has a different cost, and there will be one amongst them that has the lowest cost. This is represented by a single point on the *AC* curve at that given level of output; but it is important to realize that these boundary points are in general not at the minimum of their respective *ATC* curves. For example, taking a point on the declining part of the *AC* curve (economies of scale) we know that this is the cheapest way to produce that particular level of output. But this point also lies on the declining portion of the *ATC* curve associated with that particular plant size. That is, the firm could reduce its average total costs in the short run by increasing output. However, if this increase in output were a permanent – i.e. long-run – decision, the firm would not be operating with that size of plant. It would build a larger plant, and operate at the point on that plant's *ATC* curve coinciding with the boundary of the long-run *AC* curve as shown. In fact, the minimum of any *ATC* curve coincides with a point on the boundary only at the minimum of the *AC* curve itself. Beyond that, points on the *AC* curve will also lie on the rising portion of the associated *ATC* curves.

This means that passing through the minimum of the *AC* curve there are four curves: the *AC* curve itself, the minimum of the lowest *ATC* curve, the short-run MC_{SR} curve, and the long-run *MC* curve. As you can see, the long-run *MC* is flatter than the MC_{SR} curve. Diagrammatically this relationship can be demonstrated by the fact that the *MC* curve is nothing more than the locus of short-run MC_{SR} values at the output levels at which their particular associated plant is chosen. If, starting at any given level of output, the firm is constrained to expand its production by only increasing its labour input (i.e. moving up along its MC_{SR} curve), the rise in costs is comparatively rapid. On the other hand, if it is allowed to expand its plant as it chooses, as well as its labour input, the rise in costs for the given increase in output will be less. Hence, at any level of output the *MC* (long-run) the curve will be more elastic than the MC_{SR} curve at that point.

We define the long-run cost elasticity as:

$$\nu = \frac{\Delta TC/TC}{\Delta Q/Q}$$

$$= \frac{\Delta TC}{\Delta Q} \times \frac{Q}{TC}$$

$$= MC/AC$$

analogously to our short-run variable cost elasticity definition. Total costs (*TC*) include both labour and capital costs and, as you might expect, we see that cost is inelastic with respect to output as long as there are economies of scale (falling *AC*), unit-elastic at the minimum of the *AC* curve (the long-run minimum-cost point), and elastic if there are diseconomies of scale (rising *AC*). Incidentally, you may have inferred – correctly – that at the minimum point there are instantaneous constant economies of size, or as it is often called, 'constant returns to scale.'

3.2.2 **Changes in technology and input prices**

Technical changes

It was stated early in this chapter that the firm's cost structure was governed by technology and input prices. In order to see this more clearly, consider the effects of a technical improvement that augments labour productivity. Diagrammatically, at any given size of plant the *TP* curve shifts upwards, as though the capital stock had been increased. Therefore, with the same *FC* curve, the downward shift in the VC curve unambiguously shifts the TC_{SR} curve downwards too. This effect is also illustrated by the downward shift in the *AVC, ATC* and MC_{SR} curves (but not the *AFC* curve). The exact impact on *ATC* depends on the proportions of labour and capital in total cost. With a small plant and low capital costs the shift in *AVC* is almost fully reflected in a proportionate shift in *ATC*; but with a large plant we can see that, proportionately, *ATC* shifts relatively less.

Looking at the long-run cost picture in Fig. 3.6, where we have four distinct plant sizes for convenience, this means that the *ATC* curves of smaller plants shift proportionately *more* than *ATC* curves of larger plants. Therefore, as shown, the switch-points occur at higher levels of output. Consequently, there is a tendency to adopt more labour-intensive techniques of production: specifically, if the firm were operating inside any of the bands of output across which the switch-point moved, the firm would choose a smaller plant and correspondingly more labour input – than before the improvement in labour productivity had occurred.

Although we do not illustrate them, it is fairly easy to imagine alternative cases where:

1. capital's productivity is augmented, shifting the *ATC* curves of larger plants having relatively higher capital costs down proportionately more than smaller plants. Hence, creating an incentive to substitute more capital for labour; and
2. productivity of both inputs is equally affected (e.g. improved),

Figure 3.6 Effects of changes in costs on techniques of production

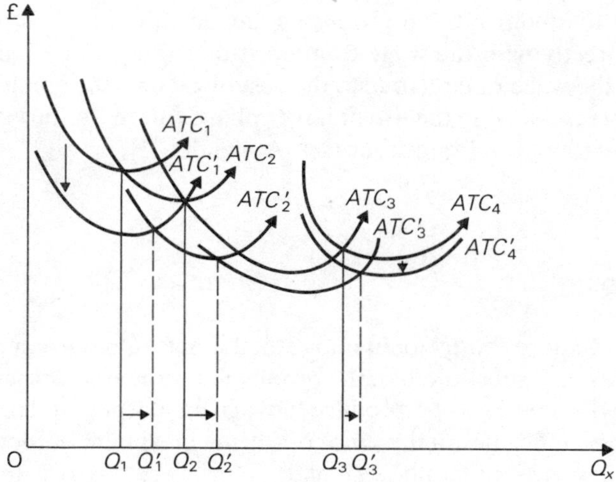

As the wage rate falls, the downward shift of *ATC* is proportionately greater for more labour-intensive techniques (smaller plants). This shifts the 'switch-points', at which the firm switches from one plant to another, to the right: diminishing capital intensivity (or equivalently, increasing labour intensivity).

so all *ATC* curves shift downwards by the same percent (proportion). Hence, no change in capital-labour ratios. ("Hicks-neutral" technical progress).

Price changes

What we have just described for technical progress can be identically attributed to changes in input prices. For example, suppose the wage rate falls whilst the interest rate remains unchanged. This shifts the VC curve downwards but not the *FC* curve, hence *ATC* falls according to the proportion of total cost accounted for by labour costs. Hence smaller, more labour-intensive plants have proportionately greater shifts in *ATC*, and therefore labour tends to be substituted for capital.

In short, extending our conclusions to the limiting case of infinite input divisibility we can say that the firm's physical capital-to-labour ratio in producing any given level of output will vary directly with the wage-to-interest-rate ratio. For example, a rise in the wage rate relative to the cost of capital (the going rate of interest) will lead to the use of larger plants (more capital) and less labour at any level of output (see Appendix 3B).

Summary

Output requires both labour and capital inputs. On the assumption that these are substitutable, the problem of economic efficiency (in production) is how to produce any given output at least cost (technical efficiency in the sense of getting maximum output out of given inputs is generally assumed). However, this is a long-run problem in that it assumes complete input variability. In the short run the firm's capital stock is fixed and only labour input is variable.

In this context we identify total, average and marginal products (for labour). Then, taking costs per unit of labour – the wage rate – as constant, we can immediately derive variable, average variable and marginal (variable) cost curves symmetric with the product curves. The latter are typically U-shaped, with the MC_{SR} curve passing through the minimum of the *AVC* curve. Adding the fixed (capital) cost curve, we then identify total, average total and average fixed cost curves; marginal costs are unaffected (by definition).

In the long run, as the capital stock varies – say, increases (equivalent to a greater money cost) – the capital ('fixed') cost component increases, but the labour ('variable') cost component decreases for any given level of output. We usually assume that at lower levels of output the latter outweighs the former effect, and vice-versa at higher outputs. These correspond to 'increasing' and 'decreasing' returns to scale, or sizes, as illustrated by a U-shaped long-run average cost curve. With infinitely divisible capital this is the smooth envelope of an infinite number of short-run *ATC* curves (with the long-run *MC* curve becoming a neat U-shaped curve as well, passing through the minimum of the *AC* curve).

Finally, we can demonstrate the nature of input substitution in response to either technological or input-price variations.

Appendix 3A Marginal labour cost (monopsony)

In deriving the *VC* curve we took the wage rate to be constant. Suppose, however, that labour is increasingly expensive as shown by an upward-sloping labour supply curve to the firm. (We are not at present concerned with how this comes about.)

Now as the firm hires more labour it must pay a higher wage to all its workers, implying that marginal labour cost (*MLC*) – the change in total labour costs per unit of labour – increases even more rapidly. The reason is that the firm pays the higher wage not only to the additional workers, but also adjusts all other workers' wages – the labour it could have hired at a lower wage – upwards. Symbolically,

$$MLC = \frac{\Delta(w \times L)}{\Delta L} = w + L\,\frac{\Delta W}{\Delta L}$$

i.e. it is equal to the wage rate plus the adjustment to wages of 'infra-marginal' workers. Alternatively, you may think of it as:

$$MLC = w \times \left(1 + \frac{1}{E_L}\right)$$

where E_L is the elasticity of the labour supply curve (positive). Note that if it is infinite the labour supply curve is a horizontal line at the level w: the firm effectively can hire as much labour as it likes at the going wage rate (perfect competition in the labour market).

The effect of this on the VC curve is illustrated by its progressive steepening compared to the fixed-wage case. Earlier we found that:

$$MC_{SR} = \frac{w}{MPL}$$

that is, the slope of the *VC* curve was equal to the wage rate divided by labour's marginal product. In this more complex case we find that:

$$MC_{SR} = \frac{MLC}{MPL}$$

As *MPL* declines with additional labour input, *MLC* is rising, hence MC_{SR} is rising doubly fast.

Appendix 3B Isoquant analysis

Techniques of production can be cast in the general form of the convex-to-the-origin 'isoquant map' shown in Fig. 3B.1. Along any given isoquant (e.g. Q_0) the same level of output can be achieved by any of an infinite number of input (L, K) combinations. (For a finite number of techniques the isoquant would be faceted instead of smooth, and in the limiting case of non-substitutability of inputs it would be right-angled.)

The convexity of the isoquants reflects the assumption of a diminishing marginal rate of substitution in production, similar to the diminishing m.r.s. in consumption assumed for indifference curves. That is, if the firm is initially using a highly capital-intensive technique (point I_A), the same output can be maintained by substituting a little labour which has a high marginal productivity, for a substantial amount of capital having low marginal productivity. As substitution progresses, however, the trade-off becomes increasingly less favourable to labour, until at point I_B it would require a lot of labour to compensate for a small decrease in the quantity of capital.

Assuming that the firm initially has a given *cost* constraint (C_0), the amounts of L and K that it can obtain are shown by the 'budget' line, representing the condition:

$$C_0 = w \times L + r \times K$$

Hence, for given wage (w) and interest (r) rates there will exist a point of tangency between this contraint and an isoquant. This represents the combination of inputs ('technique of production') that yields the greatest output for the given cost: higher output levels cost too much, and any other affordable output is lower than at I_0. (Alternatively, I_0 represents the least-cost way of achieving a given output of Q_0.)

Now, as C_0 changes the budget line, or cost constraint, is shifting in a parallel fashion, tracing a series of economically efficient – in the aforementioned sense of minimum cost – input levels. The locus of these chosen points is called the firm's

Figure 3B.1 The isoquant map and the expansion path

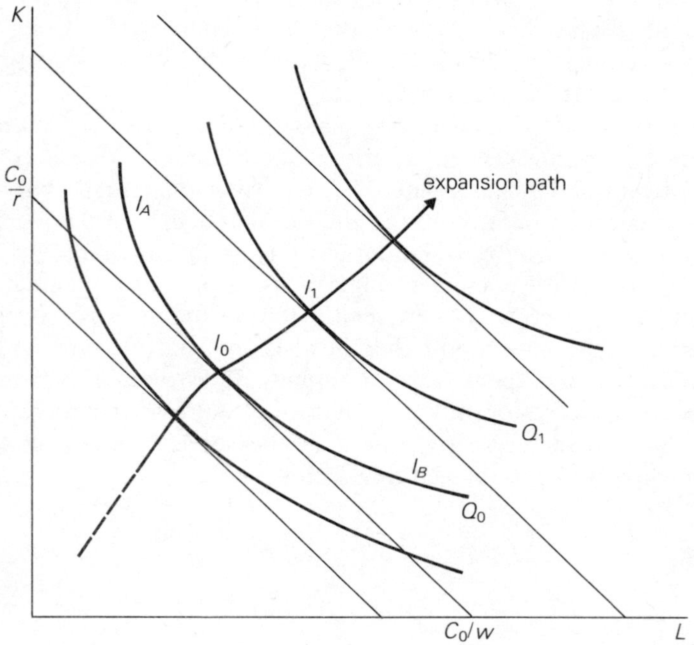

A given level of output (e.g. Q_0 or Q_1) can be produced with any of an infinite number of combinations of substitutable capital (K) and labour (L). For a given cost (e.g. C_0) the maximum output obtainable is found at the tangency of the constraint line (having slope equal to $-w/r$: verify this) with an isoquant (e.g. at I_0). As the level of cost varies – with input prices constant – the locus of the maximum output points is called the 'expansion path'.

'expansion path'. We can picture this literally as a path up a hill, altitude representing level of output.

An interesting feature of this approach is that the short run is depicted by taking a slice through the hill at a given K. The resulting cross-section has the shape assumed for the short-run total product ('*TP*') curve. Of course, if the ratio of w to r (the 'wage-rental ratio', r being identical to the rental rate per unit of capital under the assumption of a unit price for capital) changes, the constraint line swings around and thus alters the direction of this path. Typically, we expect that a higher w/r ratio (steeper constraint lines) increases the capital intensivity of production (higher K/L ratio); and vice-versa.

This has some very interesting real-world implications. Consider, for example, an economy with a labour-intensive (e.g. 'service') sector and a capital-intensive (e.g. 'manufacturing') sector. If wage rates rose relative to the cost per unit of capital this would lead to an increase in capital-intensity (capital–labour ratios) of both sectors (with manufacturing always assumed to maintain a higher ratio of K to L). In reality this might mean a rise in unemployment, but suppose that the constant available supplies of both capital and labour are eventually redistributed between sectors so as to restore full employment. You might try to verify that this will mean an expansion of the service sector, and a contraction of the manufacturing sector.

4 Output and Price Decisions

Outline

Synopsis

This chapter looks at the decisions of firms regarding price and output levels. The initial assumption is that the firm tries to maximize its profit, and on the assumption that its revenue and cost structure is stable I derive the 'MR=MC' rule, including the special cases of perfectly competitive and oligopolistic market structures. Extensions to joint production and price discrimination are discussed to provide more insight into the optimizing process.

The subject of profitability leads naturally to the consideration of competition. If there are no barriers to entry, I conclude that in the long run, profits will be driven down to zero. For imperfectly competitive firms this will mean price in excess of marginal cost; but for perfectly competitive firms this equivalence allows the derivation of an aggregate, or market supply curve to match the market demand curve, and thus demonstrates how competitive prices are determined. I also show that in the short run competitive firms may rationally choose to operate at a loss.

The next section briefly examines some alternatives to profit-maximizing behaviour, which may arise because of 'slackness' in competition. As opposed to several *optimizing* variants, I consider the possibility that firms in effect *satisfice*.

Finally, I return to consider profit maximization in a broader sense: if firms succeed in exploiting their profit-maximizing potential, this will attract entry such that this potential is severely diminished or eliminated. Therefore, firms may have as their main aim the maintenance of barriers to entry. This is a complex topic, and I introduce a simple 'limit-pricing' model to illustrate the general nature of this collusive process.

Introduction

Having investigated the relationship of total costs to output (the *TC* curve) and of total revenue to output (the *TR* curve) we are now able to consider the firm's output and price decisions. For this purpose one of our most important constructs is the *profit curve*, showing the level of profits (*H*) at each level of output. As should be apparent, diagrammatically this *H*-curve is tracing out the vertical difference between the *TR* and *TC* curves (Fig. 4.1a), since we define[1]:

Figures 4.1a and b Alternative representations of costs, revenues and profits for a monopolistic firm

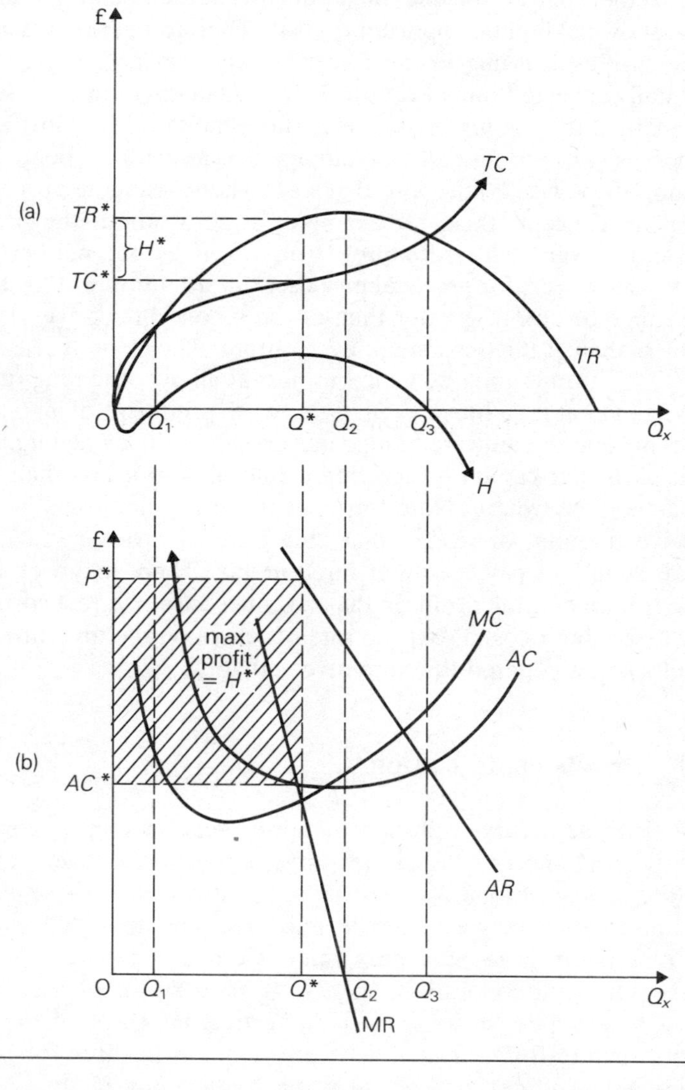

Costs, revenues and profit can all be shown as distances (Fig. 4.1a) or areas (Fig. 4.1b). At the break-even levels of output Q_1 and Q_3, the *AR* curve intersects the *AC* curve. In between, net margins ($P-AC$) are positive, and profit is at its maximum at Q^* (where $MR = MC$).

$$H = TR - TC$$

Remember that *TC* includes all input costs at their actual, or in the case of owned inputs, opportunity costs. Therefore, *H* represents a pure surplus accruing to the firm's owners over and above their normally expected rate of return. If $H = 0$, all inputs are in a sense receiving their 'going' rates, including capital. For illustrative purposes we are initially assuming a firm with a degree of monopoly power. Notice also that we are here assuming profit as a long-run concept; thus, for example, at zero output the firm is 'breaking even' with zero profit (no revenue, but neither any costs!) However, for practical purposes our attention will focus on the range of output greater than at the second break-even level, but less than at the third break-even output. The obvious reason is that if the firm is going to be in business at all over the long run, it will need to at least break even. Otherwise, producing at an output level outside the indicated range must result in the owned input(s) – in particular capital – receiving a rate of return less than that obtainable elsewhere. Note this does not mean the firm's owners receive nothing, or worse, that they have to provide still more funds simply to pay the other hired inputs. There may well be a positive 'accounting profit' in that revenues exceed direct costs (in our case labour costs), but the rate of return on the investment is insufficient compared to alternative activities.

4.1 **Profit-maximization**

A look at the *H* curve will show that profit reaches some maximum between the lower and upper (positive-output) break-even points. In fact, this must logically be so since profit is zero at these points but positive in between, hence must rise and then fall with a 'turning point' at its maximum value. Compare this with the *TR* curve for a monopolistic firm. *TR* is zero at some price high enough to wipe out demand – the vertical intercept of the *AR* curve – and also zero at a zero price, but is positive for some intermediate prices, and so must reach maximum in this range. Intuitively, it would seem reasonable to suppose that firms would aim to achieve precisely this objective, and indeed most of the analytical models in Economics assume this to be the case.

Just how a firm reaches this profit maximum is arguable. For instance, we might suppose that it learns by trial-and-error, eventually settling at a point where it knows from experience that either a rise or fall in price seems to reduce its profits. On the other hand, we can summarize this same outcome much more succinctly, in a form enabling a firm to directly achieve maximum profit once the relevant information is known. This analytical approach conceptualizes a particular trial-and-error process: start the firm at its lower break-even output and increase output marginally (i.e. by one unit). If revenue increases more than cost increases, profit increases. But this condition can be re-stated in a form which is already familiar: increase output (accomplished in this example by lowering price) in order to increase profit as long as:

$$MR > MC$$

Diagrammatically this means that if the slope of the *TR* curve exceeds the slope of the *TC* curve at the initial output level, TR is rising faster than *TC*, so *H* is increasing (see Figs 4.1a,b).

4.1.1 **General rule**

Following this procedural rule, the firm will eventually arrive at a point where the slopes are equal (since *TC* is increasing at an increasing rate and *TR* is also increasing, but at a decreasing rate; i.e. *MC* is increasing and *MR* is decreasing). This is the profit maximum, which is characterized by the condition:

$$MR = MC$$

To fully understand this, consider a slight increase in output beyond this level, so $MR < MC$. This means that over this (small) range, costs have risen faster than revenue, hence profit has decreased, even though it may remain positive.

The profit-maximization rule that output should be where marginal revenue equals marginal cost can be implemented directly, since not only should the firm have a fairly good idea of its marginal costs of production, but of its own-price elasticity of demand as well. This elasticity information can be translated into marginal revenue according to our earlier formula:

$$MR = P\,(1 + 1/E)$$

4.1.2 **Perfect competition**

For a perfectly competitive firm, with $E = (-)\ \infty$ we know that $MR = P$. This reduces the profit-maximizing rule to the simpler, special case:

$$(MR = AR =)P = MC$$

i.e. for a price-taking firm output should be determined at a level where marginal costs are just equal to the given product price. Diagrammatically, this can be illustrated in two ways. First, as before we can simply observe that the height of the *H* curve is at its maximum where the *TC* curve is parallel to the *TR* curve, which is itself now a straight line (Fig. 4.2a) with constant slope equal to *P*. Second, we can superimpose the graphs of the *AR* (and *MR*) curves and the *AC* and *MC* curves as shown (Fig. 4.2b). The same profit-maximizing output shown in the first diagram is shown in the second as the point of intersection of the *MR* and *MC* curves. The chief differences between the two presentations is that costs, revenue and profit are shown in the former diagram as vertical distances. In the latter diagram they are shown as areas: *TR* is the area under the AR curve at *Q, TC* the rectangular area under the *AC* curve corresponding to *Q* and associated *AC*, and profit, *H*, is the difference between the two. In this form of presentation it is not immediately obvious that this profit rectangle is the largest possible, yet that is indeed true by virtue of the fact that *Q* is determined where $P = MC$. Any other output must yield a smaller profit area.

Going back to the more general case of a monopolistic firm, we need to distinguish the *AR* and *MR* curves, since *MR* is less than price as we demonstrated earlier. In this case (Fig. 4.1b) *Q* occurs at the intersection of the *MR* and *MC* curves, but price – that is, average revenue – is read off the *AR* curve. Therefore, the *TR* area is the rectangle corresponding to *Q* and *P, TC* is the area corresponding to *Q* and *AC*, and *H* is the difference between these two areas.

Figures 4.2a and b Alternative representations of costs, revenues and profits (or loss) for a perfectly competitive firm

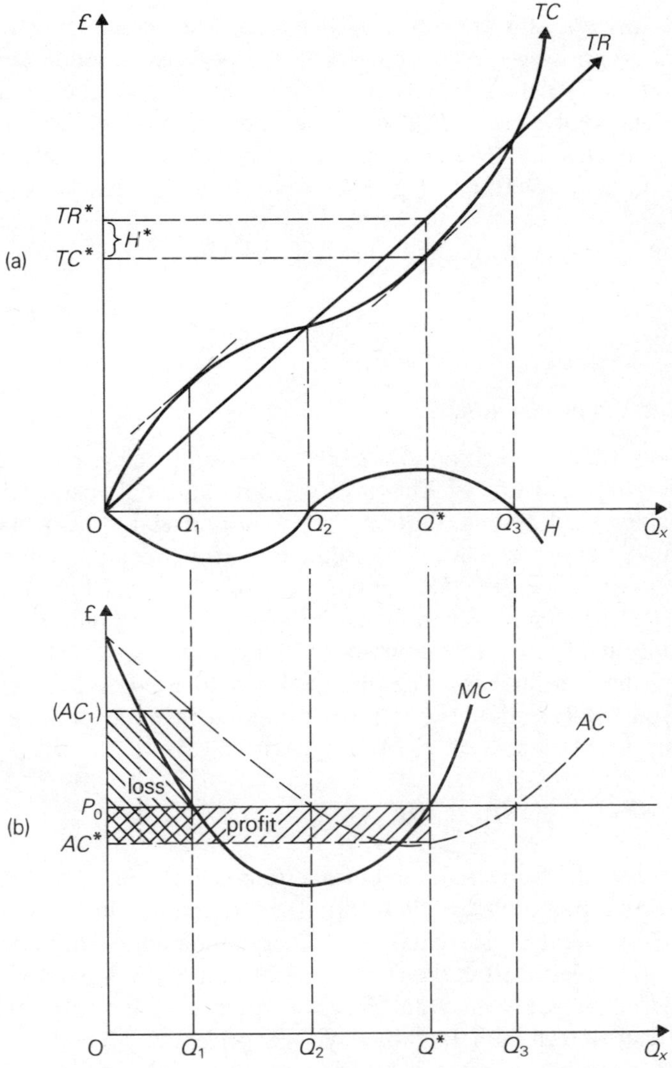

These diagrams show costs, revenues and profits both as distances and as areas for the perfectly competitive firm. Note that although $MC = MR$ at Q_1 as well as at Q^*, the former corresponds to a profit minimum (i.e. a maximum loss).

4.1.3 **Oligopoly**

For an oligopolist this profit-maximizing decision can be illustrated by superimposing the cost curves on the peculiar revenue curves (Figs 2.4a,b) which I leave as an exercise. There are no new concepts involved here, but note the interesting possibility that if *MC* intersects the *MR* curve at its point of discontinuity below the 'kink' in the *AR* curve in Fig. 2.4a, shifts in the *MC* curve, say as a result of changes in input costs, might have no effect on price or output (i.e. it stays at *Q* in Figs 2.4a,b), which is not true of the other cases.

4.1.4 **Extensions**

Jointness in production

Suppose that for each unit of 'x' the firm also produces as a joint product one unit of 'y'. This involves no additional cost, and for simplicity we'll assume that 'x' and 'y' are unrelated in demand: i.e. have zero cross-elasticity of demand. How does this alter the production decision? The answer is straightforward: marginal revenue – the (small) increment to revenue per unit increment in the output of 'x' – now consists of two components. These are, firstly, the marginal revenue obtained in selling one more unit of 'x' itself (*MRx*), and secondly the marginal revenue obtained in selling the extra unit of 'y' (*MRy*). That is:

$$MR_{x+y} = MR_x + MR_y$$

Therefore, the firm should undertake to produce 'x' and 'y' jointly up to the point where their 'total' marginal revenue (MR_{x+y} above) is equal to marginal cost. Diagrammatically, this means that the relevant MR curve is the vertical sum of the separate MR_x and MR_y curves. Notice that once the optimum joint-output level has been determined in this way, the prices of 'x' and 'y' are simultaneously determined by their respective *AR* curves. As a result it is unnecessary to use any pricing rules based upon arbitrary allocations of cost between 'x' and 'y': demand conditions fully determine the optimal pricing arrangements.

Now, suppose 'y' were a waste by-product that had no demand but entailed some extra cost to get rid of. Call this the 'total cost of disposal' (TCy), which will have an associated 'marginal cost of disposal' (MCy). In other words, each additional unit of 'x' has a 'total' marginal cost of:

$$MC_{x+y} = MC_x + MC_y$$

i.e. the direct marginal input cost corresponding to our preceding discussion plus a marginal disposal cost. A little reflection will show that for maximum profit the marginal revenue (on 'x' alone; no 'y' is sold) must equal this 'total' MC:

$$MR_x = MC_x + MC_y$$

or

$$MC_x = MR_x - MC_y$$

An equivalent way of looking at this decision is to think of MC_y – the cost of disposal – as a negative MR_y, so enabling us to re-state the profit-maximizing condition alternatively as:

$$\begin{aligned} MC_x &= MR_x - MC_y \\ &= MR_x + MR_y \end{aligned}$$

Price discrimination (market segmentation)

Suppose now that the firm produces a single product 'x' but sells in two separated, or segmented, markets. By this we mean that consumers in each market either cannot or do not effectively purchase in the other market – i.e. there is no transferrence of demand. How can the profit-maximizing firm take advantage of this situation? The easiest way to approach this conceptual problem is to imagine that there is a fixed amount of 'x' to be sold between the two markets. This enables us to ignore marginal costs for the moment, and to concentrate on how the firm can maximize its revenues for the given cost (profit-maximization in a restricted sense).

Our focus is on comparing marginal revenues in the two markets, say MR_I and MR_{II}. Initially, we may find that

$$MR_I > MR_{II}$$

i.e. the first market is yielding a higher marginal revenue than the second market (or vice versa – the argument here is unaffected by the direction of the inequality). If so, it will pay the firm to shift sales from *II* to *I*, accomplished through small changes in prices. Specifically, raise the price of '*x*' in II by enough to reduce sales by one unit. By definition this loses the firm MR_{II}. At the same time, lower the price of '*x*' in *I* just enough to increase sales by one unit. This gains the firm MR_I; hence total revenues have increased since by assumption the gain exceeds the loss.

In fact, you should be able to verify that revenue is maximized when:

$$MR_I = MR_{II}$$

(This will eventually occur because as sales increase in *I*, MR_I declines, and as sales decrease in *II*, MR_{II} rises.)

Now, consider the effect of costs on the overall output decision. For the initial given output we are realizing maximum revenue, but suppose:

$$MC < MR_I \ (= MR_{II})$$

This means that an extra unit of '*x*' costs less than it would bring in terms of revenue, whichever market it was sold in: hence, it should be produced. Again, a little reflection shows that the firm will have maximum profits when:

$$MC = MR_I = MR_{II}$$

i.e. when not only marginal revenues are equal between markets, but each is in turn equal to the marginal cost of production.

Now recall the formula:

$$MR_i = P_i \ (1 + 1/E_i)$$

This pertains to both (all) separated markets as indicated by the general subscript '*i*'. Since *MR* values must be equal when profits are maximized we see that in our particular case:

$$P_I \ (1 + 1/E_I) = P_{II} \ (1 + 1/E_{II})$$

or:

$$\frac{P_I}{P_{II}} = \frac{1 + 1/E_{II}}{1 + 1/E_I}$$

This looks complicated, but is not too hard to interpret. First, notice that $P_I = P_{II}$ (a ratio of one) if and only if $E_I = E_{II}$; i.e. if own-price elasticities of demand for 'x' are equal in the two markets. Second, we can ascertain that $P_I > P_{II}$ (ratio greater than one) if demand is less elastic in I and in II; i.e. if

$$E_I > E_{II}$$

(as for example, $-\frac{1}{2} > -2$); or in terms of absolute elasticity values if:

$$|E_{II}| > |E_I|$$

(as for example, $2 > \frac{1}{2}$)

If the second market has the relatively inelastic *AR* curve then we would expect to find $P_{II} > P_I$.

Because price discrimination increases revenue potential at every level of output – hence increases potential profit – it is clearly a desirable state of affairs. The ultimate segmentation would be the case in which every single unit of 'x' could be potentially sold at a different price. This would imply not only discriminating between different customers, but also between the units each customer buys. 'For every two you buy there is a 25% discount on your third package' might be an example of this type of discrimination. The usual instances of ultimate segmentation are in personalized services for which there is a discretionary charge; e.g. doctors' visits in the US. This complete price discrimination, as opposed to the partial discrimination examined above, aims to expropriate the whole of the (roughly triangular) 'consumers' surplus' under the whole *AR* curve. In other words, price discrimination enables a firm to at least partly capture more of what consumers are willing to pay for 'x', by escaping the 'law of one price'.

4.2 Effects of competition on profits: entry and exit

4.2.1 Long-run effects

Entry and exit as the mechanism of competition

Granted that firms attempt to maximize (economic) profit, the question naturally arises as to how competition – or lack thereof – affects this pursuit. In order to see this, first consider what the existence of positive profit means: *viz*, that the owners of the firm are receiving returns on their own inputs – in particular on the financial capital which they have provided, and which is embodied in the physical capital to which they have title – greater than is available elsewhere. This 'supernormal' return attracts entry of competitors, and as long as any positive profit remains, investors in lower-yielding activities will continue to enter the profitable 'x' industry, until profits are driven down to zero for all firms. We assume here that all firms have identical cost curves. At this point all inputs in the 'x' industry are receiving a 'normal' or 'going' rate just equal to their opportunity cost; i.e. the best rate they could command elsewhere. Conversely, positive profit can only persist if for some reason there are effective barriers to entry.

Thus, for example, a 'pure' monopolist whose product was so unique as to have zero cross-elasticities of demand (no substitutes) might be able to maintain profits (see Fig. 4.3a). However, even for the monopolist starting life fortuitously, if there are significant substitutes the profit will be eroded through the previously described process of monopolistic competition. You should be able to verify graphically that the end-result of the leftward shifts of the firm's AR curve is at a point of tangency with the AC curve. To the right, AR would exceed AC, and vice-versa if it lay to the left. Although it is not obvious, it is geometrically true that at this same level of output (Q_1) where $P = AC$, we find that $MR = MC$, as shown (Fig. 4.3b). Thus, Q_1 is a point of maximum profit (by virtue of this latter condition), but the maximum obtainable profit is zero!

As we know, this situation of monopolistic competition is such that each of the differentiated producers still retains some degree of monopoly power (i.e. the AR curve is less than infinitely elastic). If the supposed competition were from new entrants producing a virtually undifferentiated product, the individual

Figures 4.3a and b Monopoly: 'pure' and competitive

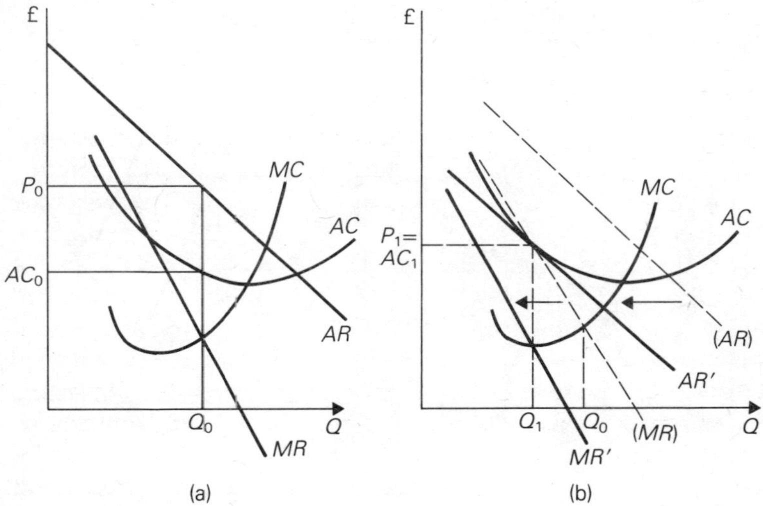

In 'pure' monopoly the lack of competitive pressure (i.e. no substitutes) enables permanent profit of $(P_0 - AC_0) \times Q_0$ to be maintained. Competition in the form of new partly substitutable products pushes the monpolists' *AR* schedule leftwards, until $P_1 = AC_1$ at Q_1.

firms' *AR* curves would simultaneously flatten. In the limiting case of 'perfect' competition the tangency of *AR* and *AC* would be as shown (Fig. 4.4a), at the minimum point of the *AC* curve. In this situation it is obvious that not only will $P = AC$ (the no-profit condition) but also that $P = MC$ (the maximum profit condition). As is apparent, the chief difference therefore between perfect and monopolistic competition is that in the former price equals marginal cost (since $P = MR$), whilst in the latter price exceeds *MC* (since $P > MR$). In both types of market structure, however, profits are nil due to unrestricted entry (and by implication, exit) of competing firms.

Figures 4.4a and b Relationship of firm and industry equilibrium (perfect competition)

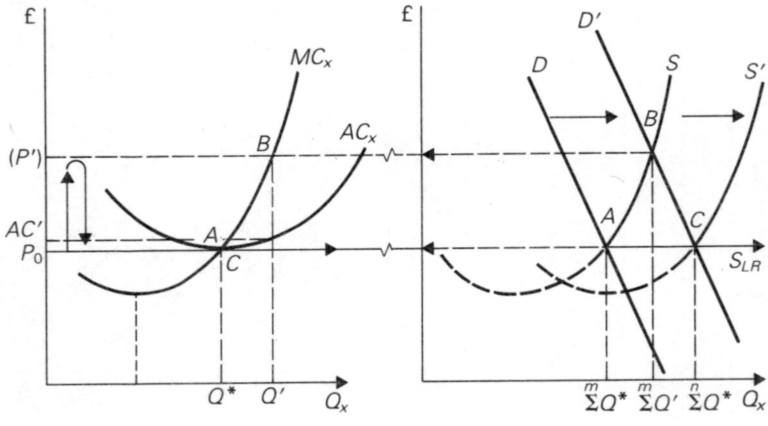

> The *process* of firm/industry adjustment is as follows: (1) An assumed rightward shift in aggregate demand for 'x' (Fig. 4.4b) – for whatever reason – raises price from P_0 to P': each of the existing firms increases output in response to Q' (from Q^*); (2) However, at Q' these firms have positive profits, which attracts entry. As new firms enter, the aggregate (industry) supply curve shifts to the right, ultimately depressing price to its original level, P_0. All firms – there are now more of them – return to output levels of Q^*. Because each firm's costs are unaffected, we call this a "constant-cost" industry. This also means that the industry's long-run supply curve (S_{LR}) – in contrast to the long-run marginal cost curve of an individual firm – is effectively perfectly-elastic, as shown.

Supply and Demand

Suppose that all firms are identical in terms of cost structure, and further imagine that each is faced with a given price of 'x' that varies according to forces outside any one firm's control over a period of time. We know that the output of each firm will consequently vary in accordance with its MC curve as shown (Fig. 4.4a). But with this happening for all firms together, we can trace out an aggregate *supply* curve (Fig. 4.4b) which shows how much 'x' will be supplied by perfectly competitive profit-maximizing firms at each potential price of 'x'. Notice that this supply curve only holds for prices at or above the minimum of the common *AC* curve. Strictly, no firm would continue producing if price were below this level in the long run; hence the dashed portion of the *MC* curve. For this particular type of market structure, price is determined by 'supply-and-demand': if market price were above its equilibrium level (P_0) there would be excess supply, which we assume depresses price. Hence, aggregate consumer demand increases and existing firms contract their output until the two match; and vice-versa for a situation in which there was initial excess demand (price too low).

In fact, with this apparatus we can trace out the full effects of the competitive process. Suppose from an initial zero-profit equilibrium, income rises shifting the demand curve to the right (Fig. 4.4b). The excess demand at the original price now pushes the price up, signalling existing firms to increase output for maximum profit, which now becomes positive (Fig. 4.4a). But this attracts entry of new firms, which is graphically represented by a rightward-shift of the aggregate supply curve (simply the horizontal summation of existing plus new firms' MC curves). At the now-higher price there is excess supply, which pushes price down until all firms are at their zero-profit points. The net result of the increased demand has thus been to enable more (identical) firms to enter and survive in the 'x' market. We ignore here the possibility that entry also affects costs. If this results in higher input prices and/or less efficient production in a technical sense, firms are experiencing external dis-economies, or simply negative externalities (of either the 'pecuniary' and/or 'technical' variety, respectively). The new equilibrium price that is reached when all profits are wiped out will be higher than before, in which case we say that 'x' is an increasing-cost industry. Our illustration is for a constant-cost industry. We leave it to the reader to show the outcome in a decreasing-cost industry.

4.2.2 **Short-run effects (under perfect competition)**

As mentioned, our notion of profit is the difference between long-run revenues and costs. In discussing the competitive mechanism of entry and exit we would not expect perceived short-run factors to count for much. Indeed, for the simpler case of a perfectly competitive firm we can illustrate precisely why it is rational not to immediately leave the industry if, say, price falls below the break-even level (Fig. 4.5). Looking at the short-run cost curves, we can see that any price above the minimum level of the *ATC* curve yields a profit, whereas a price below this level yields a loss. However, a shut-down of production will in the short-run entail a loss of the whole fixed (capital) cost. Hence the relevant short-run comparison is between this fixed cost and the amount of the operating cost. Specifically, as long as price is above the minimum of the *AVC* curve the latter will be less than the

Figure 4.5 Short-run break-even and shut-down points

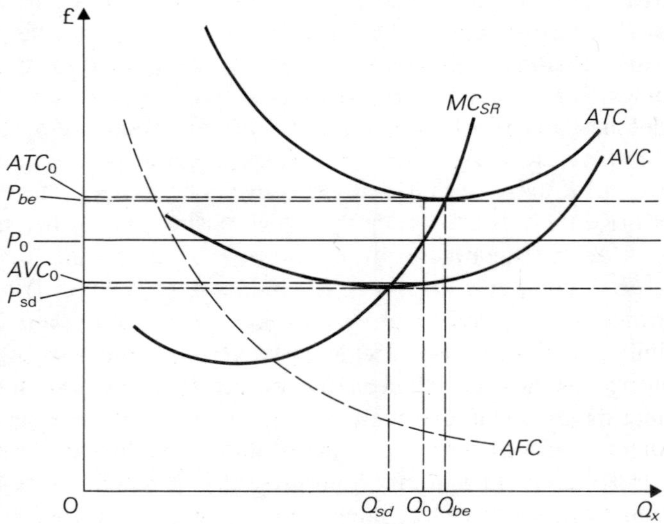

The firm breaks even at an output of Q_{be}, where $ATC = P_{be}$. At price P_0 and associated output Q_0 there is a loss, equal to: $(ATC_0 - P_0) \times Q_0$. However, this is less than $(ATC_0 - AVC_0) \times Q_0$, which would be the loss from shutting down (i.e. verify that this is equal to fixed cost). Hence, the firm continues to operate. Shut-down only occurs at Q_{sd}, when price has fallen to P_{sd}.

former. The simple reason is that the firm is in such a case making an 'accounting' profit, with revenues exceeding direct (labour, or as we often call them 'variable') costs. The difference, $P-AVC$ at the profit-maximizing level of output (this still occurs where $MC = P$, but instead of pointing to the largest positive profit it now identifies the smallest loss) is known as the (per unit) *contribution* (towards recovery of fixed costs). As long as this contribution is positive – i.e. as long as $P >$ min AVC – the firm loses less by continuing production. Of course, this begs the question of how long is 'the long run'? It clearly depends on the speed at which the physical capital can be scrapped and thereby returned to liquid (financial) form, on the rate of discount applied to future receipts and disbursements, and on how long the loss situation is expected to last. For instance, a plant which was expensive to dismantle and sell off, with product price expected to recover within a few months, and a low discount rate, would not justify shut-down. On the other hand, if you could sell off the assets quickly, the market price appeared to be depressed for the foreseeable future, and the opportunity cost of tied-up funds (our 'discount rate') was high, the decision might be immediate. However, our short-run 'snapshot' cannot capture these elements which have a time dimension.

4.3 Alternative objectives

Returning to our long-run perspective, we now consider the possibility that firms typically do not try to maximize economic profit, but instead aim at alternative objectives. However, before considering some of these alternatives, we ought to note two preconditions regarding this non-profit-maximizing behaviour. First, it requires an absence of effective competition! From our preceding discussion it should be clear that in competitive equilibrium zero profit is the best that firms can do, and this is only achieved at the level of profit-maximizing output. Any other output decision must lead to losses and eventual exit from the industry. Second, it requires separation of ownership from control. The idea is that if firms were managed purely for the sake of their ultimate owners, those owners' best interests would be served by maximizing profit. After all, profit is their source of income. Nonetheless, if owners were 'satisfied' with some lower rate of return on capital, it would be possible for the firm's managers to pursue other objectives. Typically, managerial income/status depends at least as much on sales volume, for example, as on profit performance, at least as long as the latter is 'adequate'. In fact, these alternatives can be usefully categorized as either of the maximizing type or of the satisficing type. The difference is that the former can be neatly described by mathematical (diagrammatic) tools, whereas the latter poses greater analytical problems.

4.3.1 **Alternative maximands**

Sales revenue

Following this line of reasoning, many economists have investigated sales-maximizing models of the firm. The first variant postulates that the firm pursues sales revenue maximization. Under the assumption that this occurs where profit is still positive, the firm is shown diagrammatically (Fig. 4.6a) as being at the peak

Figures 4.6a and b Alternative maximands

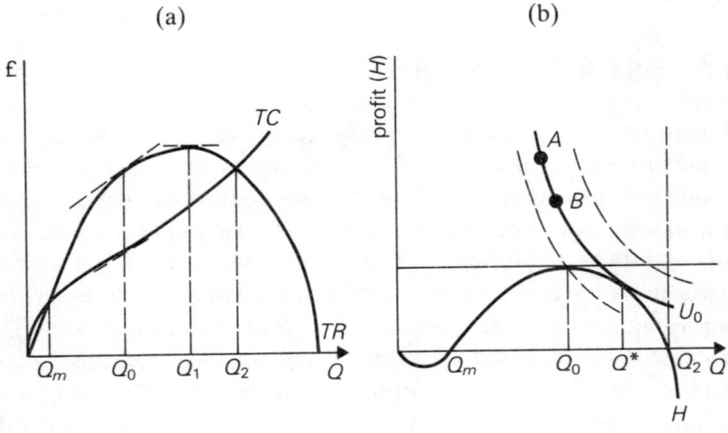

Q_0: Profit-maximizing output; Q_1: sales-revenue-maximizing output; Q_2: sales-volume-maximizing output (subject to breaking-even,); Q^* (Fig. 4.6b): managerial-utility-maximizing output (a 'two-dimensional' objective).

of its *TR* curve. As we already know, marginal revenue is zero at this point, with unit own-price elasticity of demand. This in turn implies that output will be greater than under profit-maximization, since the latter's rule ($MC = MR$) ensures that with *MC* always positive, *MR* will have to be positive also: i.e. the profit-maximizing firm operates in the region of elastic demand.

Sales volume

The second variant is that firms pursue sales-volume maximization, subject to meeting an opportunity-cost-of-capital constraint. Some constraint is necessary, since otherwise maximum volume can be achieved by setting a zero price, regardless of losses. Diagrammatically the typical position for a firm would be at the point of intersection of the *TC* and *TR* curves, which shows in this particular case that the firm operates in the region of inelastic demand, with negative *MR*. (Verify that this need not be so, e.g. the *TC* curve may shift upwards due to a rise in input costs.)

Managerial utility

A third variant focuses on the rate of growth of revenue or volume, but we will not investigate this here. Instead, we look at a two-dimensional objective function, as opposed to the one-dimensional objectives examined so far. To illustrate, suppose that the manager(s) in charge of the firm consider both profits and, say, sales volume to be important objectives. If so, it will be at least implicitly necessary for them to determine how much of one (profit) they will sacrifice for the other (sales volume) whenever the two conflict. The type of 'trade-off' function we have in mind is shown as a smooth curve, convex to the origin (Fig. 4.6b). Its interpretation is that if we start with high profit on low sales volume (*A*), this yields some particular level of managerial satisfaction, or managerial 'utility' (hence the label). Our interest is not in how much utility this combination represents, but in those other combinations of profit and sales yielding exactly the same utility (U_0), whatever it may be (see Appendix 1C).

Consider a lower level of profits, but still quite substantial (*B*). We see that this drop could be compensated by some not very large increase in sales. However, as profits fall by the same amount step by step, we assume that it will take increasingly large subsequent rises in sales volume to compensate. In economic jargon, the convex 'indifference' curve shows a 'diminishing marginal rate of substitution (m.r.s.)' between profits and sales volume. All of the infinite number of combinations on a single curve yield equal utility or satisfaction to the manager (hence he/she is indifferent as to which point actually occurs). However, points to the 'north-east' are assumed to be *preferred* to those closer to the origin (U_1 yields a higher utility than U_0). We imagine that the whole diagram space is filled with an infinite number of these curves, none of which ever cross. If they did, the assumption about more of one or both being better would be violated, as you might attempt to verify. Thus, the manager's objective is to reach the highest possible U curve. But the manager faces a constraint in the form of the H curve, showing profits as a function of – sales volume. In general, the chosen level of production will be determined by the tangency of this H-curve with the outermost U curve: anything else that is feasible is inferior (on a lower U curve); and anything superior (on a higher U curve) is unattainable.

For comparative purposes we could describe profit-maximization as the choice when the utility curves are horizontal, and sales volume maximization as the choice when they are vertical: check what these imply about the trade-off – i.e. the marginal rate of substitution – between profits and sales volume.

4.3.2 **Optimization *vs* satisficing**

This approach, whilst illuminating, can be extended without limit to encompass any number of measures from which managers might derive satisfaction, e.g. profits, sales volume, number of employees, size (value) of plant, thickness of office carpet, etc. In such a form it becomes less useful but perhaps more realistic. But however many dimensions it takes to draw the utility curves, we are still viewing the firm as an *optimizer*. That is, managers are making output choices in order to achieve their most preferred situation subject to the technical and market constraints on their ability to do so. This may sound tautological, but it is not. Just as we assumed that owners might be content with less than their firms were capable of returning to them, so it may be with managers: 'adequate' levels of profits, sales, etc. may be their only objective. This targeting behaviour is an example of 'satisficing' as opposed to 'optimizing', and it really shoves the theory of the firm out of economics into the area known as organizational behaviour. All that we will say about it here is that if the firm is in fact not controlled – either by owners or by a central management with uniform objectives – but instead functions according to the outcomes of internal conflict resolution ('office politics'), we are unlikely to see the results of any conscious optimizing behaviour. Note the relevance of game theory in reference to these internal decision processes, as well as to behaviour vis-à-vis other firms. (This also suggests that production may not be either economically or even technically efficient in the earlier sense: a condition known as 'X-inefficiency' which provides a buffer in lean times).

4.4 Profit-maximization revisited: barriers to entry

As with most awkward corners in economics, we avoid them. Just as we theorized that oligopolistic competitors would collude so all could be better off, so we imagine that all the autonomous self-seeking elements within the firm will find it to their mutual advantage to unite under the over-riding objective of profit maximization.

Carrying this argument further, as we have observed that competition wipes out profits, doesn't it make sense that competing firms should cooperate – that is, collude – to maintain mutual profitability? In a restricted context it does indeed make sense. Consider what happens when say, many small perfectly competitive firms producing a homogeneous good 'x' merge to form a monopoly with complete control over the supply of 'x'. We suspect that profit will increase – remember it is zero for the lot of them initially – but it is necessary to make a formal comparison between the two situations.

4.4.1 Merger: collusive or 'unnatural' monopoly

Returning to the competitive supply-and-demand model, we assume that costs are unchanged: the monopoly firm now has many 'branch plants' with identical cost structures. Therefore the old aggregate supply curve becomes simply the new monopoly's *MC* curve. However, because it operates on a large scale, the new firm is in a position to perceive the whole of the aggregate demand curve for '*x*' (its *AR* curve) and consequently is in a position to perceive the derived *MR* curve as shown (Fig. 4.3a). It is important to see that this does not mean that underlying demand conditions have changed; merely that for any initially small firm the aggregate demand and associated marginal revenue curve are plainly irrelevant. For the monopoly they are highly relevant, and in fact we see that the new firm will contract output and therefore raise the price of '*x*' in comparison with the perfectly competitive industry. That this does in fact increase profit – it wouldn't occur if it didn't – is shown by the common *AC* curve of all the branch plants in relation to the *AR* curve. Q.E.D.: all the original firms are able to share in the positive profits of their collusive behaviour.

The flaw in this is that it is an option available to existing firms (assuming it is legal) but requires the continuous co-option of new entrants who would be drawn into the industry by its very profitability. In fact, like the moral to be found in so many old mystery movies, there is no end to blackmail: there will ultimately be so many firms that the monopoly-profit dividends will be individually negligible. And of course the costs of expanding and maintaining the monopoly are likely to rise as the number of firms increases (reflecting diminishing returns to a third input: management).

4.4.2 **Oligopoly**

On the other hand, for an industry with only a few firms – i.e. an oligopoly – collusion might be feasible. But first we ought to consider a little more deeply exactly what makes an industry oligopolistic rather than 'atomistic', by which we mean a large number of competing firms, whether differentiated or not. The answer was known to Adam Smith writing his *Wealth of Nations* in 1776: the sustainable number of firms in an industry depends on the point at which average costs reach their minimum in relation to the size of the market. In atomistic markets this minimum efficient size is miniscule; for oligopoly it is significantly large. Even if each oligopolist were driven to its long-run break-even point, there could only be a few firms whose total output completely met demand at that price. If they were making positive profits – operating beyond the minimum AC output – the number could be smaller still. As pointed out earlier, just because there are only a few firms doesn't mean that competition – in the sense of rivalry – is absent. Each oligopolist might perceive its own *AR* as perfectly elastic ('pseudo-competitive') or, as already described, might face a kinked *AR* curve. In either case they could very likely do better by colluding.

Faced with this type of collusive monopoly, potential entrants would probably be daunted by the fact that they would have to enter this market on a very large scale. Nonetheless, although the risks are greater, the logic of competitive behaviour implies that persistant positive profits, even in such an industry, would attract entry.

4.4.3 **Limit pricing: barriers to entry**

Does all this mean that collusion to generate monopoly profit is doomed to fail because of its fatal attraction for potential new entrants? The answer is yes, and no. It depends on how we choose to view profit-maximization. So far it has been straightforwardly identified by reference to *MR* and *MC* curves. However, suppose that instead of acting effectively like a monopoly in this '*MC*=*MR*' sense, our oligopolists deliberately hold themselves to their minimum *AC* outputs. Given the number of firms, there is thus some total industry output and a price at which this output can be sold, but note that these are not the price and output implied by simple monopolistic profit-maximization. Also, we assume that the number of oligopolists is such that there is not suficient room for another firm to come in at the minimum efficient size without pushing price down to or below the minimum *AC*. This is the essence of the strategy, since if the firms restricted output to less than their minimum *AC* levels, as they would under the simple monopoly solution, there is room for the entrant to make a profit.

What this 'limit-pricing' model indicates is the important point that the firms may collude so as to maintain a smaller profit for ever, rather than a larger profit briefly. Which strategy they adopt depends on the relative sizes of these profits, exactly how long they are expected to last, and the discount rate used to compare these streams in terms of present values. This pushes our concept of profit-maximization beyond its earlier limits, wherein we considered an industry with a given population of firms, to one which admits that entry is a vital factor. Specifically, profit-maximization may take the form, not of setting *MR* equal to *MC*, but of erecting barriers to entry. These are easily observable in the real world, but not easy to model analytically. We appear to be back in the realm of game theory, in which the outcome of economic decisions depends on how the players perceive and react to each other's strategies. To take one final example: even in the above limit-pricing model the potential entrant must believe that existing firms will maintain output. If the entrant thinks for any reason that one or more existing firms will be forced to contract output, it will be induced to enter. Conversely, even if profits were huge, the retaliatory moves of existing firms – e.g. sudden price cuts and output expansion – might be believed to occur, thus discouraging entry.

Summary

With costs determined by technology and input prices (or at least, input price–quantity relationships), and revenues determined by product prices, or price–quantity relationships reflecting competitive conditions, the firm's key decision can be seen as how much to produce. By far the most common assumption is that this is chosen so as to maximize profit; i.e. simply revenue minus cost, the latter including opportunity cost elements if certain inputs are in fact not contractually hired or 'rented'.

The condition that obtains when profit is maximized is that marginal revenue be equal to marginal cost (this could also locate a minimum, but we do not worry about that at this stage). Although this is straightforward, extensions of the basic principle are sometimes much less intuitive and, partly as a result, very illuminating for many problems.

However, profit – in the economic sense – invites entry since by definition at least one input (usually capital) must be receiving a greater-than-normal return. Where there are no barriers to entry profits must therefore be driven to zero (in the long run: short-run profit can be seen as a reward for taking the initial risk). This results in operation where the *AR* (own-demand) curve is tangent to the *AC* curve. For imperfect competitors this occurs on the left branch of the *AC* curve (if at all), whilst for perfect competitors it occurs at the minimum point of the *AC* curve. I could then show that such firms might choose to operate at a loss in the short run, and that perfect competition was the only market form consistent with aggregate (industry) supply-and-demand schedules.

Some alternatives to profit-maximization are also considered. A major distinction can be made between optimizing and satisficing behaviour, but in either case these alternatives require both slackness in competitive conditions and the 'separation of ownership from control'. Finally, I looked at 'profit-maximization' in the broader sense of erecting barriers to entry (as opposed to merely setting MR equal to MC). In particular, I described a simple limit-pricing model in which oligopolists collude so as to exclude new entrants.

Appendix 4 Factor-market conditions

Short run

Since in the short run only labour input is variable, any decision regarding output must also imply a particular level of labour input. It is of interest to derive the profit-maximizing rule in the alternative context of the labour market.

Taking the general case of a monopolistic firm (i.e. it has some influence over the wage rate, or some 'degree of monopsony'), we have already established that:

$$MC_{SR} = \frac{MLC}{MPL}$$

i.e. the short-run level of marginal cost is equal to the ratio of marginal labour cost (in perfect competition simply the wage rate, w) to the marginal product of labour.

Profit-maximization as a general rule requires further that:

$$MR = MC_{SR}$$

We have examined the logic of this rule already; but now putting it together with the first condition we can derive:

$$MLC = MR \times MPL$$

In words: profit-maximization requires that marginal labour cost equal marginal revenue times marginal product of labour. The latter product is generally known as labour's 'marginal revenue product' (MRP_L) or, in the special case of a given price (perfect competition in the product market), the 'marginal value product' (MVP_L); i.e.:

$$MVP_L = P \times MPL$$

This is simply the extra revenue brought in by employing one more unit of labour. At the same time, *MLC* is the extra cost of employing one more unit of labour. Therefore, assuming the latter to rise and the former to fall (as employment increases), the firm will maximize profits when these are equalized as shown (Fig. 4A.1a,b). Before that MRP_L exceeds *MLC*: another unit of

Figures 4A.1a and b . The firm's labour market

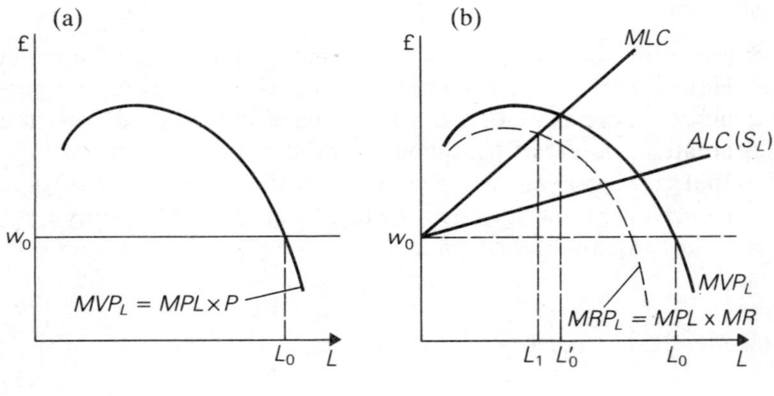

For a firm which is perfectly competitive in both labour and product markets (i.e. given wage and product prices), L_0 is the chosen level of input. Monopsony in the labour market increases the firm's marginal labour cost (*MLC*) more rapidly than labour's average cost (as shown by the labour supply, or *ALC* curve in Fig. 4A.1b). The resulting input is now L'_0. If the firm is also monopolistic, so that *MR* falls faster than *P*, input is further reduced to L_1 (i.e. where $MRP_L = MLC$).

labour brings in more revenue than it adds to costs. Beyond, MLC exceeds MRP_L. Hence, the firm should hire just the amount of labour indicated, which is of course exactly the amount implied by the profit-maximizing output rule: $MC_{SR} = MR$.

Long run

Now reverse the interpretation of labour as variable and capital as fixed. In this new 'short-run' context we would derive a marginal product of capital curve (MPK) contingent upon a given level of labour input, as well as a marginal capital cost curve (MKC) derived from the upward-sloping capital supply curve. We would then be able to establish that the $MC_{SR} = MR$ rule was equivalent to:

$$MKC = MR \times MPK \; (= MRP_K)$$

precisely as we have just done for labour.

However, in the 'long run' both inputs are variable, so both conditions must hold: a marginal adjustment of either input should generate extra revenue just equal to extra cost (per unit of output):

$$MR = \frac{MLC}{MPL} = \frac{MKC}{MPK} = MC$$

Under perfect competition this reduces to:

$$MR = \frac{w}{MPL} = \frac{r}{MPK} = MC$$

Note also that we can re-write the two middle terms as:

$$\frac{w}{r} = \frac{MPL}{MPK}$$

which is the condition for the tangency of a cost constraint line and an isoquant (see Appendix 3B).

5 Intervention: Efficiency and Equity

Outline

Synopsis

This final microeconomics chapter initially examines the concept of Pareto-efficiency, in contradistinction to both general philosophical arguments for or against intervention in market economies, and any *equity* considerations arising within a given sociopolitical context.

The major conclusion is that a perfectly competitive economy is Pareto-efficiency, except in the case of externalities, when private and social costs and benefits can diverge. Also, imperfectly competitive markets are not generally efficient; therefore, governments may pursue policies to achieve quasi-competitive results, such as direct price regulation or the removal of barriers to competition. However, so-called 'natural' monopolies present problems for the latter approach.

At the same time I caution that the policies adopted to deal with inefficiencies may themselves introduce distortions, and conclude the first section by remarking upon our ignorance in cases where overall efficiency cannot be established.

Finally, I consider policies arising from equity or redistributional, motives. These can be aimed at consumers, such as setting price ceilings (leading to black markets); or, very often, at producers in the form of guaranteed prices. I look at three forms of the latter type, all of which involve efficiency losses.

Introduction

Until now we have been describing possible behaviour of households and firms, without any implications about the desirability of such behaviour. In the language of the social sciences we have been so far engaged in positive rather than normative analysis.

5.1 Efficiency: the Paretian criterion

5.1.1 *Laissez-faire:* political and economic arguments

If we are going to try to prescribe what forms of behaviour are 'best' we need to be very careful in defining the criteria under which we rank the different outcomes. To take an extreme example, our theories of the household and the firm are infused with the idea that individuals are self-seeking (if you prefer, 'greedy'). Therefore, we can rest assured that whatever the environment, people will be making choices that they individually determine is 'best' for themselves. In other words, it doesn't matter; 'human nature' operates within any economic system, whether centrally planned, monopolistic, perfectly competitive or anything else. Strictly interpreted, this means that any governmental intervention is neutral in terms of the citizens' welfare. However, this is not a generally held belief; instead, we tend in our Western culture to see any form of coercion as damaging to individual welfare. This is a *laissez-faire political* philosophy, resting ultimately on the premise that all transactions between individuals should be freely agreed. Such *voluntary* exchanges as would then take place must reflect *mutual* advantages, and so are evidence of an improvement in individual welfare. Coercion, whilst benefiting the enforcer, clearly is to the detriment of the party whose behaviour is forced.

5.1.2 **Pareto-efficiency**

In this laissez-faire view there is an implicit criterion for judging whether we are as a society 'better off': if one or more individuals can be made better off (i.e. they would propose the action) without anyone else being made worse off (i.e. they would not oppose the action) then that action must improve society's aggregate welfare, even if we cannot always measure the improvement. In Economics, a society in which there are no opportunities for social improvement – that is, anyone's gain must lead to someone else's loss – is said to be *Pareto-efficient* (after the early twentieth-century Italian economist, mathematician and philospher). In fact, we allow a gain to one to harm another if in principle the gainer could just compensate the loser and still be ahead. In reality, compensation might of course not be paid – see below. The economic doctrine of *laissez-faire* asserts precisely that: an economy left to itself and without governing interference will be Pareto-efficient. There is nonetheless a role for government: as an enforcer of the mutually agreed contracts, and to prevent coercion by force (or other means?) of some individuals by others.

Other economists are sceptical about this claim. It is one thing to assert the political view that free exchange is a good thing, but quite another to assert the economic proposition that this produces the best of all possible worlds. Their counter-argument is typically that, although a voluntary agreement between two parties is *prima facie* evidence that *they* are better off, other parties may be directly or indirectly adversely affected. This might mean that any contract would need to involve all affected parties, which is for practical purposes an impossibility. Therefore, the government may take an active role on behalf of the excluded parties; i.e. act to protect the 'public interest' by intervening in private market exchanges. In fact, the audacity of the *laissez-faire* view is quite remarkable. It asserts no less than that the two parties to any exchange have neither any need to consider the effects of their exchange on others, nor the effects of others' exchanges on their own. Decision-taking within the market economy can be completely decentralized, and it will still be supremely efficient.

5.1.3 **Efficiency *vs* equity**

Our first purpose in this chapter is to examine this claim. In particular, we seek to establish if it could be true and under what circumstances. However, before we begin we ought to discern a second reason for government intervention in the market economy, quite apart from measures to improve its efficiency in the Paretian sense. This is often called the equity, or re-distributional function of government. Suppose that the *laissez-faire* claims proved to be true, and that no-one can be better off without harm to others. Notice that this could mean, for instance, that the income of a £100-a-month family of eight could not be increased (e.g. £1 per month) without reducing a £10,000-a-month company president's income (e.g. by £2 per month). Tough, but there it is, the poor household could not compensate the rich household without being even worse off, so the action resulting in this re-distribution is worse in terms of the Paretian criterion. Of course, governments' powers are in reality not limited to efficiency measures, but extend to this kind of 'social welfare' problem as well. Thus, in our political systems, we allow the governing authorities to re-distribute wealth – broadly interpreted – even at the cost of a less 'efficient' economy as in our example. It is important to realize that there *is* no – can *be* no – objective criterion for measuring social welfare in this way. The 'trade-offs' between individuals are necessarily a matter of value-judgements on the part of the (elected) government, just as we saw that managers might be free to pursue their own objectives at the level of the firm. Taking the analogy one step further, the electors are society's shareholders; but since their interests are often in conflict they give up discretion to the elected, who can pursue efficiency or equity as they choose, subject to the ballot box.

The second purpose in this chapter will be to look at ways in which governments intervene in markets on equity grounds, although often this is not recognized explicitly.

5.1.4 **Achieving efficiency**

Central planning

The easiest approach to the problem of attaining maximum economic efficiency – in the Paretian sense – is to imagine ourselves as central planners. We are 'revisionists' in the sense that we will allow individuals to buy and sell freely. However, our responsibility is to set the prices – letting people buy and sell what they wish – or alternatively to fix the quantities of goods supplied – letting prices find their own levels.

If we initially confine our attention to the cost and demand conditions in the '*x*' market alone, we observe something identical to the earlier supply and demand curves (e.g. Fig. 4.4b). However, the supply curve is to be interpreted for our purposes as the marginal cost curve, showing how much it costs, at each level of output, to produce another unit of '*x*'. Similarly, the demand curve can be interpreted not only as the quantity demanded at each given price of '*x*', but alternatively as the price, or 'marginal valuation' consumers place on an additional unit of '*x*'. In other words this same curve shows, at each initial level of output, how much consumers – that is, someone, somewhere – is willing to pay for one more unit of '*x*'.

Now, start with a small output of '*x*'. At this low level the marginal cost in terms of the resources (inputs) used to produce another unit is also low. But the marginal valuation consumers place on this extra unit is high. Therefore, whoever that person is who would be willing to pay a higher price for another unit of '*x*', he/she would be better off if it were produced: it is worth more to him/her than it costs in terms of used-up resources to produce! As an alternative way of seeing the same point, if supply were not in government control that person would have an incentive to produce that 'x' for him/herself. Possibly this is an explanation for the growth of the so-called 'black economy', which includes productive activities for purely domestic consumption. Following this logic to its conclusion the planner would be led to the intersection of the two curves. At that point the marginal valuation that consumers attach to another unit of 'x' just equals the marginal resource-cost of producing it. Prior to that point additional output is worth more than it costs; beyond, it is worth less. Furthermore, as central planners we can achieve this outcome simply by setting price at the appropriate level (P_0), relying upon self-seeking market buyers and sellers to establish the 'correct' level of output.

There is one problem here that we are neglecting. Although it is apparent that consumers in the 'x' market are net beneficiaries (at the 'directed' price (P_0)), anyone who doesn't purchase 'x' does so because he/she subjectively values 'x' at less than P_0; and conversely, all those who *do* buy 'x' value it at least as much as P_0; but what about consumers in other markets? Doesn't the transfer of resources from say, 'y' to 'x' involve a loss of welfare in the 'y' market?

The answer to this is 'yes', but note that the loss to the consumer of 'y' is less than the gain to the consumer of 'x'. The reason is this: if the 'y' market – and all others except for that matter – is at the point where demand price just equals marginal cost, when we transfer £1's worth of resources from 'y' to 'x' it means that someone who was just willing to pay £1 for that quantity of 'y' is thereby displaced from the 'y' market. However by assumption there is someone in the 'x' market (could be the same person!) who is willing to pay more than £1 (e.g. £2) for the extra 'x' when a £1's worth of resources are transferred to 'x'-production. If these two individuals could have bargained directly, in a hypothetical world where products could be dissolved into their constituent inputs and re-assembled, the potential 'x' consumer would have been willing to pay up to £2 for the additional 'x', whereas the actual 'y' consumer would have been willing to accept down to £1 for giving up the marginal 'y'; hence they could have traded to mutual advantage. However, the central planners accomplish all this by direct order; when they are finished no opportunities for gainful trade between any two individuals, in any pair of goods, are possible.

Free markets

This is in itself a remarkable result: when prices equal marginal costs in all markets the economy has achieved Pareto-efficiency. (This refers, as usual, to product-market conditions. For factor-market conditions, see Appendix 5.) However, as a practical matter the task of the central planners is truly enormous. They must have complete information on costs and demand conditions in every product and factor market, and then some feasible method of computing the equilibrium prices and quantities; and, of course, they have to monitor the system continuously. How much more astounding it is, then, that the unplanned market mechanism achieves the same result in a completely de-centralized and informationally efficient manner. It should be obvious that the equality of prices with marginal costs – illustrated by the intersection of aggregated *MC* and demand curves for any particular product – is precisely the outcome of perfect competition. This is the result of Adam Smith's 'invisible hand' in a very real sense. What has happened is that, as we know, in this type of market structure all participants are price-takers. It is this feature which enables everyone to calculate his/her actions independently, without regard to the actions of others. Hence all the potential interdependences, whereby many are affected by (voluntary) transactions between two traders, are effectively eliminated and the case for *laissez-faire* established.

5.1.5 **Breakdowns in competitive efficiency**

Externalities

Or are they? We have already encountered the phenomenon of externalities. A classic example is the case of a factory spewing smoke and soot into the air, which causes all the nearby residents to have higher costs for insulation/ventilation, cleaning, painting and, very probably, medical treatment. None of these is included in the producing firm's marginal cost curve. However, if they were taken into account, then the *MC* curve would have to be shifted upwards as shown (Fig. 5.1a) to reflect the negative externalities generated per unit of output. This higher curve reflects the so-called 'marginal social costs' of production as opposed to the lower marginal and private cost curve. In such a situation you should be able to verify that the Pareto-efficient level of output is

Figures 5.1a and b Externalities: taxes and subsidies

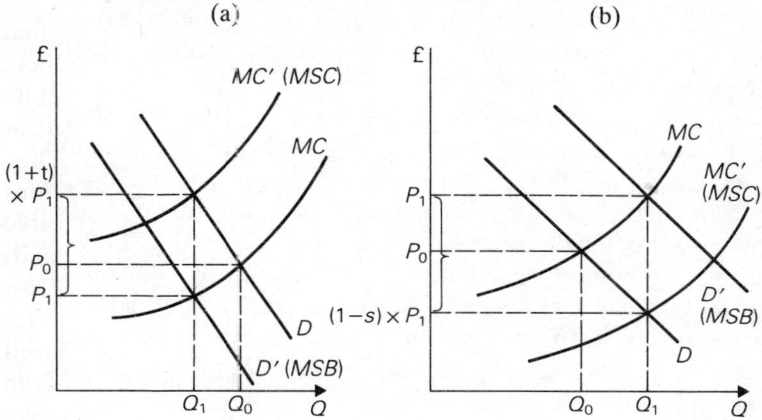

Negative externalities: the optimum output is Q_1, where the producer receives only P_1 but consumer pays $(1 + t) \times P_1$; 't' is the amount of 'damage' per unit of output (shown as either higher *MSC* curve or lower *MSB* curve). Positive externalities: the optimum output is Q_1, where the producer receives P_1, but the consumer pays only $(1 - s) \times P_1$; 's' is the amount of 'benefit' per unit of output, (shown as either higher *MSB* curve or lower *MSC* curve).

determined by the equality of price with marginal social cost (*MSC*). In order to achieve this result we can see that a tax per unit on the production of 'x' might be levied. This would drive a wedge – equal to the per unit external costs imposed – between the price consumers paid and the amount received by the firm, inducing a simultaneous contraction of both demand and supply. At the *cum*-tax equilibrium, the revenue raised by this 'pollution tax' (the rectangular area shown) is necessarily equal to the external costs imposed. Two points are of interest here. First, it makes no difference if we conceptualize the externality as a negative social benefit: that is, subtract the external cost from the market demand (*AR*) curve to yield a lower 'marginal social valuation' curve as opposed to the marginal private valuation reflected by the *AR* curve itself. Second, note that the 'optimum' amount of pollution is not zero, but remains at some positive level. To force cessation of production would mean that marginal social valuation of a unit of '*x*' – even taking pollution costs into account – would exceed the marginal cost of producing it.

Another example, of a positive externality, is health care. My good health improves your chances of good health, but the market (we are assuming there is one) does not reflect this. The marginal social valuation of any particular level of health service is shown above the marginal private valuation curve (Fig. 5.1b) – i.e. above the private market demand curve. (Alternatively, the marginal social costs curve is lower than the marginal private cost (*MC*) curve, as shown. In this situation the market can be 'corrected' by subsidizing health care by the amount of difference between the marginal private and social valuation curves. The total subsidy will in the end just equal the value of the external benefits generated at that 'optimum' level of health care. Once again, note that if health care were free, the level of service would be at a point where marginal costs exceeded marginal social benefits, even though these include positive externalities. That is, there is an 'optimum' amount of health care falling short of the amount demanded if people could consume all they wished, at a zero price.

Examples of externalities in this sense – often called public goods – abound. Their essence is the 'non-excludability' of parties not directly involved in a transaction, whether they are adversely or beneficially affected (the latter being called very descriptively the 'free rider' problem). However, proponents of the *laissez-faire* system maintain that this is not an insoluble problem. What is required is a more careful delineation of property rights in the legal sense of identifying exactly who is entitled to benefits and who is obligated to bear costs. Thus, to take our first example, the local residents would have a legally recognized entitlement to compensation. Or, if my good health – or education – benefits others, I should have the legal right to charge them for this externality. In short, there is in principle no reason why these 'social' costs and benefits cannot be brought within the market mechanism through modifications to the legal framework. In practice, however, this is unlikely to be easy – i.e. costless – since it is apparent that the number of exchanges would proliferate enormously. As another example, if I light a cigarette in a room of people who thereby experience negative externalities (i.e. they do not like smoke), theoretically I should be able to come to some agreement with everyone present about how much I will smoke and how much compensation I will pay each person. That is a free-market solution; yet it is obvious that the cost of making all these contracts is going to be rather high, probably even in excess of the total external costs suffered by the non-smokers. Therefore, it is safe to say that in many cases the market economy does generate uncompensated externalities.

Imperfect markets

Another line of criticism, which can be sustained on purely theoretical grounds, has been readily apparent ever since I established the conditions underlying a Pareto-efficient economy. Namely, if markets are imperfectly competitive – meant to encompass any structure other than 'perfect' – participants may not be price-takers. Although special circumstances might lead even large firms to perceive themselves in this way, typically it would seem that they do exercise influence over price in the manner indicated by our earlier models. The best example of this is the monopolistic firm facing a downward-sloping AR curve (e.g. Fig. 4.3a,b), hence facing an even more rapidly declining MR curve. Because it maximizes profit at the level of output where $MC = MR$, and because P exceeds MR, it follows that $P > MC$, and so we are in precisely the position that we saw to be inferior from the central planner's point of view: some consumers are willing to pay more for additonal units of 'x' than they marginally cost to produce, but the monopolist's own perception of profitability prevents this gain from being realized. In fact the net economic loss from this monopolistic restriction of output (and correspondingly higher price) is equal to the triangular area as shown.

5.1.6 **Government policies for efficiency**

Price regulation

The efficiency argument that we have developed is very important, in that it underpins governmental policies aimed at encouraging competition and discouraging monopoly behaviour. There are several forms that these policies may take. Perhaps the simplest is for the government to fix the price of 'x' as if it were a perfectly competitive industry. This would be an effective suspension of the market *AR* curve above the price ceiling (which, although it is a maximum price, clearly tends to become the normal, or 'administered' price). This would then lead to the re-establishment of the competitive-industry output as desired. But surely this is odd, since we are claiming to show that a lower price of '*x*' leads to an increase in profit-maximizing output? The logic of this behaviour provides us with a good exercise in thinking in terms of marginal conditions. Notice that together with the suspension of market *AR*, the market *MR* curve also ceases to apply down to the point at which AR equals the ceiling price. Instead, up to the quantity at which market price just becomes equal to the ceiling price, average revenue is constant and equal to the fixed price. But this means that marginal revenue is also constant and equal to the same price. Now, when the government introduces a ceiling price lower than obtains under unfettered monopoly there is of course an immediate loss of revenue, at the initial level of output. However, the crucial question is whether this is the optimum level of output after the change in price. The answer is 'no': although at the initial output MC was equal to the old market-determined *MR*, now at that same output new, administered *MR* exceeds *MC*, so the firm expands output until *MC* just equals this new *MR*, which is of course equal to the administered price.

Promoting competition

Governments often do not like to get deeply involved in this kind of close regulation, unless special circumstances warrant. As an alternative policy they usually much prefer to promote competition. In the case of smaller firms attempting to merge it is relatively easy to prevent this, but if the firm is already a large monopoly it is rather difficult to effect its break-up into smaller companies. Therefore a government may actively encourage new firms to set up, if not in the same product-line '*x*' as the monopolist, then at least in products that are substitutes for '*x*'. Usually this means the development of new products – although cheaper methods of producing existing products are also researched – which is why we often see so much government support for 'R & D'. It is interesting to see this occasionally turned around. Existing monopolies argue that they deserve high profits precisely because they go back into financing R&D. The firm needs to keep running to stay ahead, and if it cannot stay ahead it will stop running.

While we are on this subject we might also note that a pure monopoly cannot be subjected to this kind of competition. Therefore if it turns out that a monopolist can continue to extract supernormal profit indefinitely the government may intervene to break it up; or even if the monopoly is protected by patents, etc., may exercise its authority to grant licences to competitors to produce identical goods.

'Natural' monopoly

Although much of governments' activity is preferably aimed at promoting competition, there is one major class of monopoly that is not really amenable to this treatment. This is the so-called 'natural' monopoly, defined as having increasing returns to scale (size) up to the point at which it could just break even. Diagrammatically (Fig. 5.2a) at the point where the *AC* curve intersects the

Figures 5.2a and b Effects of splitting a natural monopoly into several (competing) firms

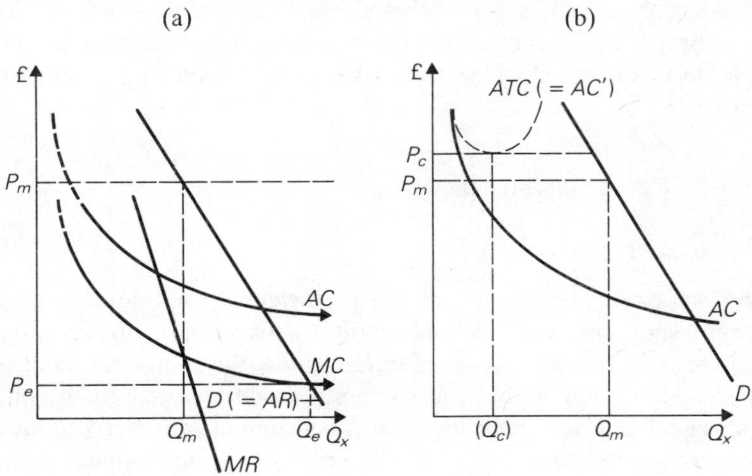

The socially (Pareto-)efficient output of '*x*' is at Q_e, which is supported by charging price P_e. In contrast, the private profit-maximizing output and price are at Q_m and P_m. However, splitting up this firm may lose economies of size: each new firm has a smaller capital stock, hence operates on a higher *AC* curve (at Q_c in the long run).

AR curve, *AC* is still falling. Therefore, *MC* must be below *AC*, although it may be falling or rising at this point. As we have established, the point of intersection of the *MC* and *AR* curves is the efficient output level, sustained by the indicated price which is relatively low. In fact it is so low that it fails to cover (average) costs: no privately owned firm would ever operate at this level. Therefore it will be necessary to subsidize production of '*x*' – the total subsidy being shown as the rectangle $Q_0(AC_0 - P_0)$ – if the socially desired output is to be achieved.

However, governments tend to feel uncomfortable politically – possibly for reasons examined below – subsidizing monopolies like this. Certainly, the monopoly could be 'de-regulated' (or 'privatized' if it were actually in public ownership) and be profitable. This is shown by the MR=MC output solution, at which price exceeds average cost; but of course this causes a considerable loss of consumers' surplus (i.e. loss of efficiency). The third option is to break up the monopoly into smaller competing enterprises (assuming they do not collude). But as shown (Fig. 5.2b), this may have even worse consequences, since the lowest price at which the smaller firms could survive is higher than the socially efficient price – society is losing the economies of scale in the production of '*x*' – and in this case higher even than the profit-maximizing monopoly price.

5.1.7 **Constraints on policy**

Lump-sum transfers

As we have just seen, achieving efficient output levels under decreasing costs ('natural monopoly') may require subsidization. There is in principle nothing unfair about this, since the idea of Pareto-efficiency is that the gainers (consumers of '*x*') can compensate the losers (taxpayers and consumers of other products generally) and still be better off. However, an immediate objection can be made: namely, doesn't the taxation itself create further distortions in the economy? Unfortunately, the answer is 'yes' except in the (very) special case of so-called 'lump-sum' transfers. To illustrate, we can take the case of a sales tax (or 'turnover', or 'value-added' tax) levied on a specific – i.e. per unit – basis on product '*y*'. This is purely for convenience. Many taxes are in fact levied on an *ad valorem* basis; i.e. as a proportion of the value or price of the good. As already seen (Fig. 5.1a), this shifts the after-tax supply schedule of '*y*' upwards, creating a divergence between the price paid by consumers (generally higher than before) and the amount received by producers (generally lower than before). In consequence, the equilibrium output of '*y*' decreases. However, although taxation of this sort improved efficiency where (negative) externalities were present, we assume that this is not the usual case. Instead, the taxation has created a distortion in the market for '*y*' as surely as if the industry were monopolistic. To extend the argument it turns out that taxes based upon levels of economic activity – whatever they may be: consumption, income, etc. – tend to affect those activities, so creating distortions. Economists have long searched for the 'optimal' tax, but have reached no consensus; except, as mentioned, for the hypothetical 'poll-tax'. That is, if we could levy taxes without regard to levels of economic activity, they would not distort economic decisions. For example, if my income is taxed I might alter my work pattern; but if at birth I had been presented with a lump-sum demand from the tax-man for £100,000, say, which had been paid on my behalf but remained as an inalterable debt regardless of what I chose to do, my economic choices would not be changed by this fact. As a simple example, consider how a firm's optimum output would change if the government levied a lump-sum tax on all businesses, regardless of their levels of profits.

Of course, you might argue that suicide is still a feasible option, but ignoring this unpleasant aspect, the reason a lump-sum tax (or subsidy, for that matter) works is because people are unable to respond. Individuals cannot choose their birth (and if you argue that parents will act on behalf of their potential children, we can extend the notion to a lump-sum tax on a whole family, including all past, present and future generations). Clearly, in practical terms, this is far-fetched, but it does suggest that if we must tax, it is better to tax activities which are least sensitive to price variations; i.e. are price-inelastic. In the limit, if the supply – or demand – of something is completely inelastic (like population in the preceding poll-tax example) no excess burden of welfare loss occurs by taxing it. Although nothing is quite so fixed, this reasoning partly explains the tendency of governments to favour taxes on earned income (work supplied inelastically) and on 'necessary luxuries' such as tobacco and alcohol (demanded inelastically). Nonetheless, there is no such thing as a 'perfect' tax system, and therefore benefits from correction of market-generated distortions must be weighed against the costs of the offsetting tax/subsidy distortions.

'Second-best'

A second cautionary point can also be raised in the present context. The ideal or 'best' situation is one where the marginal costs of all productive activities are just equal to prices. This is a slightly restrictive statement. As one economist put it: 'marginal everything should be equal to marginal everything-else'. But suppose it was impossible to achieve this, even in one industry ('*x*') only. Can we ignore this failure and proceed to set all prices equal to marginal costs everywhere else? Unfortunately, no. It has been shown, although I certainly will not try to repeat the argument here, that the existence of even one incorrigible monopolist may mean that in order to achieve our 'second-best' position it will be necessary to force systematic divergences of prices and marginal costs. This is a sobering thought, reflecting the same sort of problem as finding the 'best' tax system. To put it succinctly, if the market economy does not automatically produce a 'first-best' perfectly competitive equilibrium, it may not be possible for the government to correct it. Therefore we may need to look for ways of achieving the next-best outcome; but once we acknowledge this we have to abandon our first-best rules, and there is precious little to replace them.

5.2 Equity considerations and methods of intervention

Of course governments do not intervene in the economy only on efficiency grounds (or, as it is often called, *allocational* grounds, in reference to the fact that resources are being re-allocated between uses). As mentioned, there is very often a major equity motive, in that the government is effectively attempting to re-distribute income. Because of the impracticability of 'neutral' lump-sum taxes and subsidies the two effects cannot be separated: every re-allocation of resources in an attempt to achieve greater efficiency involves uncompensated gains and losses (compare any example of taxing to subsidize a natural monopoly); and conversely, every re-distribution of income – or more generally, wealth – in order to achieve greater equity affects efficiency, usually adversely.

5.2.1 **Interpersonal re-distribution**

Thus, for example, governments may institute ostensibly progressive systems of taxes on incomes which are likely to affect work effort, or they may impose minimum wages levels that distort the equilibrium of labour supply and demand. Alternatively, instead of legislating with respect to incomes, governments may interfere with expenditure decisions to achieve the same effect. For example, goods with high income elasticities of demand – hence consumed in greater proportion by the 'rich' – may be taxed at higher rates than 'necessities'. We have already seen, however, how in the absence of negative externalities this diminishes individual welfare (see Fig 5.1a,b). Another approach is to set maximum or ceiling prices on these income-elastic products. The effect of this is to create excess demand. This means that the available supply has somehow to be rationed, which in a free market is accomplished by a rise in price, stimulating production and discouraging demand. In the end, those who were unwilling to pay the market price – hence valuing '*x*' less than the resource-cost of producing it – would be excluded. Clearly, a black market functions in exactly this way. However, when we say 'unwilling' this is taken to include not only people whose tastes for '*x*' are less keen, but a good many whose incomes are very low. That is, you may be 'unwilling' to buy '*x*' if its price rises above the administered level precisely because you are poor. Instead, if the official price actually rules, the rationing is not in terms of willingness to pay but in terms of some other sacrifice, such as willingness to *wait*. Witness the long queues for low-priced consumer goods in planned economies, unless you are a ranking civil servant. On the face of it this may seem fairer than the market solution. The trouble is that the willingness of people to wait is unrelated to the cost of producing '*x*', so resources are not allocated efficiently. At the level of output at which available supply is exhausted, the extra *marginal* – cost of another unit of '*x*' is well below the marginal valuation (some) consumers attach to it. These 'unsatisfied' individuals would be willing to pay much more for '*x*', and at the same time some consumers who had obtained '*x*' (by queuing) would not have been willing to pay any more than the official price. Hence there would be an opportunity for gainful trade: the first group's maximum purchase price exceeds the second group's minimum selling price. But this is taking us back to the black market, explaining, in the process, why the 'underground' economy is such a normal feature of planned economies. And in some areas of market economies too. One is reminded of the scramble for tickets to the Wimbledon tennis final (rationed) and the subsequent astronomical prices for these tickets outside the gates.

5.2.2 **Industrial 'support'**

Governments do not restrict themselves to re-distributing income amongst individuals either. Especially in ostensible market economies, the type of intervention just described would rarely be applied for consumers' benefit, but it is in fact rather frequently applied for firms' benefit. As an example, suppose that the '*x*' industry is in long run, perfectly competitive equilibrium as shown (in Figs. 4.4a,b): price and quantity are determined at the point of intersection of aggregate supply (*MC*) and demand, and each firm is, at that price, at its break-even point. Now let aggregate demand shift to the left (e.g. falling income, superior substitutes) so existing firms are operating at a loss. Left to itself, firms would leave the '*x*' industry, consequently shifting the aggregate supply curve to the left, until the original price was restored. The net effect would thus be a contraction of the industry. Now imagine that the government does not wish to see this contraction, but instead determines to preserve the existing number of firms. This means that the price received by each producer must be such as to break even; i.e. P must be at least equal to AC. There are several ways of accomplishing this.

Minimum price ('buffer stock')

First, the government can simply set a minimum ('floor') price for '*x*' (Fig. 5.3a,b). If it is effective – no black market pushing price down – there will be excess supply. The government is therefore obliged to purchase this excess – otherwise price will fall – at a total cost as shown. Note that this 'stockpiling' scheme can be costly in terms of storage, etc. Hence to avoid these additional costs, and to recoup some of the subsidy, governments may sell the surplus to purchasers who are certain not to re-sell in the regulated

Figures 5.3a and b The direct cost of price support schemes

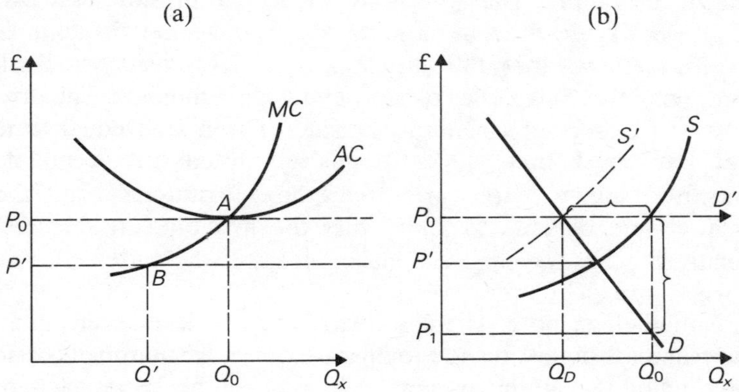

At the 'true' market price (P') the representative firm would be making losses, leading to exit of firms until P_0 is established (a reversal of the process depicted in Figs 4.4a,b). Under a buffer-stock scheme, from Q_D onwards (Fig. 5.3b) the market demand is replaced by government's infinitely elastic demand at price P_0. The direct cost of this subsidy is thus $(Q_0 - Q_D) \times P_0$. Alternatively, market price could be allowed to fall to P_1, with government making a 'deficiency' payment of $P_0 - P_1$ per unit sold. This eliminates stockpiles, but may be more costly, depending on supply-and-demand elasticities. Either scheme involves a loss of efficiency.

(domestic) market. Of course, government agencies will argue that this is merely one side of a total price-stabilization scheme. When demand shifts to the right and threatens to raise price (and induce entry), the stockpile can be sold off to hold price down. This may work in some markets, e.g. foreign exchange, but usually the weakness of market price proves to be chronic, so the scheme's effect is to permanently subsidize producers of 'x'.

Price subsidy ('deficiency payment')

A second method is to fix the price received by producers – after all, that is the point of the exercise – but to avoid the excess-supply problem by setting market price at a low enough level to just match the supply. The difference is the price subsidy, as shown. This again keeps firms in business who would otherwise fold, but avoids the awkward political problems of highly visible stockpiles and, possibly, cheap sales to 'unfriendly' governments. The direct cost of this second scheme is indicated by an area equal to the per-unit subsidy times the entire quantity; in the first scheme it is shown as equal to market price times the excess supply (Fig. 5.3b). You should be able to verify that the first type of scheme is relatively cheaper the less elastic the supply and/or demand curves, and vice-versa.

Nonetheless, both schemes clearly distort the market equilibrium and cause the industry to operate where the marginal costs of production exceed the marginal valuation consumers attach to '*x*'. The resultant income loss to society (the loss of consumers' surplus) is the measure of a government's desire to maintain existing firms in that industry.

Output restriction ('cartel')

A third type of scheme can be outlined, although there may be many variants. If all the existing firms colluded to restrict output they could all continue to break even. Of course, they would need to reduce output beyond the level where the original price could hold, since their average costs have risen as well, so price needs to be that much higher. If they all adhered to this level of output things would work out all right; but any single firm has an incentive to cheat. Taking the collusion price as given, the single firm can maximize (positive) profit at a higher level of output. Since each is too small to individually affect the market, this temptation is likely to be too great (a classic example of this is the breakdown of the OPEC cartel). That is, unless the government steps in to pay them not to produce! How much will it take to bribe them? The amount of profit they individually perceive they could have had by cheating!

Summary

The principal criterion that is used to 'judge' market results is that of Pareto-efficiency: can anyone be made better off by reallocating resources to alternative uses, without making anyone else worse off? This notion is extendable to situations where compensation might be required, in which case it can be stated as: can the gainers compensate the losers and still be better off? For a perfectly competitive economy the answer to either question is 'no', for the simple reason that there are no discrepancies between production costs and willingness to pay – at the margin – in any market. In an abstract sense the assertion is simply that if any two people can trade to mutual benefit, they will do so in a free competitive market economy; otherwise, beneficial trades are being prevented.

This suggests that breakdowns occur where 'third parties' might be affected. In principle they could enter into the trading process, but the transactions costs of increasingly wide involvement would accelerate. Hence, governments frequently tax and subsidize ('negative' and 'positive' respectively). Moreover, it is apparent that imperfect competition is not likely to be efficient. Of course, governments intervene to promote competition, but this raises other problems. Some industries are 'natural' monopolies that would seem to require direct regulation to achieve efficiency. However, the subsidy that this typically involves may be raised through taxation, which will itself distort other markets. Also, if a fully efficient 'first-best' economy cannot be achieved, it is not certain that trying to promote competition in the remainder of the economy is in fact 'second-best'.

Quite apart from the question of efficiency there is the question of equity (in principle: in practice the two are mixed). This is clearly a moral/political issue, but we can demonstrate at least the costs of redistributive measures. For those designed to aid households (e.g. ceiling prices) it is easy to show why 'black' markets arise. For those designed to aid firms – far more numerous in the West than the former type – we also are able to illustrate the creation of market distortions.

Appendix 5 Factor-market efficiency conditions

We have derived the Pareto-efficient condition that prices should equal marginal costs for product markets. Here we ask what is the equivalent rule for input (factor) markets?

You may rightly expect that it is the perfectly competitive condition: the wage rate should equal the marginal value product. That is, the general rule:

$$MLC = MR \times MPL$$

reduces in perfect competition to:

$$w \quad = P \times MPL\ ;$$

or,

$$\frac{w}{P} = MPL\ ;$$

the 'real' wage rate should be equal to the marginal product of labour (and similarly for capital). If a central planner decided to employ labour (in industry '*x*') at some lower level, MPL exceeds *w*/*P*. What this means is that someone, somewhere, is willing to work for that real wage – reflecting his/her subjective choice between leisure and more income – and at the same time, by employing more labour in '*x*', society could gain in the sense that consumers of '*x*' could compensate that extra work and still be better off. Indeed, if production were not in planners' hands those workers would have an incentive to increase their output of '*x*' precisely because the additional revenue was worth more to them than the subjective cost of their additional labour. This gain continues to accrue until, at the margin, the marginal valuation consumers attach to the output of another unit of labour just equals the subjective valuation in terms of the wage that workers attach to their marginal labour. Beyond the efficient point the subjective cost of additional labour exceeds the value consumers place on the goods it produces.

It is interesting to note that this restriction of employment, together with the implied lower wage rate – as compared to perfect competition – results from monposonistic behaviour. Therefore it can be corrected either by encouraging competition, or by price regulation as indicated. Note that the fixing of a minimum of 'floor' wage in this case induces a rise in employment. You should be able to verify that this counter-intuitive result occurs because, although the wage is higher, the marginal labour cost (MLC) is lower up to the equilibrium level.

Part II Macroeconomics

6 Macroeconomics: The Basic Equilibrium Model

Outline

Synopsis

This chapter begins by considering the element of simultaneity that distinguishes macroeconomics from microeconomics, including the fundamental issues of existence, uniqueness and, especially, stability of general market equilibrium.

Three measures of nominal income (product, income and expenditure) are identified and related in the concept of 'circular-flow', initially for a stationary economy with no saving. The Quantity Theory of money is introduced in order to highlight the determinants of these nominal levels.

The determination of output (real income) levels is then considered in terms of four aggregated markets: consumption goods, labour, capital goods and bonds. Together with the money market these constitute our basic general equilibrium supply-and-demand model. Non-stationary (growth) equilibrium is introduced by adding a savings–investment model. These are also incorporated into the 'shorthand' model of circular-flow equilibrium.

The final stage is to allow household consumption behaviour to alter (in favour of saving) and to compare equilibria. We conclude that in terms of orthodox Classical analysis the rate of interest must fall; whereas, although money wages and prices might fall in the short run, under certain special – but non-essential – assumptions they retain their original levels in the new long-run equilibrium.

Introduction

In microeconomic analysis the focus is on the decisions made by individual firms and households concerning the supply and/or demand for certain inputs (e.g. labour, capital goods) and outputs (e.g. goods '*x*', '*y*') under certain constraints such as price–quantity relationships and competitive conditions. Although this may have some operational relevance at the individual level, the chief concern of the economist as a social scientist is to deduce or predict the resultant prices and quantities of inputs and outputs, and to establish whether these correspond to an efficient use of limited resources in the special 'Paretian' sense of not being able to make anyone better off without necessarily making anyone else worse off.

In macroeconomic analysis we take the logical next step of looking at the entire economy, not as a multitude of separate markets, but as an interconnected whole in which it is literally true that 'everything affects everything else'. For example, in a micro context an assumed change in consumer tastes concerning good '*x*' shifts the demand curve for 'x', thus altering equilibrium price (P_x) and quantity (Q_x). Also, we know that this will affect the demand for inputs in 'x' and therefore alter the prices of hiring both labour and capital in that industry. However, this is only a partial analysis, which ignores many important ramifications, including: (1) a change in P_x shifts all other product demand curves, hence alters both output and input prices in those sectors as well; (2) because homogeneous (identical) units of labour and capital must ultimately receive the same wage and interest rate, these inputs will shift between sectors as long as differentials persist, thus affecting cost and supply conditions; and (3) at these new wage and interest levels income may have altered from its earlier level, generating a further source of change in the pattern of demand.

At first it might seem that any attempt to determine the eventual equilibrium set of prices and quantities would be hopelessly complex: there are just too many simultaneous conditions that have to be met. In a sense this objection is well-taken, insofar as it applies to our inability to mentally juggle a large number of items at once. However, when these conditions are expressed as mathematical equations, it is certainly within the capability of modern computers to solve very large systems.

Indeed, for many applications such as macroeconomic forecasting, computers are absolutely indispensable when it comes to crunching out the numbers. But with each degree of 'disaggregation' – i.e. the more sectors that are included in the whole model – there is inevitably some further removal from easy comprehension. That is why, at least at an introductory level, we take the opposite approach of extreme aggregation in analysing simultaneous, or general equilibrium. All consumer goods are heroically aggregated into a single 'consumption good'; all labour is supplied and demanded in a single 'labour market'; etc. In fact, we will be dealing mainly with just five of these aggregate markets; *viz*: labour, consumption goods, capital goods, bonds and money markets. The latter two are financial markets, and could be considered the feature of macroeconomics that distinguishes it from being simply microeconomics on a broader scale. However, although it is the case that money demand in particular is not usually dealt with on the level of introductory microeconomics, the two subjects are definitely two facets of the same edifice.

Ironically, there may be a temptation to dismiss this focus on a mere five markets as too macroscopic, but in fact generations of economists will testify to the subtle difficulties of grasping simultaneity even in this context. There are in fact three distinguishable problems surrounding the study of general equilibrium. First, there is the problem of whether or not any set of equilibrium prices actually exists; i.e. *can* all markets simultaneously clear? This is not so obvious as it seems; for instance, with the usual U-shaped average and marginal cost curves it is not generally possible to prove it. Second, there may be more than one set of equilibrium prices: the problem of *uniqueness*. And third, obviously related to both of these, is the problem of stability: if the economy is out of equilibrium, can we rely on automatic market mechanisms to restore it; and, as a secondary but practically very important question, how long might this process take? As we shall see, it is this last issue that generates most of the well-known controversies in economics.

6.1 An overview

6.1.1 Measures of product, income and expenditure

In the simplest type of market economy firms produce final consumer goods and services using labour and capital inputs. The value of this final output – taken at current market prices – is called the gross product (Y_g). (More usually, gross national product (GNP) or gross domestic product (GDP). The difference is that the former includes the value of output produced in the rest of the world (RoW) with inputs owned by domestic residents and excludes output produced domestically but with inputs owned by foreigners. Vice-versa for GDP.) 'Gross' because some of the stock of capital goods is used up in production (indicated by depreciation or capital-consumption allowances) and this is in a sense embodied in the value of the final goods and services. If the stock of capital goods were to be kept intact, a fraction of total output would have to be devoted to replacement: hence, net product (Y_n) is gross output minus depreciation. In fact, for present purposes, and in keeping with our earlier microeconomic treatment, we will ignore depreciation as though capital goods were infinitely durable. Thus, gross and net product can be represented by the same symbol (Y).

Whatever the value of output might be, we must also be able to account for it in terms of the 'value-added' by each of the input components: *viz*, labour and capital. Specifically, total wage payments at the going rate, plus total interest payments at the going rate, plus profits in the economic sense (positive or negative) must be equal to the market value of the goods produced. It is akin to the fact that a single firm's revenues can be distributed as wages, interest, and profit (in fact, in the perfectly competitive environment usually assumed, the last item is zero).

Firms might decide as a matter of convenience to retain some of the income due to capital – if it had been provided by shareholders – but in principle both wage and capital payments (including normal interest and profits, if any) can be seen as wholly distributed to the households who ultimately have provided both the labour and the capital. In other words, we can think of the value of output as being identically reflected in the amount of current income received by households.

Finally, it is up to these households to decide on their spending and saving patterns. Here we shall initially make an enormous simplification by excluding any saving: all income must necessarily be devoted to current consumption! This means that our simple economy is by assumption in macroeconomic, or 'circular flow' equilibrium: the value of consumer goods produced or supplied is necessarily equal to the value of consumer goods demanded. Symbolically, letting C_S stand for the former and C_D for the latter, equilibrium can be written in shorthand fashion simply as:

$$C_D = C_S$$

Of course, at this stage we have assumed that the sole type of product made by firms is a consumer good, and that the only use for the income arising from production is spending on consumption. Nonetheless, even in this artificial model it is possible to examine several interesting features.

First, note that it is possible to measure total product (Y) in three different ways:

1. As the market value of all the goods and services actually produced. For a single good 'x' this is simply $P_x \times Q_x$, but since we are aggregating all of these individual goods conceptually into a single 'good', the value of the output of this one good is generally written as:

   $$Y = P \times Q \ (= C_S \text{ in this case})$$

P is the price level, and Q is the quantity of the consumption good physically produced (in reality, P is weighted average of the prices of a 'basket' of many goods and services and Q is often residually calculated as Y/P. For example, suppose nominal income (Y) remains at £100B, and the price of a 'unit' of consumption – a pound of meat plus a shirt plus a day's rent, etc. – changes from £100 to £200. 'Units' of consumption (Q) would thus have declined from 1B to ½B (500M). Also, Y and P themselves are often expressed as indexes, ($\bar{Y}$ and $\bar{P}$); e.g. the index of nominal income would remain constant at $Y = 100$ while the price index would rise from $P = 100$ to $P = 200$. In consequence, the index of output (Q) would fall from 100 to 50.)

2. Alternatively, total product can be measured as the value of incomes received by the (household) owners of labour and capital. If there are no economic profits this is just:

$$Y = w \times L + r \times K$$

where w and r are the wage and interest rate, and L and K are the aggregate quantities of labour and capital (the latter in nominal, or money terms)

3. As the value of total expenditure, which in this case is just C_D: i.e.

$$Y = C_D$$

Taking (1) and (3) together we see that

$$C_S = C_D$$

is guaranteed.

6.1.2 **Nominal income and the Quantity Equation**

The second item of interest centres on the fact that these are all measure of nominal, or money, income.

This suggests that the amount of money (M) in the economy might have some bearing on the level of income (Y), an idea that is encapsulated in the so-called 'Quantity Equation' of money:

$$Y = M \times V$$

V is called the income-*velocity* of money for the obvious reason that if we divide income (taken over some period of time) by the average stock of money during that period, then Y/M shows the average turnover of one unit of currency (e.g. £1) over that period.

So far this is merely definitional and asserts nothing about the level of income as it may be related to the quantity of money. If M were to vary, then clearly Y would change not only depending on the change in M, but also on any change in V. Formally, there is no limit: Y might even move in the *opposite* direction to M if V altered sufficiently.

In contrast, the so-called 'Quantity Theory' of money holds that V is not subject to wide fluctuations: hence, changes in the level of nominal income are fairly closely correlated with changes in the quantity of money.

The 'old' Quantity Theory held that the near-constancy of velocity was due to institutional factors. For example, my bills fall due at a uniform rate each month, say £20/day. If I am paid a monthly (30-day) salary of £600, my average balance over the month is £300, which implies a velocity of two (£300 supports £600 of expenditure). However, if I am paid £150 weekly (4 weeks in a month!) then my average money balances will be £75 over the whole month: a velocity of eight! In short, velocity for the whole economy was thought to be an average of conventional periods for receipts and disbursements.

The 'new' Quantity Theory asserts much the same, but argues that the stability of V is due to the desire of households to hold a fairly stable proportion of their total wealth – taken in the broadest sense – in liquid form. In abstract, we can think of their 'wealth' as the discounted, or present, value of their entire lifetime earnings (seen from the perspective of youth). During the household's lifetime this wealth will be partly embodied in real fixed assets like a house, semi-fixed assets like a car or consumer durables, a stream of current consumer non-durables such as vacations, food and clothing, and financial assets of equally variable longevity, ranging from a pension to stocks and bonds, to money balances. The argument is that the composition of these lifetime asset holdings, though responsive to changes in relative prices (e.g. house prices rise and vacation costs fall) is not volatile: i.e. does not alter sharply. Hence, desired money balances remain reasonably constant relative to households' planned expenditures.

When this quantity-theoretic view is combined with the belief that M can be controlled by the central bank (acting as the agent of government), we obtain the policy doctrine known colloquially as 'Monetarism': i.e. the control of the level of nominal income (Y) via control of the quantity of money (M).

There is, as you might expect, an opposing view which argues that either: (1) velocity is much more unstable than quantity theorists suggest; and/or (2) in any event the quantity of money cannot be adequately controlled, at least in modern financially sophisticated economics where 'near-money' assets can be readily created. In either case, the level of total expenditure, income or product – call it what you will – is not controllable by central bank action.

We will return to this controversy a bit later, after we have taken up and completed the orthodox, 'Classical' (or 'neo-classical' which is a term applied often to the standard microeconomic theory of Part I) view on the mechanisms of the circular flow, of which the Quantity Theory is usually considered a part.

We begin therefore with Fig. 6.1, which shows how nominal income (Y) is determined by the quantity of money, or 'money supply' (M_S). For instance, with a comparatively high interest rate (e.g. r_1), velocity would be greater (at V_1) as households – and business firms – economized on their non-interest-bearing money balances. Hence, a higher level of total expenditure (Y_1 or Y_0) could be sustained by the given money supply. A fall in the rate of interest (to r_2) would lead to a somewhat greater willingness to hold money balances, and the consequent *fall* in velocity (to V_2) would thus be consistent with a fall in nominal expenditure (to Y_2) (see also Fig. 6.5).

However, the crucial question is how the composition of nominal income is determined between the price level (P) and the volume of output, or real income (Q) – which in the stationary context is identical to Q_c, the quantity of consumption good produced.

6.2 The general equilibrium of supply and demand

The short answer to this is that Q, like every other quantity in the economy, is determined by the forces of supply-and-demand. In

Figure 6.1 The money market

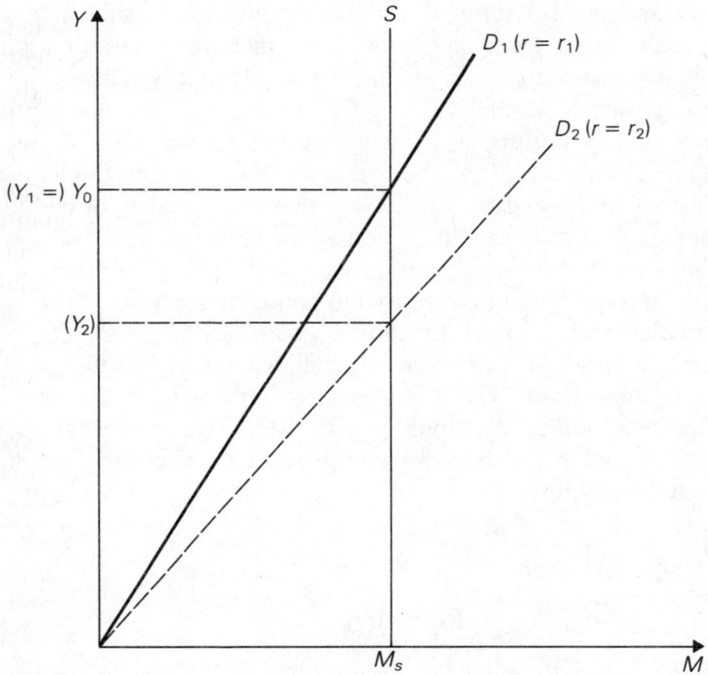

> Desired money balances as a proportion of current income ($M/Y = 1/v$) depend partly upon the rate of interest: as r falls, these are shown to increase. That is, the velocity of money decreases. A given quantity of money, M_s (supplied by the Central Bank) is thus consistent with a particular level of nominal income, for each rate of interest.

the context of general, simultaneous equilibrium in which labour and capital markets must also clear, this means that output is always at its 'full employment' level. By 'full employment' we mean that no inputs – and especially no human workers – that are willing to be employed at (or below) the going rate are unable to find a job. Conversely, any inputs that are not employed can only be so if they are only willing to be hired at more than the going rate: i.e. their 'unemployment' is in that sense voluntary rather than involuntary.

6.2.1 Consumption-goods market

The assumed situation of general equilibrium is shown in Figs 6.1–6.5. As we have seen, Fig. 6.1 depicts the determination of nominal income (Y_0) according to the Quantity Theory (given money supply, M_s and velocity V_1). In Fig. 6.2 this total nominal level of expenditure is depicted by the (hyperbolic) aggregate demand schedule (D_0): the area ($P_c \times Q_c$) under this curve is constant and equal to Y_0 showing that any number of combinations of P_c and Q_c could be consistent with this amount of total *money* expenditure. (Note that we use P_c and Q_c to denote the price and quantity of consumption goods, respectively. The same variables with respect to capital goods are P_K and Q_K. The aggregate price level, P, is a weighted average of P_c and P_K; while aggregate output, Q, is a weighted average of Q_c and the *additional* output of capital-goods, ΔQ_K (Q_K representing the *stock* of capital goods previously produced). Therefore, we have the relationships:

$$\begin{aligned} Y &= P \times Q \\ &= P_c \times Q_c + P_K \times \Delta Q_K \end{aligned}$$

In the assumed case where $\Delta Q_K = 0$, P and Q are identical to P_c and Q_c.)

The same diagram (Fig. 6.2) shows that equilibrium in the consumption-goods market occurs (at Q_{C_0}) where this demand intersects the supply schedule(s): i.e. where C_S – the area under the supply schedule – equals C_D, the area under the demand schedule. We show both the short-run schedule reflecting short-run marginal costs of production aggregated over the existing number of firms, as well as the long-run industry supply schedule in which firms may enter or leave the consumption-goods sector. As is apparent, we assume that this is a 'constant-cost' industry such that variations in the number of firms affect neither the technical nor the pecuniary (per unit labour and capital cost) conditions facing the representative firm. Note, however, that this constant long-run supply price depends on factor prices; in particular the wage rate (w).

Figure 6.2 The consumption-goods market

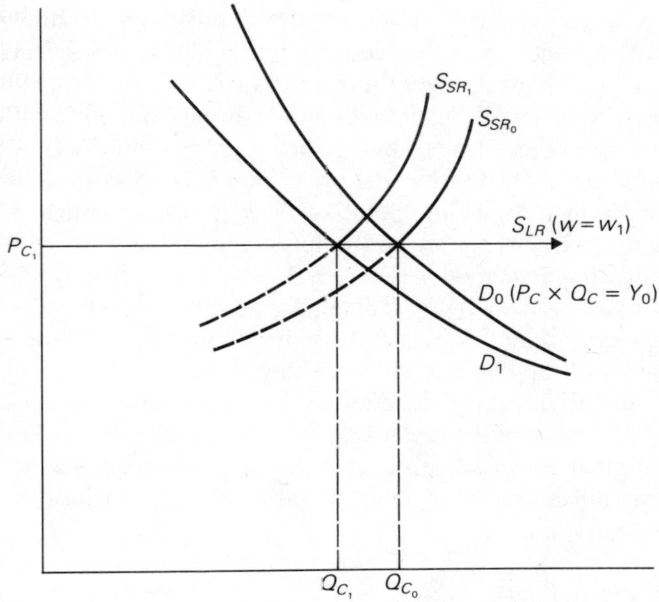

In a stationary economy all income is spent on consumption: the area $P_c \times Q_c$ under the demand curve D_0 is constant and equal to Y_0. The equilibrium level of output (Q_{c_0}) is therefore determined by supply conditions, in both short- and long-run situations. Keeping nominal income at Y_0 (= Y_1), but allowing for savings means that the consumption–demand curve shifts to the left. On the simplest assumption that money prices remain the same – especially the money wage rate – this translates into reduced consumption-good output to Q_{c_1} but also to simultaneously increased capital-good production. Remember, however, that this higher investment level will lead to higher *future* consumptions, in contrast to being permanently at Q_{c_0} in the stationary state. (i.e. D_1 will shift rightwards continually).

6.2.2 **Labour market**

Fig. 6.3a shows the supply and demand for labour in terms of the *money* wage rate (w). Each of these schedules is drawn in particular on the *ceteris paribus* assumption that the price level (P) is fixed. If it changes, then these curves will shift in response. (A minor point concerns the definition of P. From firms' point of view it is an average of the things they produce and sell: i.e. a combination of P_C and P_K, the prices of consumption and capital goods. From households' point of view it is an average of the things they buy, which are consumption goods and, instead of the machines (capital goods) themselves, the bonds that confer indirect ownership of them. Taking P_B as the price of bonds, we shall assume that it varies in proportion to P_K, so there is no possibility of the two schedules shifting unequally.)

The underlying 'real' schedules, expressing labour supply and demand in terms of the real wage rate (e.g. the demand schedule is the marginal (physical) product of labour curve aggregated over firms in both consumption- and capital-goods sectors) are shown in Fig. 6.3b.

6.2.3 **Capital-goods market**

The market for capital goods is shown in Fig. 6.4a. As with consumption goods, all the supply-and-demand schedules for different types of goods are aggregated in this single diagram. The price variable here is similarly a weighted average of these many actual equipment prices ('the' price of capital goods, P_K). Again, the short-run supply schedule S_{SR} reflects short-run marginal costs, whereas the long-run schedule again illustrates that the entry or exit of firms has no effect on the level of costs. (Incidentally, capital is used in its own production when we consider it in an aggregative sense.)

Capital is peculiar in that it is both an output – like consumption goods (denoted by Q_K) – and an input, like labour (denoted by K). Hence, its supply is similar to the former, whereas its demand is similar in nature to the latter. The difference is that capital goods are *durable* inputs yielding a marginal product over time, rather than instantaneously. To put it as briefly as possible (see Appendix for an elaboration), the future stream of net revenues (the market value of the additional output less operating costs such as labour and maintenance) that is expected to flow from an additional unit of capital – a 'representative machine' – has a present value

Figures 6.3a and b The labour market: determination of money and real wage rates

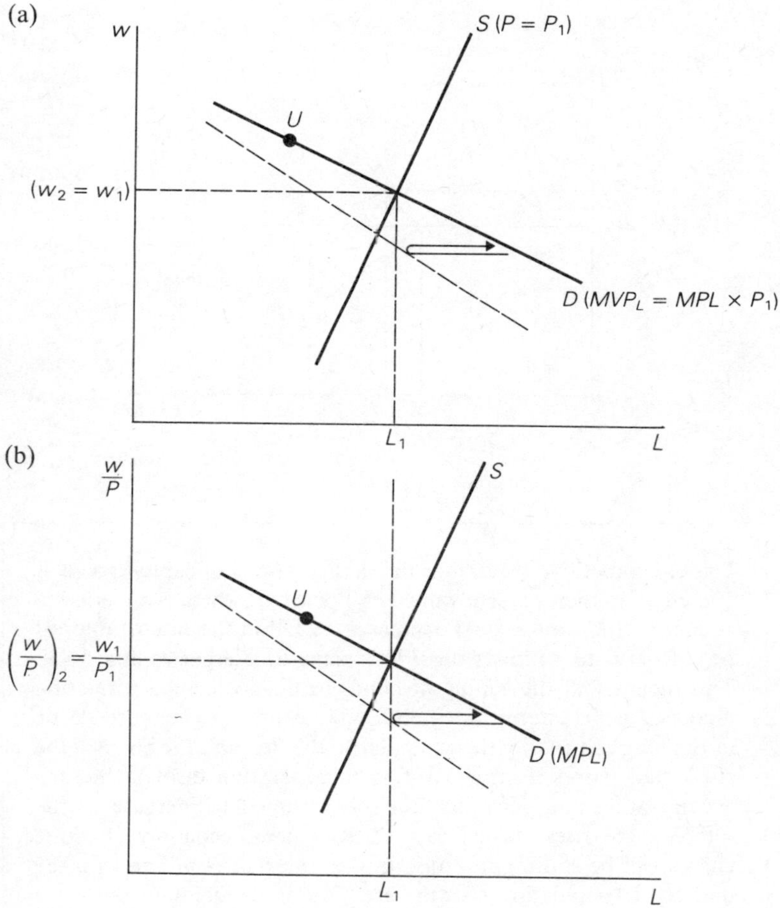

The real wage rate is determined by the real forces of supply (the rate at which households are willing to trade leisure for goods) and demand (the marginal productivity of labour, with a given capital stock). The money wage rate at which the labour market is in equilibrium therefore depends on the price level, which it also serves to determine. At a point like U the money wage rate is above its market-clearing level, given the price level at P_1; i.e., the real wage rate is too high. Decreased consumption-good demand will shift the labour demand curves temporarily to the left, but in (neo-)Classical theory the concomitant increase in capital-goods output will reverse this, as shown by the reversing arrows.

Figure 6.4a The capital-goods and (derived) bond markets

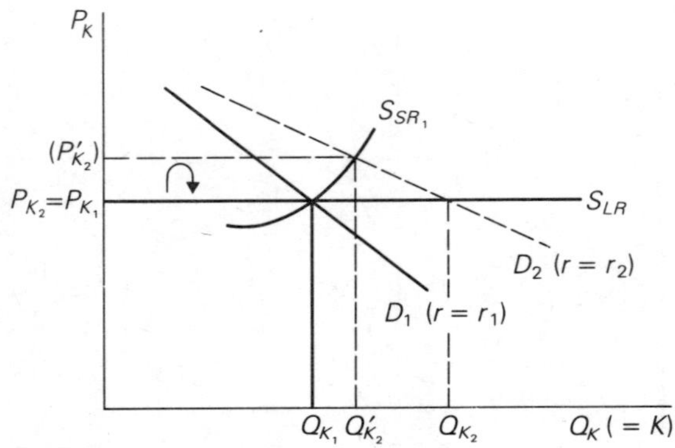

Under competitive conditions the demand price of capital goods is just equal to their present value (*PV*) per unit, which is assumed to decline as the capital stock increases. A fall in the rate of interest (e.g. from r_1 to r_2) raises this *PV*, leading to a larger capital stock. This means that the supply of bonds to finance capital formation increases as the interest rate falls, and is assumed to be more elastic in the long run (verify this). Similarly, the demand for bonds – the stock that passes from generation to generation through lifetime accumulation and decumulation – is assumed to increase as the interest rate rises. In a steady-state dynamic economy all these curves will be shifting in proportion to the right – in line with the underlying population growth rate – so as to maintain the same equilibrium interest rate (e.g. r_1).

depending on the market rate of interest (r). This present value (*PV*) indicates just how much a firm would be willing to pay for this unit of capital, and is therefore, in a competitive economy, the demand price for capital. The demand schedule of Fig. 6.4a is based on the assumed constancy of the interest rate (*ceteris paribus* once again), and shows that as the size of the capital stock increases, this demand price declines. Why? Because we assume that either additional units of capital yield successively smaller increases in output (diminishing marginal productivity of capital) or operating costs are rising, or both. In other words, the *PV* of additional units of capital is falling.

6.2.4 **Bond market**

The next diagram (Fig. 6.4b) relates the *value* of the capital stock to the rate of interest (r). The assumption, familiar from microeconomics, is that this represents borrowing, so the value of the capital stock is identically expressed as the market value of the stock of bonds which have been issued by firms to finance their physical capital formation. Thus for example, equilibrium B_1 is equal to $P_{K_1} \times Q_{K_1}$, and corresponds to an equilibrium interest rate of r_1 as shown.

The upward-sloping demand schedule for bonds is a reflection of the accumulation behaviour of households. Although there is by assumption no net saving, each household presumably saves in the earlier periods by building up a holding of bonds which it then lives off in later, 'retirement' periods. Thus, there is some stock of bonds (e.g. B_1) which in theory passes from generation to generation forever. What the demand schedule shows is that the size of this stock increases with a (permanent) increase in the rate of interest (households assumed to build up larger bond-holdings in earlier periods) and vice-versa. (This implies that the substitution effect of a change in the rate of interest outweighs the income effect. See Chapter 1 on saving behaviour.)

The downward-sloping *supply* schedule for bonds is derived from Fig. 6.4a. In particular, the demand schedule in this preceding diagram is drawn on the *ceteris paribus* assumption of a given rate of interest. But if, for example, this rate were to fall (say, from r_1 to r_2), this would raise the present value (*PV*) of capital goods (see Appendix), and shift the demand schedule in Fig. 6.4a upwards as shown. This would mean that the cost of the desired capital stock – the value of the stock of bonds issued to finance it – increases. As shown in Fig. 6.4b, depending on whether we move along the short- or long-run (industry) supply schedule the supply of bonds will be less or more elastic with respect to the rate of interest. (Although we usually interpret the rate of interest as determining a particular quantity of bonds (associated with a particular quantity of capital goods), it is perfectly possible to reverse direction: in this interpretation we read for any given quantity of bonds (capital), the rate of interest that just equalizes the present value of the capital with its price (see Appendix). Looked at in this way, the long-run schedule in Fig. 6.4b is called the 'marginal efficiency of capital' (m.e.c.) schedule, while the short-run schedule is called the 'marginal efficiency of investment' (m.e.i.) schedule.) This increased demand for a larger capital stock is exactly what is reflected in the increased stock of bonds being supplied. (Note, of course, that this is hypothetical, since at the initial equilibrium prices where all markets simultaneously clear there are no forces tending to alter the rate of interest from its initial level of r_1.)

To summarize, observe the circular flow of income and expenditure as illustrated through our simplified set of more-or-less familiar diagrams: total product – consisting of consumption goods entirely – is shown as $P_{c_1} \times Q_{c_0}$ $(=Y_0)$ in Fig. 6.2. The area under the supply schedule is C_S; and this is equal to the sum of the areas $w_1 \times L_1$ (the aggregate wage bill shown in Fig. 6.3a) and $r_1 \times B_1$ (total interest payments shown in Fig. 6.4b). In turn, this is equal to aggregate consumption expenditure which is also shown by the area $P_{C_1} \times Q_{C_0}$ in Fig. 6.2. The area under the demand curve is C_D, so it is apparent that the point of intersection between supply and demand schedules is where $C_D = C_S$. Finally, we can observe that this total expenditure must equal $M_s \times V_1$, which is shown as a *distance* along the vertical axis in Fig. 6.1; i.e., Y_0.

Finally, we can 'close' this model of the economy with Fig. 6.5. Here we reverse the *ceteris paribus* assumption of Fig. 6.1 and show how the demand for money balances varies with the rate of interest, for given levels of income. At the initial income level Y_0 $(=Y_1)$ households and business firms will just be willing to hold the existing quantity of money (M_s) at r_1.

6.3 A dynamic economy: saving and investment

So far, we have been looking at a long-run 'stationary' economy; literally, one that maintains the same prices and quantities period after period. The key distinguishing feature of such an economy is that it is not accumulating capital goods – i.e. there is no (net) investment – and equivalently, there is no net saving. As mentioned, younger households buy an unchanging stock of bonds

Figures 6.4b and 6.5 Relationship of bond and money markets

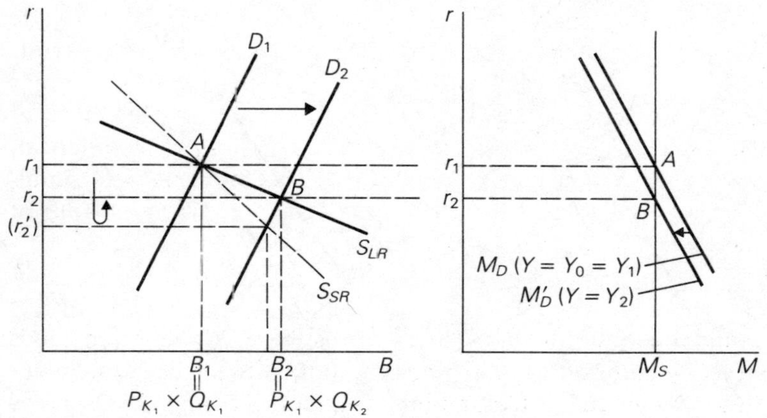

At the initial interest rate (r_1) and income level (Y_1) the supply and demand for both the stock of bonds and the stock of money are in balance (at B_1 and M_s respectively). In a steadily-growing economy r_1 could be maintained as all the relevant curves shifted proportionately to the right – including M_s, notice!

An increased desire to save shifts bond demand (and the associated savings schedule of Fig. 6.4d) from D_1 to D_2. The fall in the rate of interest to r_2 is consistent with a fall in nominal income to Y_2 (see Fig. 6.1). The economy has moved from *A* to *B*, and can continue to grow, or expand, from this new 'starting' position.

(B_1) from older households, and sell them in turn, as they themselves age.

6.3.1 'Steady-state' growth

However, if the number of households is increasing over time this population growth will be consistent with an ever-increasing aggregate demand for bonds: the upward-sloping schedule of Fig. 6.4b will shift continuously to the right, (as will the labour supply and the consumption-good demand schedules), as shown in Fig. 6.4c.

Figures 6.4c and d The bond market in a dynamic context: saving and investment

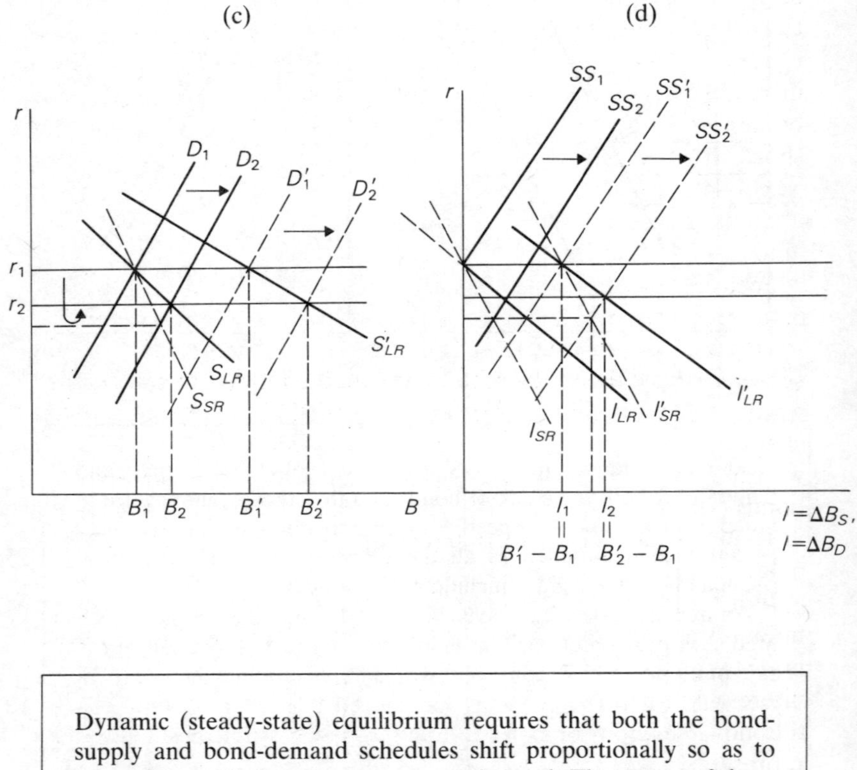

Dynamic (steady-state) equilibrium requires that both the bond-supply and bond-demand schedules shift proportionally so as to leave the equilibrium interest rate unchanged. The extent of these shifts can be diagrammed separately (in Fig. 6.4d): the change in bond demand is, for any given level of r, saving; the change in bond supply is investment. These two diagrams thus show that equilibrium of supply-and-demand for the existing stock of bonds is maintained over time by the equilibrium of savings–investment flows.

A shift of preferences in favour of savings can be shown as an additional rightward shift of the bond-demand curves in Fig. 6.4c. Note that although this leads to a long-run rate of interest at r_2, in the short run it may fall even further (to r'_2). In terms of the changes in bond demand and supply – i.e. saving and investment as shown in Fig. 6.4d – in each subsequent period savings will be greater than before.

Of course, one apparent possibility is that this will drive both the interest and the wage rate continuously downwards. Indeed, this was the (in)famous conclusion of the Rev. Thomas Malthus in the early nineteenth century (and which led the historian Thomas Carlyle to dub Economics 'the Dismal Science'). Fortunately, this is only half the picture, since population growth can also mean increased demand for consumption goods, and therefore, for both more labour and additional capital goods to produce them. In short, it is possible to see change as a process of so-called 'steady-state' growth in which all the schedules of Figs. 6.1 to 6.5 are continuously shifting to the right in exactly proportional amounts, so that the equilibrium prices remain unchanged.

Focusing, for example, on the bond market described by Fig. 6.4c, this can be shown as an equal shift of both S and D schedules, leaving the rate of interest the same (at r_1). In subsequent periods these schedules would continue to shift rightwards, but it is sufficient for our purposes to concentrate on the changes occurring over a single representative period. Specifically, we can now show the resulting positive change in the demand for bonds (ΔB_D) and the positive change in the supply of bonds (ΔB_s) in terms of the savings (SS) and investment (I) schedules of Fig. 6.4d.

In a stationary economy, these schedules can be thought of as intersecting precisely along the vertical axis at r_1. In the assumed non-stationary growing economy they intersect at the same rate of interest, but at a positive level. Fig. 6.4d represents equilibrium in the 'flow' of additional bond supply and demand, just as Fig. 6.4c represents a sequence of 'stock' equilibria.

6.3.2 Savings–investment equilibrium

In terms of the simple model of circular flow, we see that the value of total production is now composed of two elements: the value of consumption goods (C_S) and the value of the additional capital goods, or investment (I); i.e.:

$$Y = C_S + I$$

As before, this amount is the value of the aggregate income received by labour and capital, which are ultimately owned by households. Now, however, households are allowed not only to spend on consumption (C_D), but also to save (S); i.e.:

$$Y = C_D + S$$

This second equation can be thought of as the 'uses' of income, in contrast to the 'sources' of income expressed in the first equation. In fact, it must be true that:

$$\underbrace{C_S + I}_{\text{'sources'}} \equiv \underbrace{C_D + S}_{\text{'uses'}}$$

where the triple-bar indicates an identity.

It is important to distinguish this from the equilibrium condition that:

$$C_S = C_D$$

i.e. equilibrium in the consumption-good market occurs when the (value of) goods supplied is matched by the (value of) goods demanded.

An evident alternative way to express the same equilibrium condition results from subtracting the last equation from the preceding identity: i.e.

$$I = S$$

which we recognize as the condition that the change in the supply of bonds equal the change in the demand for bonds; or simply, investment equals saving.

Figs. 6.1–6.5 can now be conceived as representing the general equilibrium of a simple non-stationary (growth) economy with positive savings and investment.

Strictly speaking, as Fig. 6.4c relates to Fig. 6.4b, we ought to show two pairs of supply-and-demand schedules in each of the other diagrams, Figs. 6.1 to 6.4a (but not for Fig. 6.4d which illustrates changes): a 'before' (leftward pair) and 'after' (rightward-shifted pair, designated by primes). However, rather than make a mess of the diagrams, we can imagine that the schedules in their original positions are a 'snapshot' of a growing economy taken at, say, the beginning of some arbitrary period. Fig. 6.4d shows how much savings and investment is about to occur; and therefore how much the schedules in Fig. 6.4c are about to shift; and, since the economy is growing smoothly, this shift will be matched by exactly proportional shifts in the other schedules – including, note, the exogenous supply of money – that we do not attempt to illustrate.

6.3.3 The real level of consumption: short- and long-run considerations

Apart from that, the one significant re-interpretation of our original stationary-state diagrams concerns the consumption-good demand schedule.

We are making the explicit assumption that nominal income is the same in this dynamic context as in the stationary context. That is, $Y_1 = Y_0$. Furthermore, we assume for convenience that the quantity of output, Q, is also the same. Hence, the price level, P, is also the same.

However, because new capital goods are now being produced in addition to consumption goods, for output to remain constant it must be true that Q_C is less than in the stationary state. This is shown by the new equilibrium level Q_{C_1} in Fig. 6.2. The new demand curve (D_1) lies inside D_0 because some of the income is being saved, in the net sense that the greater number of younger households want to accumulate assets (bonds) in excess of the amounts being sold by the smaller number of older households in order to finance their retirement consumption. This excess demand for bonds is met by the increase in the capital stock, which it finances. Note also that the area under D_1 may not be constant, as it is under D_0; in fact, we show roughly that the proportion of income saved declines with the price of consumption goods (P_C).

The critical reader might well wonder why people would save at all if their consumption level declined as a result. The answer is that we are again taking a 'snapshot' of an economy that is steadily growing, as compared to an unchanging level of activity in the stationary state. Thus, the demand curve (D_1) in Fig. 6.2 will be continuously shifting to the right, indicating higher levels of *future* consumption. (This raises an interesting issue: more savings will finance more capital, hence raising output (per capita). On the other hand, more saving means less consumption out of any given level of total output. Hence, there would appear to be an 'optimal' savings rate that would just balance these two tendencies. This is called the 'golden rule' rate, but there is no guarantee that it will be established by a perfectly competitive market economy.)

6.4 A comparison of long-run equilibria

A change that affects macroeconomic equilibrium can originate with households (a change in tastes), with firms (a change in technology), or indeed, with government itself (a change in fiscal or monetary policies).

This section wil be primarily concerned with the first type of change: specifically, a shift in household preferences away from consumption towards increased saving (i.e. greater acquisition of bonds).

6.4.1 Interest-rate adjustment

In terms of our diagrammatic apparatus a comparison of long-run equilibria is easy. We shift the consumption-good demand curve still further to the left (D_2), and the bond-demand schedule – together with its associated change in bond-demand (saving) schedule, since both the desired stock as well as the flow of desired net additions to it have increased – to the right, more than would occur simply due to growth (to D'_2 and SS'_2). As is apparent from comparing the initial long-run equilibrium (subscripted '1') with the new long-run equilibrium (subscripted '2'), the quantity of the consumption good has decreased (to Q_{C_2}) and vice-versa for the capital good (to Q_{K_2}). These are consistent with the increase in the level of saving and investment, and the fall in the rate of interest.

6.4.2 Real- and money-wage rate adjustments

This much is straightforward, but an immediate question is why we have omitted any mention of the labour market. The answer is that we have implictly assumed that the contraction of the consumption-good sector, and the expansion of the capital-good sector, is just such that the aggregated marginal product schedule (the weighted demand schedule for labour in Fig. 6.3b) is unaffected.

Therefore, with the equilibrium real wage rate unchanged, and the price level unchanged, neither does the equilibrium money wage rate change! In short, the shift of demand and, thus, resources from consumption-good to capital-good production has no net effect on the aggregate labour market(s). This is shown by the notional (dashed) demand schedules that would apply if we only considered the fall in consumption-good demand. The original schedules are restored (reversing arrows) by the simultaneous expansion of the capital-goods sector.

Relaxing these simplifying assumptions would of course have an effect on the labour market(s), but increasing the complexity of the analysis – involving, for example, the consideration of relative sectoral capital intensivities (capital–labour ratios) – is at this stage not worth the effort. In any case, the important fact remains that depending on these underlying technical data, the real wage rate might fall, or it might rise.

Concerning the money wage rate, however, one final point ought to be made. In the 'old' Quantity Theory velocity is constant by virtue of institutional factors; therefore, with the same quantity of money being supplied by the central bank, nominal income remains constant. Since we have just assumed that the overall (aggregate) price level (P) is unchanged, so it must be that aggregate output (Q, the weighted sum of Q_C plus ΔQ_K) is also unchanged; since:

$$\begin{aligned} Y &= P \times Q \\ &= P_C \times Q_C + P_K \times \Delta Q_K \\ &= C_S + I \end{aligned}$$

However, in the new (or, 're-stated') Quantity Theory, velocity is not completely invariant. In particular, a fall in the rate of interest may lead to a fall in velocity, as households (and firms) decide to hold slightly larger money balances. If so, the new pivoted money demand line of Fig. 6.1 would imply lower nominal income. However, with unchanged aggregate physical output (less consumption but more capital-goods production recall) this means that the price level (P) must fall, and in turn, that the money wage rate (w) must fall in order to maintain the same real wage.

In fact, not only w, but all other money prices would have fallen in proportion as well. Diagrammatically, all supply and demand schedules expressed in money terms would have to shift in proportion to the change in P: downwards in Figs. 6.2, 6.3a and 6.4a, and leftwards in Figs. 6.4b, c, d and 6.5. However, we do not depict this.

6.4.3 A description of 'circular flow'

Although the diagrammatic approach is clear enough by itself, we can reinforce our understanding of this by referring to the two 'circular-flow' conditions:

$$C_S + I \equiv C_D + S \quad \text{(an identity)} \tag{1}$$

and

$$C_S = C_D \quad \text{(an equilibrium condition)} \tag{2}$$

which together imply:

$$I = S \quad \text{(an alternative equilibrium condition)}$$

Now the change in household's consumption–saving pattern initially causes:

$$C_D < C_S$$

and therefore:

$$S > I$$

i.e. deficient consumption-good demand is necessarily matched by excess saving (excess additional bond demand). This is of course precisely what is shown at the initial prices (P_{C_1} and r_1, respectively) immediately after the shift in the two schedules. Therefore, downward pressure exists on both P_C (excess supply of consumption goods) and on r (excess demand for bonds, bidding bond prices up).

Both of these movements will tend to stimulate consumption and discourage saving, until equilibrium is restored as shown.

Note, however, that under the assumed conditions of constant costs (i.e. perfectly elastic long-run supply when firms are free to enter or leave either sector) the fall in P_C is a short-run phenomenon which will serve only to force some firms out of the consumption goods industry, until P_{C_1} is restored. This leaves the rate of interest as the sole long-run price-adjustment mechanism.

Summary

The economy can be seen in aggregate as a 'circular flow' in which the value of the goods produced is received as income by households, who then decide to spend or save. Equilibrium is established when their planned demand for consumption goods is equal to the supply, which in a static context occurs by definition. In a dynamic context net (positive) saving is occurring, which means that in order to sustain this flow there must be an equal amount of net investment taking place. This constitutes a source of income in addition to the original production of consumption goods; so if the demand for these goods matches their supply, then with income necessarily being spent (on goods) or saved, saving must equal investment. Equivalently, savings and investments constitute the demand and supply of bonds, so this market also clears whenever the goods market is in equilibrium.

The increase in the supply of bonds (to finance net investment) is itself a derivative of the desire to increase the physical capital stock. In steady-state growth – the simplest form of dynamics – this is just proportional to the increase in the labour force, period by period. This population growth also produces the net saving (the increase in the demand for bonds) that matches the increased supply of bonds. All quantities grow at the same rate and all prices remain unchanged over time.

However, if some underlying technical or behavioural condition alters – in particular, say a shift in preferences toward greater saving and less (current) consumption – equilibrium prices and quantities will also change. What happens to the real wage rate depends on the relative input intensities of the consumption-goods and capital-goods sectors (see Appendix 3B), but we can conveniently assume that it is virtually unaffected. Likewise the money, or nominal, wage rate may in fact fall (leading to proportionately lower price level and proportionately greater total output level) but we may assume it does not (implying a full contraction of consumption-goods output to make room for increased capital-goods output, rather than a net increase in total output). This allows us to focus on the key price adjustment: i.e. the decline in the rate of interest.

Appendix 6 Present value

The present value (*PV*) of an investment – i.e. an asset yielding net revenues over more than one period – is given by the formula:

$$PV \text{ (in period 0)} = \frac{\text{Net revenue in period 1}}{1 + r_1} + \frac{\text{Net revenue in period 2}}{(1 + r_2)^2} + \ldots . + \frac{\text{Net revenue in period } n}{(1 + r_n)^n}$$

where r_k is the rate of interest, in period k, and $1/(1 + r_k)^k$ is the 'discount factor' applied to net revenues in the kth period.

Net revenue is gross revenue minus any operating costs incurred by ownership of the asset (e.g. associated additional wage costs, maintenance and repair of a machine).

In the special case in which: (1) all the r_k are equal (a long-run 'prevailing' rate, r); (2) net revenue is constant; and (3) the asset has an infinite life ($n = \infty$), this formula reduces to:

$$PV = \frac{\text{Net revenue}}{r}$$

The *PV* of an asset, whether financial or physical, is its *demand* price, in the sense that the buyer would be willing to pay just up to that amount. If he/she can purchase for less, it means that the implicit rate of return (say r') is greater than r, the 'going' rate.

7 Extensions of the Basic Model: Foreign and Government Sectors

Outline

Synopsis

Using the simple circular-flow model to express macroeconomic equilibrium in terms of either goods-market or, alternatively, bond-market equilibrium, we first introduce the possibility of either type of flow occurring between the domestic economy and the rest of the world (RoW). In fact, with a simple model of supply-and-demand in the foreign exchange (forex) market we can show that any excess outflow of goods (current-account surplus) is necessarily balanced by an excess outflow of savings (capital account deficit). In case of initial disequilibrium – e.g. deficient demand worldwide – we show that not only the interest rate and the domestic price level (the latter being a short-run phenomenon) will tend to fall, as in the purely domestic case; but also that the exchange rate will tend to fall.

Introducing a government sector, we then show how the existence of a budget deficit – a positive public-sector borrowing requirement (PSBR) – will displace any or all of consumption, investment or exports by maintaining any or all of these prices: consumption-good price, interest rate, exchange rate; higher than would otherwise prevail.

Introduction

In the previous chapter I distinguished two types of economy: stationary, in which all income is consumed and there is no net saving nor investment; and non-stationary, in which there is positive saving and investment. In the first type of economy there was no problem of disequilibrium in the consumption-good market, but in the second type of economy the possibility of goods-market disequilibrium could be considered, leading to a (price and) interest rate adjustment mechanism. The former effect was, in the context of our assumptions, a short-run phenomenon, serving to drive firms out of the consumption-goods sector.

In both instances the economy is entirely 'private', as well as 'closed': i.e. there is no trade with the rest of the world (RoW). In this chapter I shall add both sectors to this basic model of Chapter 6, beginning with the foreign sector. I continue to assume that there is positive savings and investment.

7.1 Foreign sector

When we consider two economies – domestic and foreign (RoW) – the diagrammatic supply-and-demand approach which was illuminating in a closed context becomes unwieldy, except in limited instances.

Instead, it is much easier to apprehend the nature of equilibrium in an 'open' economy through the same circular-flow analogue that we used to clarify our earlier discussions.

As a preliminary, we assume that all of our domestic economy's exports (the value of which we denote by X) as well as imports (the value of which we denote in this treatment by F, for 'foreign' goods) are consumption goods. Trade in capital goods is like that in labour – i.e. as an input – and although we allow free trade in products, factors of production are taken to be immobile.

7.1.1 **Circular-flow equilibrium with net exports**

As before, domestic firms continue to produce consumption goods and new capital (investment) goods, but part of the former may be exported. Also, domestic households continue to produce consumption goods and to save, but now part of the former may consist of imports. Overall, it is still necessarily true that:

$$Y \equiv \underbrace{C_S + I}_{\text{'sources'}} \equiv \underbrace{C_D + S}_{\text{'uses'}}$$

but now it is no longer required that $C_D = C_S$. This is an unnecessarily restrictive condition that forces domestic production to match domestic consumption, and therefore forces exports to equal imports.

Instead, the appropriate equilibrium condition is:

$$C_S = C_D + (X - F)$$

In words: the consumption-goods markets in both countries are jointly in equilibrium when domestic demand, together with net exports of consumption goods, just equal domestic production. What we buy, plus what they buy net from us, adds up to what we produce. Notice that net exports can of course be negative; i.e. we would have net imports if domestic consumption exceeded domestic production.

Current- and capital-account balances

In order to find an alternative, equivalent way of expressing the same condition, we can again subtract this last equation from the preceding identity to give:

$$I = S + (F - X)$$

Notice the difference between this and the closed-economy condition that $I = S$. In an open economy investment is matched by the sum of saving plus net imports $(F - X)$ (or minus net exports).

At first this may seem particularly hard to interpret, but recall for a moment the situation in the previous chapter when we had deficient demand $(C_D < C_S)$. This had as a counterpart excess saving, or excess demand for bonds $(S > I)$. Together these triggered a falling price level (P) – in the short run – and interest rate (r). In an open economy, however, these adjustments may not be needed. Why? Because the mirror-image of these circumstances might obtain in the RoW: they might have excess demand for goods, so that total world supply and demand are in balance; and correspondingly, deficient savings such that the world supply and demand for bonds are equal. In fact, this is precisely the condition we have derived. Rewrite it as:

$$S - I = X - F$$

In this form it says that equilibrium obtains as long as the domestic economy's excess savings (demand for bonds) is equal to its net exports.

In the terminology of international trade the term on the left – the demand for bonds in excess of the domestic supply – constitutes a 'capital account deficit', or simply a 'capital outflow' in view of the fact that domestic households are necessarily acquiring foreign as well as domestic bonds. For equilibrium to obtain this outflow must be matched by an inflow. Thus, the term on the right is called the 'current account surplus', or simply 'net exports' as above. But is this not a net outflow of goods? Yes it is, but it represents a net inflow of money, or in the language of international economics, 'currency'.

The foreign-exchange market

In other words the equilibrium of capital outflows with net exports, or capital inflows with net imports, corresponds to equilibrium in the foreign-exchange ('forex') market depicted in Fig. 7.1. As long as the supply and demand for our domestic currency is in balance, the above equilibrium condition is fulfilled!

The way it is drawn, supply and demand for our domestic currency (say £) are shown as related to the exchange rate (R) which we take to be the number of \$ per £ (i.e. the RoW uses \$).

Figure 7.1 The foreign exchange (forex) market

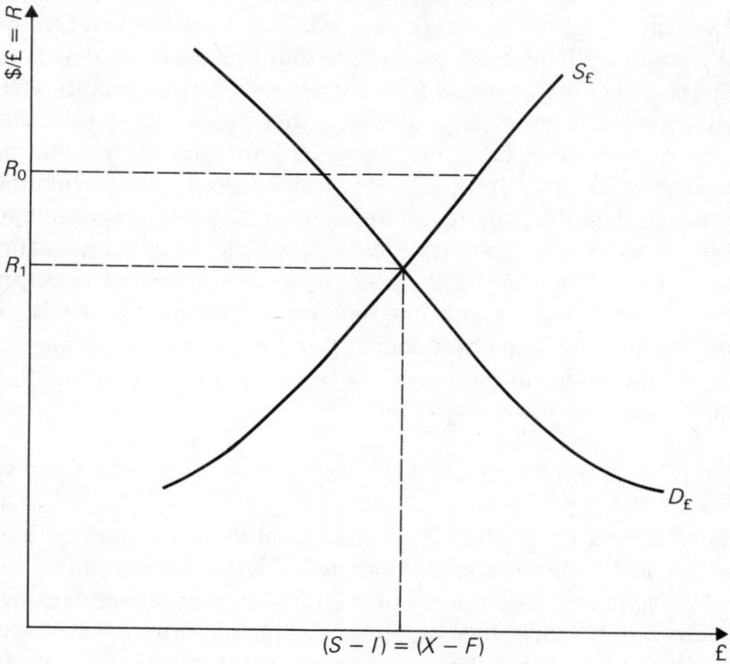

The excess supply of £ (i.e. excess demand for $) shown at R_0 is consistent with a capital outflow in excess of any trade surplus: $(S-I) > (X-F)$. Both curves are drawn on the assumptions of fixed price levels and interest rates (in both regions).

Looking at the supply schedule for £, we see that the number of £ supplied increases as the number of $ *per* £ increases, in the normal manner. This is because as the pound sterling (£) appreciates, £1 buys more dollars ($); or equivalently, any goods priced in dollars require fewer £ from the domestic consumer's point of view. Now, although it is conceivable that in total fewer £ would be spent even though more physical goods – or bonds – were being purchased (verify this), we are ruling out a backward-bending supply schedule for present purposes.

As for the demand curve, this shows that as our domestic goods (or bonds) become more expensive to foreigners (their dollars are depreciating against sterling), they would in total demand fewer £. (We ought perhaps to mention here that it is assumed that every purchase of goods or bonds from foreigners ultimately requires the conversion of £ into \$. Specifically, either the domestic purchaser must go to his/her bank and buy the \$ to send abroad, or the foreign seller must take the £ received to his/her bank and exchange them for \$ there, and vice versa. From the point of view of the banks' forex dealers it matters very little, since eventually all the orders to buy and sell on either side will flow through the market. The major exception is when foreigners might wish to hold £ instead of converting them (as has happened to sterling and latterly the dollar in the twentieth century). In this case the 'full' equilibrium condition would be:

$$(S - I) + (F - X) = \Delta H_{£} - \Delta H_{\$}$$

where $\Delta H_{£}$ = the change in foreigners' holdings of sterling; and
$\Delta H_{\$}$ = the change in domestic holdings of dollars.)

As is apparent, there is a single equilibrium exchange rate (R_1) which will balance the supply and demand for sterling (and simultaneously, for dollars). To repeat, it is perfectly possible for this to be consistent with excess supply or demand for goods – and corresponding excess supply or demand for bonds – in the domestic economy. Indeed, equilibrium in the forex market signifies that these domestic imbalances are matched by excess demand or supply for goods – and corresponding excess demand or supply for bonds – in the RoW.

7.1.2 **Interest- and exchange-rate adjustments**

Now, in order to investigate the adjustment mechanisms in an open economy, suppose that we start with:

$$C_D + (X - F) < C_S$$

i.e. total domestic and net foreign demand for the consumption good are together less than domestic production.

The corollary 'capital-account' condition that is associated with this 'current-account' imbalance is therefore:

$$S + (F - X) > I$$

or alternatively,

$$S - I > X - F$$

That is, our capital outflow exceeds our trade (current account) surplus (or capital inflow is less than the trade deficit).

In diagrammatic terms (Fig. 7.1) this is seen as an excess supply of £ – since we are trying to buy more £'s-worth of bonds from the RoW than they are buying £'s-worth of goods from us. As shown, this means that the exchange rate is at R_0, above its equilibrium level, and should tend to fall.

However, let us look first at the other price-adjustment mechanisms that characterized a situation of deficient goods demand in the closed economy; *viz*: falling domestic consumption-good price (P_C) – in the short run – and interest rate (r). In fact, the same pressures exist in this situation. Faced with deficient demand domestic firms will tend to reduce their prices (eventually driving out some firms until price is restored in the long run) and if there is an excess demand for domestic bonds the interest rate will also tend to fall. Thus we would expect the following to increase: domestic demand (C_D), domestic investment (I), and exports (X) since our goods are now relatively cheaper to foreign buyers; and we would expect the following to decrease: domestic goods production (C_S), domestic saving (S), and imports (F) since foreign goods are now relatively more expensive to domestic buyers.

All of these are changes in the right direction, towards the restoration of circular-flow equilibrium. However, they are not the whole story. Looking again at Fig. 7.1 we observe that the supply and demand schedules for £ in terms of the exchange rate (R) are constructed on the implicit assumption that P and r are constant (*ceteris paribus* as usual). When these do in fact vary, these schedules will shift, but in which directions?

Consider first the fall in the price of consumption goods, P_C. As we have just stated, this stimulates exports and depresses imports, which on the diagram means a rightward shift of the demand and a leftward shift of the supply schedule. By themselves these would tend to restore equilibrium in the forex market without the need for change in the exchange rate. Of course, this may be a temporary (short-run) effect. On the other hand the fall in the domestic (£) rate of interest will shift the demand schedule leftwards and the supply schedule rightwards as foreign bonds become increasingly attractive relative to domestic. (Recall too that these effects are all being reinforced by the opposite price movements in the RoW; e.g. the dollar interest rate is tending to rise.) This long-run shift works against the short-run effects of the price movements, and although it may transpire that the net effect is sufficiently dominated by the change in P_C to leave the exchange rate unchanged or even higher for a while, eventually this rate will tend to fall to establish equilibrium (as shown). (We might mention the common observation that a fall in a country's exchange rate feeds through into a higher price level. This applies only insofar as the final consumption good(s) produced by domestic firms uses imported intermediate goods in its production. As long as there is any domestic value-added component the change in P_C must be proportionally less than the change in R. In fact, recalling that we assume that all production is undertaken with (domestic) labour and capital inputs only, this connection is entirely omitted. If we allowed for imported intermediate goods the conclusion that R falls in both short and long run is strengthened.)

In summary, we expect in the case of an open economy reductions in all three of P_C, r and R, the latter being longer-run effects.

7.2 Government sector

The final extension that we make is to include a domestic public sector alongside what until now has been a wholly private-sector economy. Implicitly, this has been the case all along insofar as the quantity or supply of money has been assumed to be under central bank control. However, our chief concern is now to examine the effects of direct governmental command over real resources in the form of expenditure (the amount of which we denote by G) and taxation (the amount of which we denote by T). In so doing, three things ought to be mentioned. First, we exclude pure redistributional activities from our definitions. For example, if a social security programme taxes a younger worker and spends this to subsidize an older retired worker, this is regarded as a transfer not involving any direct command of resources. Second, this implies – at least on the basis of what we have established in microeconomics – that the government's spending and taxing (its 'fiscal') activities are motivated by a desire to achieve a more efficient allocation of resources in the light of market imperfections. Third, although either of these interventions is bound to have consequences for total output (Q), in aggregate, or macroeconomic analysis we shall simply ignore them (if you like, the improvements on efficiency grounds just offset the distortions arising from intervention on equity grounds).

7.2.1 **Circular-flow equilibrium: 'injections = withdrawals'**

With this background we can again approach the problem of characterizing equilibrium by way of the circular-flow; only now, the value of total product consists of consumption goods (C_S) – for domestic sale or export – investment, or new capital goods (I), and public goods (G). (A slight definitional problem can arise here. Suppose for example that the government partly subsidizes purchases of health care on the grounds of positive externalities. Some of the total expenditure on health care is therefore privately financed, and we would classify this as part of C_S. The remainder is publicly financed, and we would classify this as part of G, even though it is in reality the same service in both instances.)

Hence, aggregate income will now be:

$$Y = C_S + I + G$$

Matching these sources of income will be three uses: spending on consumption (C_D), saving (S), and in addition, taxes (T); so:

$$\underbrace{C_S + I + G}_{\text{'sources'}} \equiv \underbrace{C_D + S + T}_{\text{'uses'}}$$

(Remember from the last section that C_S includes exports and C_D includes imports.)

That is, the income flowing to households from the employment of their labour and capital in the public and private sectors – the latter divided into consumption-good and investment-good sectors – will be taxed away (leaving them with 'disposable' income), spent on consumption or saved.

The key element is as always the condition(s) for equilibrium in the 'goods' market. Fortunately, this remains exactly as it was in the case of an open, private economy; *viz*:

$$C_S = C_D + (X - F)$$

i.e. the consumption-goods market is in equilibrium when domestic production is just balanced by domestic demand plus net exports.

Therefore, subtracting this from the 'sources = uses' identity we obtain the alternative, equivalent condition:

$$I + G = S + T + (F - X)$$

In turn, this has two commonly used forms:

$$\underbrace{I + G + X}_{\text{'injections'}} = \underbrace{S + T + F}_{\text{'withdrawals'}}$$

This states that whatever households do not spend on domestically produced goods (savings, taxes and imports being in that sense 'withdrawals' or 'leakages' out of demand) will equal that part of gross output that is not sold on the domestic-goods market (investment, public spending and exports being 'injections' or 'additions' to domestic goods sales). Conversely, this means that in equilibrium the amount of consumption goods that firms are attempting to sell in the domestic market is matched by the amount of domestic goods that domestic households are planning to buy. Alternatively,

$$G - T = (S - I) + (F - X)$$

With a balanced budget, such that the government's deficit or 'public sector borrowing requirement' (PSBR) is zero, this reduces to exactly the same condition as in the open private-economy sample. Specifically: the excess domestic demand for bonds (excess saving) spills out as a capital outflow, which in forex-market equilibrium is balanced by a current-account surplus (net exports): a positive first term on the right will imply a negative second term, and vice-versa.

However, with an unbalanced budget these two (bracketed) terms may or may not have opposite signs. Suppose there is a government deficit (written as $G - T > 0$). Then this provides an outlet for the otherwise excess domestic saving. In fact, the deficit, or 'PSBR' for short, could be so large that the domestic economy became a net importer, hence requiring an additional, balancing capital inflow which would go towards financing the deficit. Similarly, a government surplus ($G - T < 0$) means in effect that the government becomes a net lender (an admittedly peculiar role). Thus, its demand for bonds would tend to exacerbate any situation of excess domestic saving, leading to a still-larger capital outflow (or reduced inflow) and a correspondingly larger trade surplus (or reduced deficit).

7.2.2 **Price-adjustment mechanisms and 'crowding-out'**

In order to see the consequences of having an unbalanced buget, recall that in an earlier example we considered the adjustments that occurred when:

$$(S - I) > (X - F)$$

(corresponding to: $C_D + (X - F) < C_S$; i.e. deficient demand for goods). To be precise, it was found that one, or more likely all, of the three prices – P_C, r and R – would tend to fall (although the fall in P_C may be only temporary).

But notice that this condition occurs whenever $G - T > 0$; i.e. whenever there is a deficit. This implies that a positive PSBR will be associated with at least one of these prices – and unless elasticities are extreme, all three – being higher than would otherwise occur. Indeed these effects are often perceived in classical economic analysis as 'crowding out' the private sector in the following ways:

1. to the extent that the price of consumption-goods (P_C) is higher, domestic goods consumption is reduced;
2. to the extent that the rate of interest (r) is higher, domestic investment is reduced; and
3. to the extent that the exchange rate (R) is higher, exports are reduced.

Obviously these simple statements neglect cross-effects, such as the fact that a higher level of P_C will also reduce exports, but the idea is clear enough.

Summary

Adding a foreign sector to the basic model of circular flow allows the domestic supply and demand for consumption goods to diverge; and correspondingly, the levels of domestic savings and investment. Indeed, the magnitude of the difference in one of these markets is equal (and opposite) to the difference in the other. This is summarized by the equilibrium condition:

$$X - F = S - I$$

The term on the left is the domestic economy's trade surplus: the amount by which our domestic demand falls short of supply, being matched in equilibrium by the rest of the world's (RoW's) excess consumption. The term on the right is our capital outflow: the excess amount of savings that we transmit abroad. This gives rise – by itself – to an excess demand for the RoW's currency (e.g. \$); but this is balanced by the RoW's excess demand for our currency (e.g. £) in order to buy goods. Hence, the condition is effectively a statement about the foreign-exchange market. This introduces the exchange rate (e.g. \$ per £) as another price variable, and assuming an initial balance-of-payments deficit (excess supply of £) both this and the rate of interest will tend to fall (the price level might in fact also fall, but we assume as in the preceding chapter that in the long run it is unaffected).

With government fiscal – taxing and spending – activity, the condition for equilibrium becomes:

$$G - T = (S - I) + (F - X)$$

This shows in particular that a government deficit corresponds to a situation where the terms on the right sum to a positive number rather than zero as before. Comparing this to the assumed situation of forex market dis-equilibrium when exchange and interest rates (and possibly, domestic prices) fell, this implies that these are all – ignoring possible perversities – to some extent higher than would otherwise occur: this is the mechanism by which government spending crowds out private spending (I, X, and C_D).

8 The Process of Adjustment: Classical and Keynesian Perspectives

Outline

Synopsis

This chapter elaborates the Keynesian criticism of the preceding Classical model of the market adjustment process; *viz*, the inability of the interest rate to fall so as to stimulate an expansion of the capital-goods sector sufficient to absorb resources from a contracted consumption-goods sector.

In the extreme case of no additional investment, the chapter examines how the initial fall in goods demand does translate into lower labour demand, which leads to a still-further drop in goods demand, etc. As part of this analysis I show that whether or not the money wage rate falls, income still declines. As a simplification, however, I introduce the assumptions of both a fixed money wage and fixed goods prices. Together with the constancy of the interest rate – derived from the Keynesian theory of liquidity preference, in which money is held speculatively as a substitute for interest-bearing bonds – this turns the Keynesian theory into an effective 'fixed-price' model. Using this simplified approach, I then construct the basic theory of income determination; i.e. as an 'injections equal withdrawals' condition in circular-flow equilibrium. I initially derive this for a closed, private economy but expand it to include a foreign sector and then a government sector which can actively manage its deficit so as to maintain full employment.

Introduction

A clear lesson that emerges from the preceding orthodox ('Classical') analyses is that complete price flexibility will always work towards equilibrium. In short, a 'free' market economy is an automatically self-stabilizing system.

The particular occurrence that we have had in mind as causing this adjustment is an autonomous shift in household preferences in favour of saving and away from consumption. Starting at the equilibrium points subscripted '1' in Figs. 6.1–6.5 we can show this change as a spontaneous leftward shift of the consumption-good demand schedule (from D_1 to D_2 in Fig. 6.2) and an associated rightward shift of the long-run bond demand schedules (from D_1 to D_2 and D'_1 to D'_2 in Fig. 6.4c) and the savings (single-period net bond demand) schedule (from SS'_1 to SS'_2 in Fig. 6.4d). As expected, this leads to lower r and P_C, the latter forcing out firms until P_C has risen to its original level. This is the end of the story in Classical terms.

8.1 The Keynesian 'revolution'

On the other hand, these conclusions apply to a fully-functioning price system. If for some reason the price-adjustment mechanism were to fail, then the economy could conceivably remain in disequilibrium indefinitely. (This raises the interesting question of whether we should not call this an 'equilibrium' – on account of its being a state of rest from which there is no tendency to move – even 'though markets are failing to clear.)

In fact, it is precisely this objection that has been raised by so-called 'Interventionists', or as they are often known, 'Keynesians'. J. M. Keynes was one of the first – and certainly most influential – economists to advocate the use of fiscal policy in order to stabilize a market economy, which he saw as lacking any strong corrective mechanisms (hence the term 'interventionist'). Writing his major work in 1936, the context of his arguments was the so-called 'Great Depression' which had apparently been triggered by the stock market collapses of 1929–30.

Although economic cycles had been observed for a long time, and were not considered especially inconsistent with Classical notions of equilibrium this particular depression was deeper and seemingly longer-lasting than its predecessors. Also, and this is an important historical point to keep in mind, there was a considerable amount of political foment during the decade of the 1930s. From that point of view Keynes' own prescriptions can be seen as merely pragmatic. However, he was at the same time deeply concerned to win over the Classical economic establishment to his radical theories; a victory that was almost complete, and lasted for three decades or more.

As with other important works and ideas, there have been numerous re-appraisals and interpretations over the years. Hence, the views expressed here are in a sense similarly interpretative.

8.1.1 Excessive wages *vs* structural maladjustment ('deficient demand')

To start with, the principal attack was on the widespread belief that the massive (up to 20%) unemployment experienced during the Depression could be eliminated by money wage reductions, much as a drop in the price of bananas would serve to correct a situation of over-supply. This simple analogy would be more apt if we were investigating a temporary – and inexplicable? – perturbation or displacement from an unchanged initial equilibrium (e.g. point *U* in Fig. 6.3a). In such a situation, having arisen because somehow money wages rose above their equilibrium level to begin with, it is hardly surprising that their fall should serve to restore full employment.

However, in the type of disequilibrium that we considered in the previous chapters it was the case that the true equilibrium had in fact changed. There is considerable evidence that Keynes was addressing himself to this type of problem, which had arisen either: (1) from a sudden fall in investment intentions due to pessimistic expectations (a downward shift in the *I*-curve of Fig. 6.4d) and/or (2) from a shift in consumption patterns in favour of increased saving. Both of these can be seen as symptomatic of a stagnation in spending behaviour on the part of either firms or households, or both, perhaps indicating that the long phase of Western industrial expansion had lost momentum by the second quarter of the twentieth century.

Focusing on the second possibility, as we have done throughout, we should be struck immediately by the conclusion – directly from Classical analysis – that the change in real wage rates – if any – is of little relevance. Ultimately, when the shift of resources from consumption-goods to capital-goods production has been accomplished, these may have moved up or down. Instead, Keynes was concerned with the inability of the market economy to achieve this shift at all.

In fact, although we have previously compared equilibria, the essence of the Keynesian approach is to look at the dynamics of moving from *A* to *B*, so to speak (or from '1' to '2' in our case), although even this is kept to a fairly simple level.

Consider first the situation that can develop if the decline in consumption spending occurs before the expansion in the capital-goods sector. The leftward shift of the consumption-goods demand schedule (to D_2) now translates into a corresponding leftward shift of the demand schedule(s) for labour (dashed curves). This latter shift is of course supposed to be eventually reversed, as indicated by the reversing arrows in Figs. 6.3a,b. In the meantime, however, because of the fall in income from reduced employment, shown in Fig. 8.1a as a move from point *A* to point *B*, there will be a *further* drop in demand; but, as the demand schedule shown in Fig. 8.2

Figures 8.1a and b Fall in employment and wage rate due to deficient demand

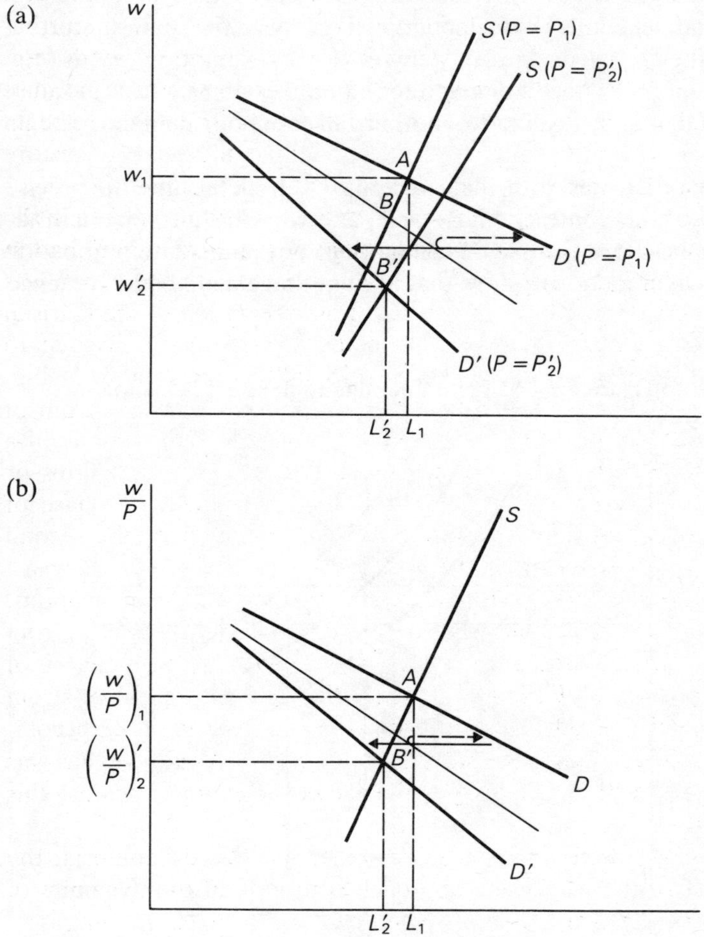

In orthodox Classical theory the real – as well as money – wage rate can be unchanged as factors of production shift from the consumption-goods to the capital-goods sector (shown by reversing arrows). However, as with consumption demand, if the former sector contracts before the latter expands, there will not be a reversal but a continuation of decline in labour demand. With 'normal' supply conditions this leads to lower wages – in real and money terms – but also to less employment (e.g. L'_2).

thus moves successively leftwards beyond D_2, so too does the demand schedule(s) for labour in Figs. 8.1a,b. That is, starting with the initial decline in demand for consumption goods, the consequent decline in demand for labour results in a further fall in goods demand, leading to another fall in labour demand, and so on.

One of Keynes' principal concerns was to determine the precise extent of this contractionary cycle, and we will shortly be describing his model of income determination. For immediate purposes it is sufficient merely to show that at some stage demand has reached

Figure 8.2 Fall in output due to deficient demand

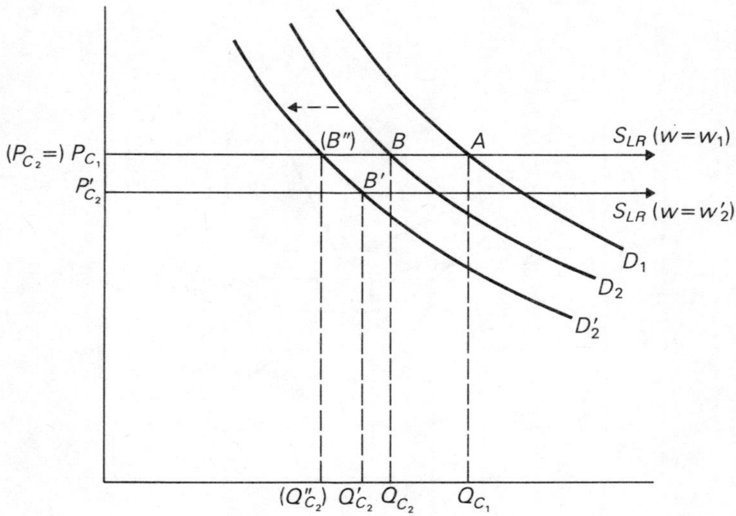

The assumed initial fall in consumption-good demand is shown as a shift from D_1 to D_2. However, the failure of capital-goods production to expand means that reduced income (e.g. $P_{c_2} \times Q_{c_2}$ being less than $P_{c_1} \times Q_{c_1}$) leads to still further cuts in demand until the position P'_{c_2}, Q'_{c_2} is reached. In the 'simplified' Keynesian model the short-run supply curve can be taken as perfectly elastic (fixed money wage), hence coinciding with the long-run supply curve. In this case output suffers even more, declining to Q''_{c_2}.

a limit of its decline. This is depicted in Fig. 8.1b at point B', with lower employment and a lower real wage. Notice that the labour market is in equilibrium, but has contracted because of the fall in (real) demand occurring because consumption-good producers are being forced out of business, with no corresponding expansion of opportunities in the capital-good sector. This same level of employment (L'_2) is also shown by Fig. 8.1a, in terms of the money wage. Because there has been a fall in the money wage, the long-run supply prices of both consumption- and capital-goods will also have fallen. We do not attempt to illustrate the latter (in Figs 6.4a–d) but in Fig. 8.2 we do show that P'_{C_2} is consistent with wage rate w'_2. Note that this shows that a cut in the price of the consumption-good mitigates but does not eliminate the decline in demand. At the same time, this fall in P_C translates into a lower price level (P'_2), so both supply and demand schedules in Fig. 8.1a shift downwards, with the demand schedule also showing the added effects of the decline in real demand.

As can be seen, the fall in the money wage exceeds the fall in the real wage. A simple example will help to show why this is so. Suppose that wages comprise 60% of total unit costs, so that a 1% cut in w can lead, in a competitive environment, to a 0.6% cut in output prices. On this basis, a 28+% (2/7) fall in the *ratio* of w to P is consistent with a 50% fall in the money wage rate, which roughly corresponds to the illustrated case.

Clearly, the source of the problem is the failure of investment – i.e. the production of new capital goods – to increase at the same time as consumption decreases. In the orthodox Classical theory it is apparent that this should be occurring. The rightward shift of the saving and associated bond demand schedules is supposed to push the interest rate down, and thus stimulate capital goods production (i.e. greater investment).

As this occurs, we should witness some revival of labour demand, which will then feed through into higher income and greater consumption; in turn leading to still more demand for labour, in a reversal of the contractionary cycle until the new 'full employment' equilibrium is attained.

8.1.2 **Price insensitivity of savings/investment**

Now, one possible objection to this story is that it assumes a fair degree of sensitivity of savings and investment (and their counterpart long-run bond demand and supply) to the interest rate. If, on the contrary, these are rather interest-inelastic then it is possible that the interest rate would have to fall drastically to equate them. Conceivably, the downward-sloping *I* curve of Fig. 6.4d could intersect the horizontal axis short of the point where the upward-sloping *SS* curve began, implying that the interest rate would have to become negative. That is, even when the interest rate is zero the amount that firms wish to invest is still less than the amount households wish to save.

This is not so unbelievable, especially in the context of the 1930s. As we have shown, the responsiveness of investment to changes in the cost of borrowing is less elastic than the long-run supply of bonds itself due to the steeper short-run rise in the marginal cost of producing additional capital goods. If at the same time this long-run supply is not very elastic, this possibility of 'investment exhaustion' arises.

In fact, one of the major elements in Keynes' attack on Classical economics was precisely this insensitivity of the desired capital stock to interest rate changes: i.e. the demand schedule of Fig. 6.4a barely shifts even with substantial changes in *r*. This is in turn due to the overwhelming dominance of expectations regarding future net revenue streams. Put succinctly, firms operating in the present must form some view of these future yields, including a subjective measure of the risk attached to them. In depressed times this 'risk premium' – which can most easily be thought of as an added component to the market rate of interest used to discount future yields – is likely to be much greater than normal. Indeed, some interventionists take the stronger view that even in 'normal' circumstances when the economy is seemingly operating near full employment, these decisions on the desired size of the capital stock – as well as the shorter-run timing of investment – reflect the 'animal spirits' of businessmen.

8.1.3 **Interest-rate inflexibility: liquidity preference**

An interest-rate 'floor'?

The second line of objection to the Classical model is that, regardless of the interest sensitivity of investment, it may not in any case be possible for the interest rate to fall by enough to restore full employment. Although the demand for bonds (and hence the corresponding flow of additional net demand; i.e. saving) may be fairly interest-inelastic at higher interest levels, it may become perfectly elastic at some 'floor' rate of interest. Diagrammatically, this would be shown in Fig. 6.4d by the savings schedules (SS_1, SS_2) becoming infinitely elastic at r_1; i.e. the section below r_1 would disappear.

What this means is that households do indeed prefer to save more and consume less, but only at a rate of interest at or above its initial level (r_1). The result is that investment will be stuck at its original level; so the countervailing increase in income and, hence, demand for consumption goods and labour that is supposed to reverse the contraction occurring in the rest of the economy, is prevented. As income thus declines without impediment, the savings (and bond demand) schedule(s) will themselves be shifting to the left until, as I shall soon demonstrate, income has fallen by enough to wipe out the excess saving that households had originally attempted: a Keynesian unemployment 'equilibrium'.

The immediate question that this raises is why households should in effect stop buying bonds when the interest rate goes below its floor level (r_1). In the Keynesian theory this phenomenon is a manifestation of the close substitutability of bonds, which yield interest, and money, which does not. To be more specific, it might happen that at relatively low rates of interest households (and firms) would prefer to 'save' – using this term now in the broader sense of income minus consumption expenditure – by the accumulation of liquid money balances rather than bonds. This shift in the pattern of savings flows would also be associated with a longer-run shift in asset portfolios out of bonds and into money.

This phenomenon is known as 'liquidity preference' and is illustrated in Figs 8.3a,b, with a perfectly elastic demand for money occurring at some (low) rate of interest (the 'liquidity trap'). The theory of the demand for money that this represents is a major feature distinguishing Keynesian from Classical economics.

The demand for money: three components

Keynes himself identified three components of this demand for money. First, the *transactions* demand (M_T) arising from the level of the income–expenditure flow. In effect this is the 'old' Quantity

Figures 8.3a and b Components of money demand: Keynesian view

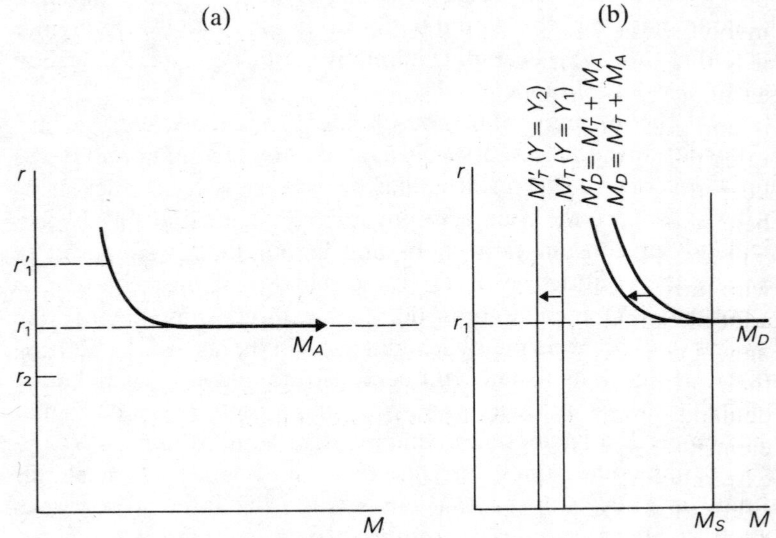

Keynesian theory identifies total money demand as the sum of transactions demand (M_T) related to income, and 'asset' demand (M_A) related to the rate of interest. In the extreme, this latter component becomes infinitely elastic at some 'floor' rate of interest (e.g. r_1). This means that a leftward shift of the M_D schedule has no effect on r_1 and consequently ensures that the fall in income is the result of a decrease in physical output. (In the Classical theory of Fig. 6.5 the ability of r to fall implies instead that any fall in income is purely nominal.)

Theory based on institutional characteristics, carried over and represented by a given line or ray emanating from the origin in our original Fig. 6.1. Second, the *precautionary* demand arising from the uncertainty of these expenditure flows, at least at a micro-level. Because any given household (or firm) may not know the timing of its receipts (income) and disbursements (expenditure) it has an incentive to hold excess money balances. In particular, if it held only as much money as on average would suffice to meet expenditure, and then found that occasionally its income was delayed (or expenses accelerated), in such circumstances it would be necessary to cash in some of its bond-holdings. This would involve inconvenience as well as more direct transaction costs, and it is these that have to be weighed against the foregone interest earnings. At higher interest rates the tendency would be to 'chance it' and keep money balances to a near-minimum; whereas at lower rates the tendency would be to avoid awkward situations and to keep fully-adequate money reserves. (This is precisely how firms behave regarding inventories of goods. With customers arriving at a predictable average rate, they are faced with holding low stocks with the possibility of delayed delivery, or large stocks which tie up a lot of capital.) Although at the time this was an innovation, the 'new' Quantity Theorists have subsequently incorporated this into their own analysis, as part of the acknowledgement that money demand is in fact dependent on the rate of interest. However, this element has never been seen as responsible for anything so extreme as the liquidity trap of Fig. 8.3a.

For that we need to consider Keynes' third component of money demand: the *speculative* motive. Suppose for instance that the rate of interest were considered to be higher than normal: i.e. above its expected longer-run rate, say as r'_1 is above r_1 in Fig. 8.3a. This simultaneously implies that the majority of savers expect that the rate will fall, and as a corollary, that interest-bearing asset prices (that is, bond prices) will rise. This perceived opportunity to realize a capital gain, or equivalently, the opportunity to lock-in at a 'good' rate of return, would thus prompt savers to acquire bonds; and in so doing they would tend to reduce their 'idle', not-required-for transactions, balances. Now suppose that the interest rate does fall as expected. As it does so we would expect that some bond-holders will sell, thereby realizing their gains. Unless market expectations are completely uniform, the numbers selling out will increase continuously as the rate falls, as shown. Ultimately, virtually no-one will be expecting further rises in bond prices, or equivalently, further declines in the rate of interest. At such a level (e.g. r_1 in Fig. 8.3a) the willingness to hold money balances may become unlimited. The corresponding infinitely elastic portion of this interest-related money demand schedule (M_A) thus illustrates a *liquidity trap*: the rate of interest which would generate sufficient investment (e.g. r_2) is below the rate at which anyone would be willing to lend!

When we add this interest-related, or 'asset' demand for money to the transactions demand we obtain the total money demand schedule (M_D) shown in Fig. 8.3b. Observe that when income now falls, reducing the transactions component, the leftward shift of M_D has no effect on the equilibrium rate of interest, which remains stuck at r_1. Moreover, whereas in the Classical model this fall in income would be purely nominal – all prices fall in proportion, but Q remains the same, albeit consisting of less consumption- and more capital-good output – in this extreme Keynesian model it is prices that are unchanged and the whole brunt of the contraction is borne out of physical ouput.

8.1.4 **Fixed money prices: a simplifying assumption**

It should be evident that the Keynesian critique of Classical (price) adjustment mechanisms rests fundamentally on either the insensitivity of investment to the interest rate, or the inability of this rate to fall sufficiently due to 'liquidity preference'.

Equally evident, although in the latter case the interest rate is downwardly inflexible, there is no presumption that either the wage rate or the price of the consumption good cannot fall.

Of course, it might be that workers would resist money wage reductions. If so the consequent worsening of unemployment might be attributable to 'money illusion' as Keynes called it – not realizing that the fall in goods prices had made their labour more expensive in real terms – or simply to the basically correct belief that if and when full employment were restored, wage rates would also be restored to their initial level anyway.

Whichever, these both imply that labour supply might be perfectly elastic with respect to the money wage rate, as shown in Fig. 8.4a. If w did not fall, then neither would the (long-run) supply schedule of Fig. 8.2, and we would end up at B'' instead of B'; and if the price level did not fall – not only consumption-good, but bond prices being stuck as well – this would mean that the supply of labour was also effectively perfectly elastic in real terms, as shown in Fig. 8.4b.

The result of this behaviour is obvious. Instead of having labour-market equilibrium in the true sense – albeit reduced from its original level, note – we now see a considerable amount of *un*employment ($= L_1 - L''_2$) in the sense that these workers cannot find jobs at the going rate.

Figures 8.4a and b Fall in employment due to deficient demand (fixed wage rate)

(a)

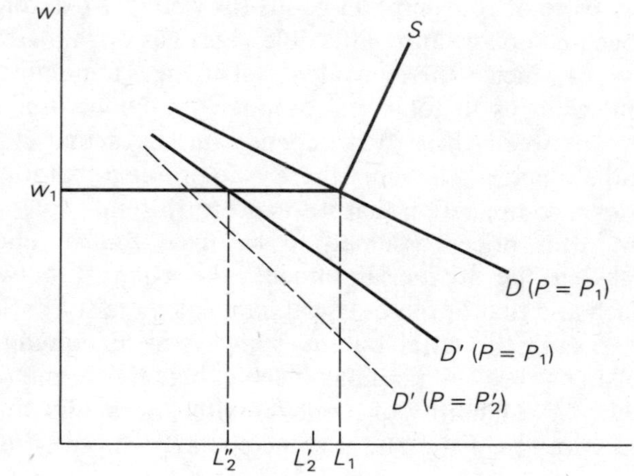

(b)

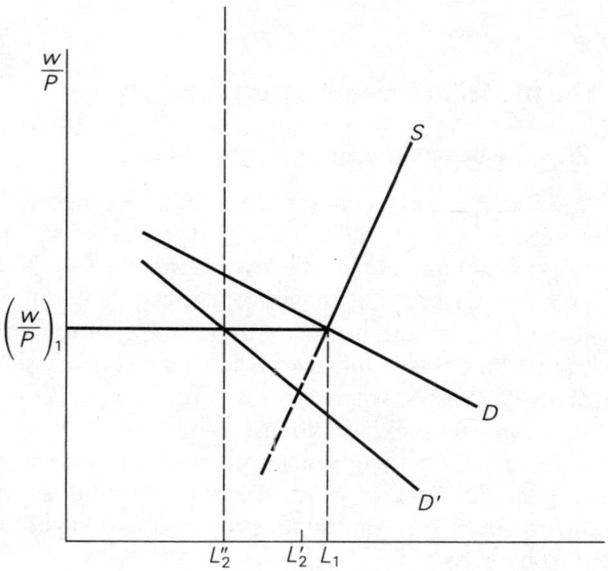

Under the Keynesian assumptions of fixed real and money wage rates, a decline in labour demand will result in unemployment.

Now, the point of introducing this somewhat special assumption is that it does transform the Keynesian model into one of fixed prices. Not only the interest rate, but also the money wage rate and the price of consumption goods (as well as P_K and hence, P) have become downwardly inflexible. This has certain advantages, not least of which is the equivalence of changes in nominal income (Y) and changes in total real output (Q). Otherwise, the relationship between these two depends on the actual supply and demand elasticities: in theory there is no problem, but for practical purposes a complication that we henceforth remove.

Now, with prices assumed to be fixed for all intents and purposes in the Keynesian model, the contrast between this approach and that of the Classical model is quite stark. Specifically, whereas in the latter output is always at its equilibrium 'full employment' level – nominal income being determined subsequently by the quantity of money – with prices adjusting, in the former prices are fixed and it is income and output together that adjust.

8.2 The model of income determination

8.2.1 Effective demand: income = expenditure

To see how income is in fact determined in the Keynesian analysis, consider Figs. 8.5a,b. In the first diagram aggregate savings (S) is shown as a (linear) function of the level of income (Y). Notice that at low incomes this is actually negative: the economy is too poor to be capable of supporting its current consumption out of current income. (Just how this is financed is left unanswered, since in all the cases investigated saving is positive. In an open economy it is of course very easy to explain this).

The slope of this 'saving function' shows the rate at which S changes, related to the rate at which Y changes. This is a graphical depiction of the m.p.s. (marginal propensity to save), which is assumed to be constant.

The 'investment function' is even simpler: we assume that the level of investment (I) is invariant with respect to the level of income (Y). As it is commonly expressed, investment is exogenous, or autonomous in contrast to the fact that saving is endogenous, or induced (by the level of income).

Figures 8.5a and b The determination of equilibrium level of income

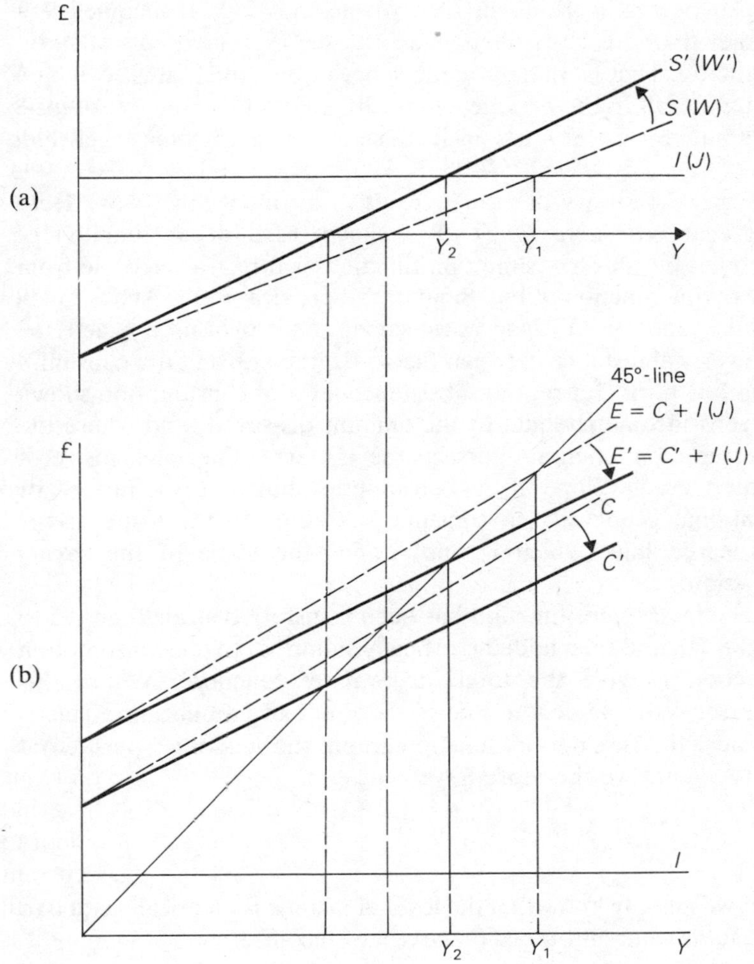

Taking initial income (Y_1) to be at its full employment level, the Keynesian theory predicts that a rise in the average savings propensity (shown as a pivoting of the withdrawal curve, which therefore implies a rise in m.p.s. also) will merely result in lower income and employment (Y_2). This is shown alternatively as a clockwise pivot of the expenditure curve in Fig. 8.5b to intersect the 45-degree line at Y_2.

The intersection of these two schedules is clearly where $S = I$, and it occurs at a unique level of income (Y_1). If income were higher than this level, then as we can see: $S > I$, or equivalently, $C_D < C_S$. That is, there is a deficiency of demand that is corrected not by a fall in the price level, but by a fall in income (Verify the alternative case of a rise in income at a *lower* income level than Y_1.)

Fig. 8.5b shows the same result in an alternative way. Here aggregate *consumption* (C_D) is shown as a linear function of income, but this 'consumption function' is directly derivable from the saving function of Fig. 8.5a; or rather, vice-versa. At any given level of income (Y), aggregate saving (S) is measured exactly by the vertical distance between the 45-degree line and the consumption function. Hence, the subsistence level of consumption shown at zero income is equal to the amount dis-saved; and where the consumption function intersects the 45-degree line, saving is zero. Moreover, the slope of the consumption function (the m.p.c., or 'marginal propensity to consume') is equal to the slope of the 45-degree line (which is one) minus the slope of the saving function.

The investment function has been transferred straight across to Fig. 8.5b, and then added (vertically summed) to the consumption function to give the total '*expenditure* function'. Where this intersects the 45-degree line is the point of equilibrium. This is because the expenditure function graphs the sum of C_D plus I, and at this point we therefore have:

$$C_D + I = Y$$

But we already know that the level of income is identically equal to the total value of output ('sources' of income):

$$Y \equiv C_S + I$$

so this is simply another way of demonstrating that $C_D = C_S$.

As an interpretation of equilibrium, this highlights the fact that investment is both an output (a component of net product) and an input (a component of expenditure). Fig. 8.5b thus shows that the equilibrium level of income is determined at the point where the level of expenditure that it generates, or induces, is just enough to support that level of income. Any other level of income is unsustainable in the sense that it generates a level of spending which is either too little to support it (income then falls) or which exceeds the level of income itself (income then rises).

The postulated change in consumer behaviour – a preference shift away from consumption and towards saving – can be shown in Fig. 8.5a as a pivoting upwards (counter-clockwise rotation) of the savings function (to S') or as a parallel shift upwards, or some combination of the two. In Fig. 8.5b these would correspond to a downward-pivoting (clockwise rotation to C′) or a parallel downward shift of the consumption function, or again as some combination of these shifts. This clearly decreases the equilibrium level of income, and in terms of Figs. 6.2 and 8.2 this translates into a leftward shift of the consumption-good demand schedule. If we adhere to the simplified extreme assumption of absolutely fixed money prices – the infinitely elastic supply schedule in Figs. 6.2 and 8.2 – then the whole of this decrease in income ($Y_1 - Y_2$) is absorbed as a decrease in total physical output.

8.2.2 **Comparison with Classical price-adjustment mechanisms**

The Classical adjustment mechanisms can be demonstrated easily on the same diagrams. The fall in the consumption-goods price (P_C) tends to shift or pivot the consumption function upwards, and vice-versa for the saving function of Fig. 8.5a. However, this can only partly restore full employment and may be a short-run effect. Remember that the underlying preferences of households have altered, and it is therefore necessary for the output of consumption goods to decrease with the slack taken up by an increase in the output of investment (new capital) goods. Therefore, in addition to the shifting of the consumption and saving functions, the investment function must also shift upwards. This, as we have seen, relies on the interest-rate mechanism, which will also reinforce the direction of shift in the other two schedules (e.g. a fall in the rate of interest should tend to reduce saving at any given level of income as well as stimulate investment as shown in Fig. 6.4d). These are, of course, the mechanisms that Keynes disputed.

8.2.3 **An extended model**

When we expand the model to encompass foreign trade the Classical theory introduces a third price-adjustment mechanism: *viz*. the exchange rate. Put briefly, if domestic households are saving too much, they can acquire more foreign bonds. This increased capital outflow will tend to depress the exchange rate and stimulate more output for export. Furthermore, if the domestic price level does fall, even though by itself this is not wholly sufficient to restore full employment, this will also tend to stimulate foreign demand and, therefore, domestic employment.

The interventionist arguments regarding these mechanisms fall into three categories, two of which are very similar to arguments *re* domestic mechanisms.

First, there may be an international, forex-market liquidity trap similar to that encountered in the domestic money market. At a 'high' exchange rate – a 'strong' domestic currency – in comparison to its expected longer-run rate, traders will have every incentive to shift from domestic-currency (£) balances into foreign-currency ($) balances. This is because they implicitly expect sterling to depreciate, and in so doing to be able to make gains by re-exchanging $ for £. If the £ depreciates to a level sufficiently below its 'normal' level the reverse may now occur: the demand for £ will become virtually infinite because there will be virtually unanimous opinion that it must appreciate. Hence it may be that the exchange rate cannot fall sufficiently, as in the case of domestic interest rates.

Second, as in the case of domestic investment, and to some extent domestic saving, interventionists are sceptical regarding the price sensitivity of international trade and finance. That is, the supply and demand schedules of Fig. 7.1 are very inelastic, so that even a large change in the exchange rate – or alternatively, the domestic price level – would have little impact on the level of domestic activity.

Third, and perhaps most salient in the light of the twentieth-century interdependent world economy, the problem of persistent unemployment is not usually confined to a single economy. To the extent that it is international, attempts to improve one economy's position through improving competitiveness vis-à-vis the RoW will only tend to 'beggar thy neighbour' as indeed occurred in the 1930s. In short, the problem to which Keynes addressed himself was for all intents and purposes within the context of a closed – albeit international – economy.

Imports (F) and exports (X) can be easily incorporated into this model if we wish. The latter is an autonomous or exogenous element; whereas the former is usually assumed to be a linear function of income. The (constant) slope of this function is the 'marginal propensity to import' (m.p.f.). We add this schedule vertically to the savings schedule to obtain a 'withdrawals' schedule (W) having a slope equal to m.p.s. + m.p.f. Likewise, the vertical summation of the I and X schedules gives us a total 'injections' schedule (J). These are indicated in Figs 8.5a,b by the parenthetical labels.

With or without this extension it is apparent that the equilibrium level of income may be below its full-employment level. But if this contractionary adjustment is occurring instead of the alternative (Classical) price adjustments, how can full employment be restored?

From the preceding, the solution is almost obvious. Taking the equilibrium condition we derived inclusive of the government sector:

$$S + F + T = I + X + G$$

it is possible for taxes (T) and public expenditure (G) to be varied at will in order to achieve the target level.

Figs. 8.6a,b illustrate how this can be accomplished. Tax revenues are assumed to be a (linear) function – the 'tax function' – of income, with a constant slope: the marginal tax rate (m.t.r.). The withdrawals function is now the vertical summation of all three schedules, having a slope equal to: m.p.s. + m.p.f. + m.t.r. (where m.p.s. and m.p.f. are the changes in savings and imports related to the changes in *total* income, Y, rather than *disposable* income, $Y - T$).

At the same time, government spending can be fixed at any desired level regardless of the level of income. Thus, G is shown as being just sufficient to ensure that income stays at Y.

Recall that this corresponds to the equivalent condition that:

$$G - T = (S - I) + (F - X)$$

which says that whatever the PSBR (government deficit), it will be financed by a combination of excess domestic saving or foreign saving in the form of a net capital inflow (i.e. a current deficit on trade).

The multiplier

What has happened is that the increased spending over tax revenues has served to raise income. This increase in income has in

Figures 8.6a and b Government expenditure and the multiplier process

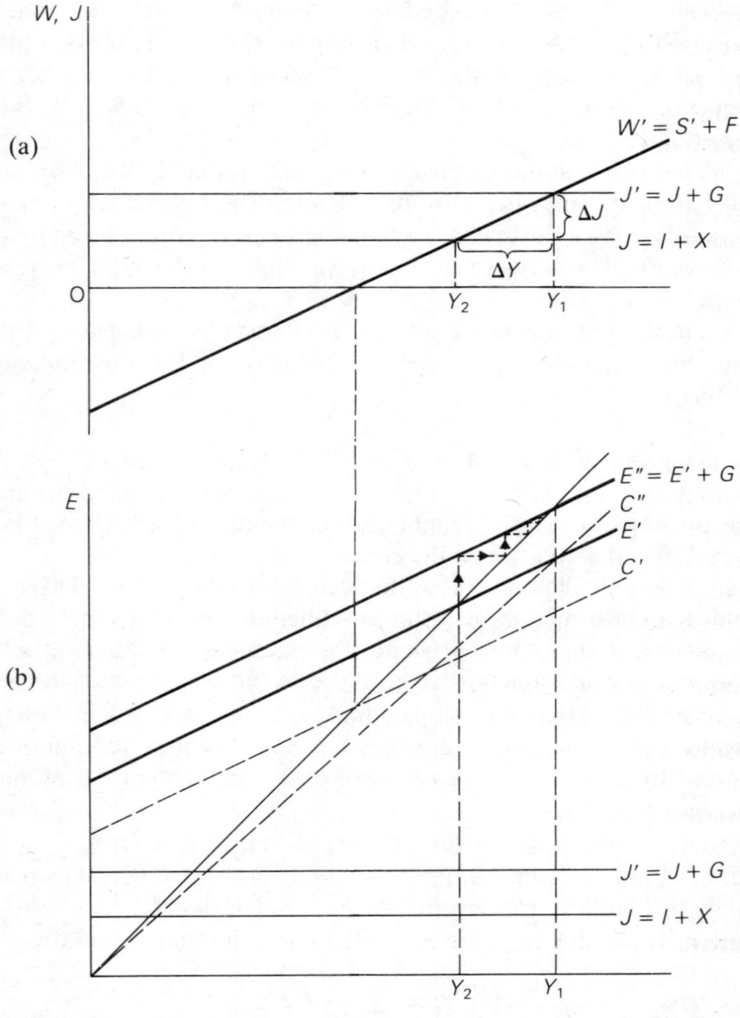

The introduction of government spending (*G*) raises the 'injections' curve of Fig. 8.6a and thus raises income. The changes in these magnitudes are clearly related through the slope of the withdrawals curve (note: no taxes). Alternatively, *G* raises the expenditure function of Fig. 8.6b. The multiplier process, whereby a rise in expenditure (vertical distance) generates an equal rise in income (horizontal distance), which then generates a fractional subsequent rise in expenditure, etc, is shown by the dashed steps.

turn generated increased saving (S) and increased imports (F) just up to the point where they are sufficiently greater than investment (I), and exports (X) to finance the required deficit.

This is literally a 'bootstrap' operation: more spending means more income means more saving (domestic and foreign) to finance itself. In fact, the extent to which income must rise as a result of an increase in G is, conversely, determined precisely by these requirements. As shown in Fig. 8.6a the total change in income (ΔY) deriving from a given change in J ($\Delta J = G$) is equal to one divided by the slope of the withdrawal function. Formally, it must be that:

$$\frac{\Delta Y}{\Delta J} = \frac{1}{m.p.s. + m.p.f. + m.t.r.}$$

the term on the right is known as the 'expenditure multiplier' for obvious reasons. Note that its value is lower – less of an impact on income from spending – the higher is our propensity to save or to buy imported goods, or the higher is the marginal tax rate. As we have asserted, all these elements constitute 'leakages' (or 'withdrawals') from the circular flow, in the sense that they reduce the proportion of each £1 earned which will be spent on domestically produced goods. Conversely, if we save a smaller fraction of our income (a fall in the m.p.s., say), the change in G will have a larger positive effect on Y (illustrating the so-called 'paradox of thrift'), simply because more of each additional £1 will be spent on domestic goods! (For a more detailed exposition, see Appendix 8A).

Summary

The essence of the Keynesian argument as presented is that, at least in the short run, the failure of the capital-goods sector to expand enough to absorb factors (labour) from the contracted consumption-goods sector results in a loss of output and employment that wage reductions may be powerless to prevent, even if they were to occur.

They might not occur either because workers suffered from 'money illusion'; or because they (correctly) perceived that when the capital-goods sector did expand wage rates – real and money – would be restored to their original level (as we have conveniently assumed to be the case). If wage reductions did occur then the employment situation would be improved somewhat; even so, the new equilibrium would be at a lower level of employment and output, with a much lower real wage bill, than before. Also, in the circumstances of the 1930s this might have had disastrous political consequences.

One possible explanation for this failure to adjust is extreme price (interest rate) insensitivity of capital-goods demand. If firms invest upon 'animal spirits' a few percentage points on the cost of borrowing will have little effect. This is one way in which self-reinforcing negative expectations prevent recovery.

The other way in which expectations play a role has to do with the willingness of people to lend. In particular, if they are not willing to lend at a sufficiently low rate of interest that will induce more investment, recovery will be inhibited just as effectively. This reticence is manifested as an increasingly strong and ultimately complete preference for liquidity (money) over bonds, due principally to speculative motives.

With price mechanisms ineffectual, it must be income that bears the brunt of adjustment. Assuming for convenience that money wages and prices are downwardly inflexible, and that the rate of interest is initially at its 'floor' level, the Keynesian theory can be presented as a simple model of income determination. Taking *I, X* and *G* ('injections') to be fixed, and *S, F* and *T* ('withdrawals') to be linear functions of income (*Y*) it is immediately apparent that the equilibrium condition:

$$I + X + G = S + F + T$$

occurs at a single level of income (output). Furthermore, any given level of income can be attained by varying *G* and/or *T*.

Appendix 8A A general multiplier example

A generalized multiplier process is described in the following table. We assume arbitrarily that there have been increases in *I, X* and *G* of 30, 20 and 50 respectively. We take the marginal propensities (out of gross income) to be as follows:

Marginal propensity to consume (*m.p.c.*) = 0.70

Marginal propensity to import	$(m.p.f.)$	=	0.20
(foreign-produced goods)			
Marginal propensity to save	$(m.p.s.)$	=	0.10
Marginal tax rate	$(m.t.r.)$	=	0.20

(Note that the 10% saved out of additional gross income is therefore 12½% out of disposable, after-tax income. Also, the marginal propensity to consume domestically produced goods is 0.70 − 0.20 = 0.50.)

	$\Delta Y =$	$\Delta C_D +$	$\Delta F +$	$\Delta S +$	ΔT
		ΔC (= $\Delta C_D + \Delta F$)			
$\Delta I + \Delta X + \Delta G = \Delta J =$	100	50	20	10	20
30 + 20 + 50					
	50	25	10	5	10
	25	12.5	5	2.5	5
	.	.	.	.	.
	.	.	.	.	.
	200	100 +	40 +	20 +	40
			$\Delta W = 100 = \Delta J$ (= 40 + 20 + 40)		

Here J stands for injections, W for withdrawals, and F for the value of imports.

Often, the consumption of domestic and foreign goods is aggregated into a single 'consumption' variable; i.e. assuming all imports (F) are of consumption-goods total consumption-good demand is:

$$C = C_D + F$$

as indicated. In reckoning aggregate income (Y), the associated formula is often given as:

$$Y = C + I + G + X - F$$

which reduces in our terminology to:

$$Y = C_S + I + G + X$$

where $C_S = C_D$ is assumed to hold.

Another way to see this equivalence is simply to note that the excess of total consumption over domestic supply is equal to imports:

$$C = C_S - F$$

or: $C_S = C - F$

Returning to our example, we have finally:

$$\begin{aligned} G - T &= 50 - 40 = 10 \\ I - S &= 30 - 20 = 10 \\ X - F &= 20 - 40 = -20 \\ \hline \text{Therefore} \quad J - W &= 0 \end{aligned}$$

This says that the counterpart of the public sector's deficit (10) plus the domestic business sector's excess borrowing requirement (also 10) is a capital inflow (net lending by foreigners) of 20, which is manifested as a trade deficit of the same amount (−20).

An interesting phenomenon is the 'international multiplier'. Note that the initial, completely exogenous injection of 100 raised imports by 40 units; but this is in turn an exogenous increase in exports for the rest-of-the-world (RoW). Suppose that the RoW has no taxes, nor saves anything, but has a propensity to import of 0.50 (and by implication a propensity to consume their own domestically produced goods of 0.50 also). Then the rise in injections of 40 will raise income ultimately in the RoW by 80 units (a multiplier of 2), which will consist of a 40-unit increase in their goods production, and a 40-unit increase in imports.

However, this is a second round of injections into our domestic economy; and in fact it is apparent that this sub-sequence will also continue for ever: the initial injection of 100 causes a second injection of 40, causes a third injection of 16, etc. (verify). Therefore, total injections will rise by 166⅔ (also verify).

With a domestic multiplier of two, the total rise in domestic income will thus be 333⅓ rather than 200. We leave it as an exercise to determine: (1) by how much foreign income has risen; (2) what the flows of funds will be; e.g. how is the domestic trade deficit/surplus financed?

This international 'repercussion' obviously increases our subjective estimate of the power of the multiplier. At the same time we ought to recognize two qualifying aspects: (1) the full value of the multiplier depends on unlimited time. In reality, perhaps only one or two rounds of spending might take place within the relevant policy horizon such as a year. In fact, if a discretionary injection of public spending impacted significantly later than when the appropriation was made, it could well turn out to be 'pro-cyclical' rather than 'contra-cyclical; (2) Although it is assumed that the m.p.c. is an average value, there may be distributional deviations. Specifically, if the better-off received the income, the multiplier impact would be diminished by their greater saving propensities and vice-versa.

Appendix 8B The accelerator mechanism

A special model of the business cycle is the so-called 'accelerator' mechanism, which relies on the constancy of capital per unit of output.

This connection means that any change in the level of income will induce a change in the (desired) capital stock, and in turn affect income through the multiplier process.

In order to trace this process it is often assumed that the response of investment occurs in the period following a change in income, but that the multiplier impacts fully in the same period as the investment.

For convenience, we take the capital–output ratio equal to one. Initially, both the capital stock and output are equal to 100, but in the first period some exogenous force (e.g. a rise in X or G, but not I) raises the permanent underlying level of income to 110. The multiplier has a value of 2.

Period	*Income*	*Desired K*		*Actual K*	*Investment*
0	100	100		100	0
1	110	110		100	0
2	130	130	–	110	10
3	150	150	–	130	20
4	150	150	–	150	20
5	110	110	–	150	0
6	(30)	(30)		(110)	(−40)

In words, the rise in income in period 1 stimulates an investment response of +10 in period 2, which through the multiplier adds another 20 units to the underlying income level of 110. This second-period income of 130 now induces investment of another +20 units in period 3, generating income of 150 (= 110 + 2×20). Once again, firms add +20 to the capital stock in period 4, thus maintaining the level of income at 150. However, there is consequently no desire to invest in period 5 and income therefore falls to its base level of 110.

Although investment in period 6 would be −40, this may not be feasible: the maximum run-down would be dictated by depreciation, say at a 20% rate. Therefore, the next section of the table looks like:

Period	*Income*	*Desired K*	*Actual K*	*Net investment*
6	50	50	120	−30
7	62	62	96	−24
8	71.6	71.6	76.8	−19.2
9	99.6	99.6	71.6	− 5.2
10	166	166	99.6	28
.	.	.	.	.
.	.	.	.	.

In period 6 investment is limited to −30 (20% of 150), so actual *K* falls to 120 instead of 110 and income to only 50 instead of 30. In periods 7 and 8, *I* is similarly limited, but in period 9 we find that although *dis*-investment is still occurring (desired *K* less than actual *K* in the previous period) it is not at the maximum possible rate.

The important thing to observe is that even though investment is negative, as the size of the disinvestment decreases, income is rising since there is a smaller negative multiplier effect. Thus, at some point there is a shift to positive investment intentions.

Likewise, even though investment may be positive, if it does not continually increase then income will start to fall and thus lead to disinvestment as shown.

9 Synthesis and Comparison: The Role of Money

Outline

Synopsis

This chapter begins with the 'synthesis' of Keynesian and Classical theories in terms of the *IS–LM* framework. In the former theory public expenditure increases translate almost fully into income increases because of the high elasticity of money demand (large excess balances); whereas in the latter the inelasticity of money demand (small or nil excess balances) means that this change in spending 'crowds out' the private sector.

These differing views on the substitutability of money for bonds are also indicative of a difference in the substitutability of money for goods. This argument can be expressed in terms of the velocity of money – in short- and long-run senses – or equivalently, in terms of the consumption function. I then briefly elaborate the New Classical (Friedmanite) notion of permanent income.

9.1 The IS–LM Framework

A more general yet concise presentation of the Keynesian system is shown by Figs 9.1a–c: the so-called '*IS–LM*' diagrams. Each of these schedules is in fact merely constructed from our earlier diagrams as follows (for a closed economy).

9.1.1 Derivations of stock and flow equilibria

IS (Fig. 9.1a)

This construction starts in the second (north-west) quadrant showing investment related to the rate of interest; while the third (south-west) quadrant graphs an equilibrium 45–degree line along

Figure 9.1a The *IS* curve

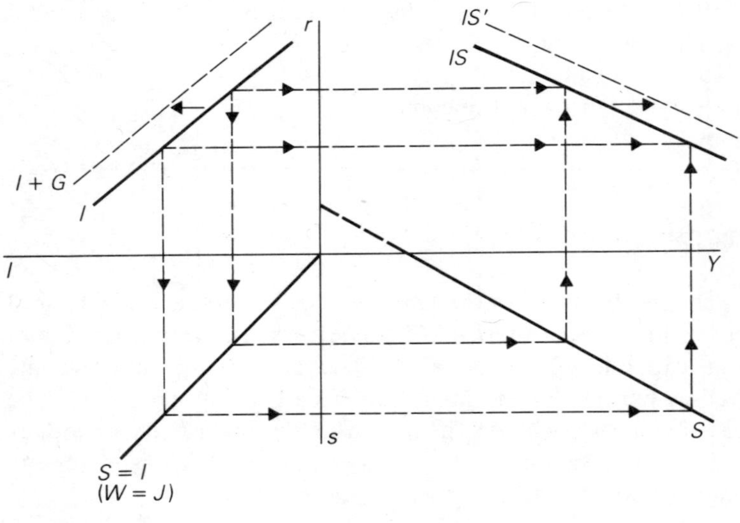

> An autonomous 'injection' of spending (e.g. increased *G*) shifts the second-quadrant curve outwards, hence *IS* shifts outwards.

which savings is equal to investment. The fourth (south-east) quadrant graphs the savings function of Fig. 8.5a, and with this we are able to trace a relationship between the rate of interest and the level of income: the *IS* curve of the first (north-east) quadrant.

In simple terms, lower interest rates will stimulate greater investment, but for this to be an equilibrium level it must be matched by saving. However, savings will increase only if income rises. Therefore, the goods market can be in equilibrium at any combination of lower interest (r) and higher income (Y) as shown. (Remember that in this context $S=I$ corresponds to $C_D = C_S$).

LM (Fig. 9.1b)

This construction utilizes the Keynesian separation of money demand into transactions and interest-related (precautionary plus speculative) components. The latter is drawn in the second quadrant as in Fig. 8.3a, including the liquidity trap at some low

Figure 9.1b The *LM* curve

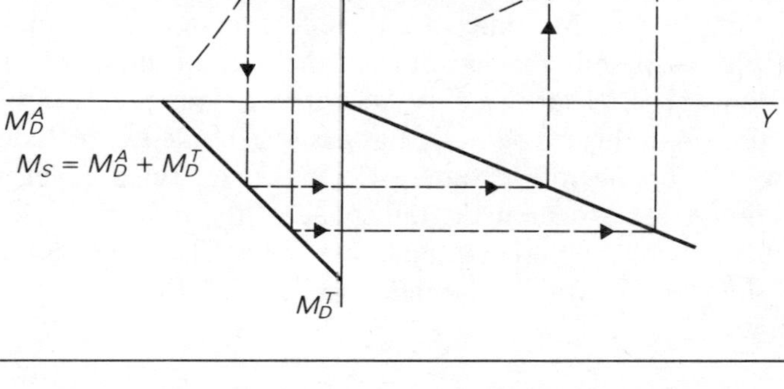

> The existence of a 'liquidity trap' means that the *LM* curve becomes infinitely elastic. In contrast, the Classical view is that money demand is not so interest-sensitive.

rate of interest. For comparison, the Classical money-demand schedule of Fig. 6.5 is also shown. The third quadrant shows that equilibrium in the money market requires that the total demand for money equal the (given) supply, labelled M_S. So, if at a lower rate of interest more money is demanded for precautionary/speculative purposes (M_A), for equilibrium the other component – transactions demand (M_T) – must be less. But, as shown by the straightforward schedule of the fourth quadrant, this is consistent with a lower level of income as well. Therefore, as the *LM* curve of the first quadrant shows, money market equilibrium obtains with any number of combinations of lower r and lower Y and vice-versa.

The intersection of *IS* and *LM* curves in Fig. 9.1c thus indicates a unique combination of r and Y such that both goods and money markets are in equilibrium. Furthermore, if both of these balance, it must be the case that the bond markets also clear; since the equality of C_D and C_S implies that the flow of additional bond supply and demand is equal ($S = I$), while the equality of M_D and M_S implies that the supply and demand for the existing stock of bonds are also equal.

In the somewhat simplistic but conceptually convenient world of fixed prices, like that for which we have developed the preceding 'withdrawals equals injections' models of income determination, if the equilibrium income level is less than its full-employment level (Y_1), there are no automatic corrective forces at work. Hence, government must undertake expansionary *fiscal* policy (i.e. raising G and/or reducing T) to restore full employment.

Within the *IS–LM* framework the effect of an increase in G, for example, is to shift the schedule in the second quadrant in Fig. 9.1a outwards. That is, this becomes a graph relating total injections – in this case $I + G$, but easily extended to include X if we wish – to the rate of interest. Of course, since government spending is set exogenously, the shape of the new schedule is in exact conformity with the original, as shown. The end result of this is to shift the *IS* curve to the *right* (verify this), thereby increasing income.

9.1.2 'Keynesian' *vs.* 'Classical' ranges

Two special cases deserve mention here. First, if the economy is in the liquidity trap this increase in government expenditure has no

Figure 9.1c The *IS-LM* framework: 'Classical' and 'Keynesian' effects

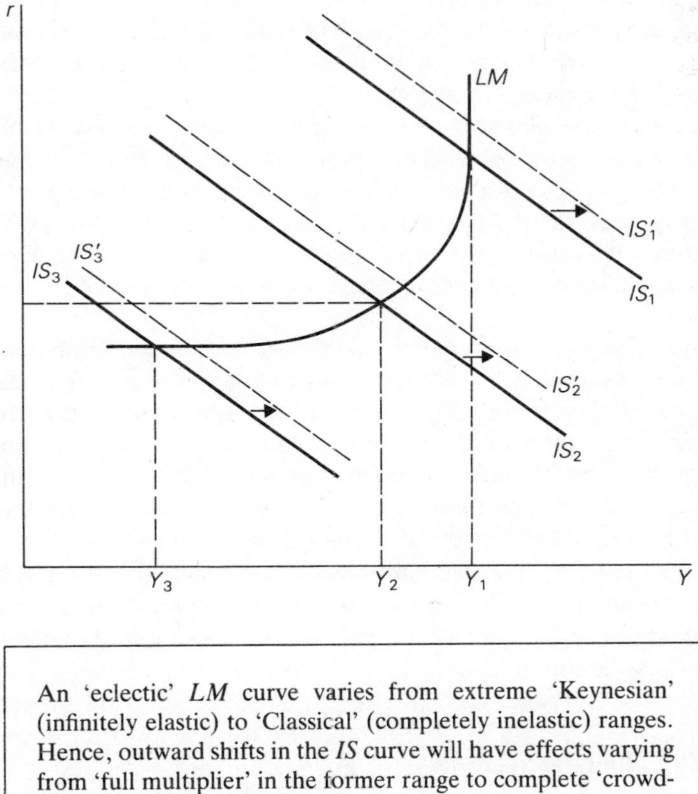

An 'eclectic' *LM* curve varies from extreme 'Keynesian' (infinitely elastic) to 'Classical' (completely inelastic) ranges. Hence, outward shifts in the *IS* curve will have effects varying from 'full multiplier' in the former range to complete 'crowding out' in the latter range.

effect on interest rates. The government is able to borrow from, or 'tap' the existing pool of idle – i.e. speculative – balances without exerting any upward pressure on interest rates. This money can then be spent, having a full multiplier impact as derived in the earlier model of income determination.

In the second case it may happen that equilibrium occurs where the *LM* curve is not infinitely elastic. If so, the increase in public sector borrowing will displace some private investment through the rise in the interest rate. In other words, government spending 'crowds out' private spending, partially but not completely. This extreme incidence occurs when the *LM* curve has become vertical, in which case there is no possibility of a rise in income. You might recognize this as the Classical case of (automatic) full employment wherein an unbalanced budget necessarily implies a contraction in the level of private-sector output.

In fact, the elastic part of the illustrated *LM* curve is often referred to as the 'Keynesian' range, in contrast to the inelastic, 'Classical' range. In the latter the literal interpretation is that the transactions demand is virtually the sole motive for holding money. Therefore, any government borrowing must be at the expense of private spending; there is no pool of 'idle' balances at all!

As we know, the interventionist theories of Keynes are based on the conclusion that the economy can be stuck at a level like Y_3 in Fig. 9.1c. This is a curious form of unemployment 'equilibrium' where households (and firms) are holding excess money balances in preference to interest-bearing bonds, due to expectational factors. The implied failure of the interest-rate mechanism therefore prevents any expansion of the capital-goods sector to absorb the unemployment caused initially by our assumed contraction of the consumption-goods sector. As a result, income – together with real output and employment – will decline until desired saving just matches the initial level of investment once again.

9.2 The role of money

This Keynesian perspective focuses exclusively on the substitutability of money and bonds. However, if idle balances do exist, then households are also holding money as an implicit substitute for goods. In commonsense terms, excess money balances are being neither lent nor spent.

It is precisely this aspect of the situation that has been emphasized by the Classical school. Specifically, even if households wished to spend less and save more (out of any given income), the absence of acceptable savings opportunities would not simply result in the build-up of larger money balances, but would substantially reverse the initial change of intentions.

Therefore, in diagrammatic terms, the saving schedule of Fig. 9.1a (fourth quadrant) would shift to show a reduced proportion of income saved, resulting in a rightward shift of the *IS* schedule. Also, to the extent that firms were holders of money balances, they would spend on additional capital goods (i.e. investment) rather than sit on 'cash mountains' indefinitely. This would show up as an outward shift of the injections schedule (second quadrant of Fig. 9.1a), thus reinforcing the equilibrating tendency.

As an important point, observe once more that this works through the *IS* schedule, and hence does not appear to depend on the elasticity of the *LM* schedule. However, the two are not independent: the inelasticity of the latter curve implies that there is a limited degree of substitutability between money and bonds, and therefore that money is a closer substitute for goods; conversely, an extremely elastic LM curve indicates high substitutability of money and bonds, to the implied exclusion of expenditure (*IS*) effects.

9.2.1 **Velocity of money**

Another way to summarize the differences – and one which is popular in contemporary discussions – is by means of the concept of velocity V (= Y/M).

It is readily apparent that the Keynesian theory of money allows for a sharp change in this measure. Income can fall with no change in M; and conversely, M can be increased with no change in Y (V therefore falls in either case). When government borrows 'idle' balances and spends them, the reverse occurs and V rises.

This contrasts with the views of the modern Quantity Theorists, or as we shall henceforth call them, the 'New Classical' school. Admittedly, velocity can vary with the rate of interest (the *LM* curve is not strictly vertical) but not to the great extent – and especially, not for the length of time – that Keynes suggested. As we have stated before, velocity is 'stable'.

Although much of the discussion concerning the demand for money is technical, the underlying approach of the New Classical analysis rests on the premise that households and firms form 'rational expectations' about future prices and quantities. What this means is that although they do not know ('perfect foresight') what these will be, neither is there any reason for systematic bias to creep into their expectations about them. That is, the same (full) information about the determinants of equilibrium prices (and quantities) is available to everyone, and although certain individual firms and households may err in their judgements, aggregate markets will tend to be highly efficient in establishing the 'true' equilibrium prices and quantities.

This may seem a long way around to assert that, in general, there is no reason for economic agents (firms, households and governments) to persistently expect any outcome other than the Classical market equilibrium predicted by the set of underlying supply and demand schedules. But if these agents generally – and correctly, in an aggregative sense – expect these markets to clear (i.e. they expect 'full employment' to be maintained) then they also have no reason to drastically alter their planned behaviour, regarding either investment (firms) nor consumption (households).

9.2.2 **'Permanent' income**

One of the principal authors of the New Classical theories is M. Friedman, who summarized this perspective in the concept of a household's 'permanent' income (Y_P). Without going into detail, the basic idea is that the given (present) endowments of both human and non-human (physical or financial) capital that are possessed by the representative household represent a potential present and future stream of consumption. As we first saw in microeconomics, the planned pattern of work, saving and ultimately consumption – as well as the current composition of household assets – is based on the household's preferences and tastes, conditioned by prices.

In looking to the future, the household must form some expectation, even if only implicitly, about these prices; and therefore about its future income. Now although in reality this stream might well be irregular, it can be thought of as equivalent to some lifetime stream of equal incomes ('annuities'): i.e. 'permanent' income. Looked at in another way, the present value or net worth of our household in the current period is just the net value of its human and non-human wealth. 'Permanent' income is the annuity that could be purchased (presumably from an insurance company) if they could cash in all at once.

The 'Friedmanites' would certainly admit that the level of permanent income, together with its planned division between consumption and saving and the division of its assets between real, physical assets such as a house and financial assets such as money and bonds, is influenced by changes in prices. This includes the rate of interest, and explains for instance why the demand for money is not completely interest-inelastic. However, these changes are in theory predictable, and certainly not catastrophic. Thus, for example, if there were a fundamental shift of resources from consumption to capital goods as a result of a change in demand, the response would be stable; muted, so to speak, by the tendency of households and firms to absorb changes over a lifetime horizon.

Now if, as Keynesians contend, income were to suddenly fall as an immediate result of this change in behaviour, the New Classical view would hold that: (a) in general, market participants would be able to perceive the new equilibrium prices and quantities, and therefore tend to establish it fairly quickly; and (b) consistent with this, households would treat the immediate change (drop) in income as a purely transitory component, and therefore not react in the emphatic manner suggested by Keynes.

We can use Fig. 8.6b to illustrate this difference. The Keynesian consumption function is fairly flat, indicating that a change in income will be accompanied by a considerable change in the proportion of income consumed (the 'average propensity to consume' or a.p.c. declines due to a 'fundamental psychological law', according to Keynes). But if this change is seen as transitory, then what we may be observing is instead Friedman's predicted low response in terms of consumption. To see this, suppose the change in income were seen as permanent. In that event, the permanent income hypothesis suggests that the response of consumption would be much more substantial, as shown by the steeper (dashed) ray, C''.

Indeed, studies of short-run consumption have often revealed the kind of small-ish m.p.c. characteristic of the Keynesian consumption function, whereas studies over longer time periods usually show a much higher proportion of income consumed, in conformity with the Friedmanite view.

In addition, note how these differing schools explain the money market. If we ask Keynesians what has happened to money holdings as consumption drops with income, the answer is that as there is significantly less spending, so average balances must have increased (velocity falls). From the New Classical point of view, the fact that permanent income has hardly changed is likewise consistent with the fact that desired money balances have not varied much (velocity is highly stable).

Although for money demand the general empirical evidence is far less clear-cut than for consumption behaviour, the income velocity of money (V) has usually been found to be more stable over longer periods of time. This is again consistent with the New Classical (Friedmanite) view that agents are responding to more permanent, equilibrium features of the economy. Thus, for example, if we define 'permanent income velocity' (V_p) as:

$$V_p = Y_p/M$$

this is in theory a measure with a very limited degree of variation. Comparing this to the more conventional, current income velocity measure we see that:

$$V = Y/M = Y/Y_p \cdot V_p$$

so we might expect that 'observed' income velocity (V) varies to the degree that current income changes in proportion to permanent income: as the time period lengthens the two should more closely correspond.

Ever since Keynes' arguments were first published as a 'general theory' in 1936, there has been a continuing process of synthesis between Keynesian and Classical models. From a contemporary perspective it now appears that the basic price-insensitive/price-inflexible model of the former school is of a rather short-run nature, whereas the latter school's model is more relevant to longer-run adjustments. However, despite a unifying theoretical perspective there remain obvious and important issues of practical implementation. Undoubtedly Keynes himself recognized this problem in his famous pronouncement: 'In the long run we are all dead'.

What has been achieved by all the intervening research and discussion is a clarification of the nature of the division between short-run disequilibrium and long-run equilibrium, centring on the role of expectations. At one extreme is the belief that nearly as quickly as economic agents are able to perceive equilibrium, they act in aggregate to bring it about. At the other extreme is the belief that lack of information and inertia can generate indefinite stagnation. We might almost characterize the two approaches as self-fulfilling optimism *vs* self-fulfilling pessimism!

The truth undoubtedly lies somewhere between, but modern Economics does not yet have sufficiently detailed models of dynamic adjustment processes to identify it. (On a hopeful note, the investigation of expectation and price formation will probably continue to grow at a rapid pace.) Nevertheless, with the weight of evidence from studies of consumption and money demand leaning towards the side of the New Classical school – although frequently questioned and criticized – and perhaps far more important, given the contemporary resurgence of libertarian political philosophies, their beliefs have once more gained ascendancy in economic policy-making.

Summary

The *IS* curve illustrates 'flow' equilibria (income and the rate of interest inversely related) such that the goods and savings-investment markets both clear. The *LM* curve illustrates 'stock' equilibria (Y and r directly related) such that the markets for the existing quantities of money and bonds both clear. An outward shift of the *IS* curve, such as occurs when G increases, has an effect depending on the slope of the *LM* curve. If the latter is flat ('Keynesian' range) the rise in G has a full multiplier effect. If it is vertical ('Classical' range) the rise in G has a full crowding-out effect.

The implied Keynesian view is that strong liquidity preference means that there is a large pool of 'idle' money balances not being spent (or lent) that can be tapped by government borrowing. The Classical view is that money is not held idly – i.e. the speculative motive is transitory – and therefore its transfer from private to public balances is merely financing a displacement of activity.

However, even a vertical *LM* curve is misleading of the Classical case, in that it focuses on the substitution of money for bonds. For example, crowding out occurs through higher interest rates; but if money is seen as a substitute for goods as well, then the Classical argument is also that increased government borrowing displaces private spending – such as for consumption, and not just investment – directly. Thus, the economy is not susceptible to Keynesian remedies.

This Classical notion was expressed originally by the assumed constancy of money velocity. In the 'New' Classical theory it is not constant but 'stable', reflecting limited shifts in money demand in response to long-run changes in equilibrium prices. In fact, if aggregate market expectations are similarly 'rational' there is in any case no reason to believe that the phenomenon of unemployment is anything but transitory, eliminated through appropriate price adjustments. The evidence for this is the long-run ('longitudinal') consumption function: households have expectations about their normal or 'permanent' income levels and behave accordingly; i.e. in a stable and predictable fashion. This empirical evidence on consumption behaviour – supported by evidence that velocity fluctuates less as the time period increases – lends some weight to Classical views. Nonetheless, their contemporary dominance undoubtedly owes much to the resurgence of political conservatism as well.

10 Policy Issues: Unemployment and Inflation

Outline

Synopsis

This chapter attempts to explain the unemployment and inflation experiences of the Western world since the 1930s from overall New Classical and neo-Keynesian perspectives.

The former school interpret the shock which caused the Depression not as a fundamental shift in spending behaviour, but as a monetary contraction which required price and wage deflation. Likewise, the 'stagflation' of the 1970s was due to excessive monetary expansion, upsetting expectations to such an extent that only in the 1980s are markets re-adjusting. The moral is that real economic activity levels can at worst be adversely affected, and at best be unaffected by discretionary government fiscal or monetary policies.

In contrast, the (neo-)Keynesians see the recent experience as evidence of 'cost-push' inflation. Although the quantity of money may matter, as a policy 'Monetarism' is irrelevant since the control of the money suppy is very imperfect and perhaps impossible.

Finally, I briefly consider the extent to which contemporary unemployment is structural: i.e. having microeconomic foundations. To the extent that it is, the argument shifts to one between industrial planning (an interventionist approach) *vs* 'supply-side' removal of market distortions (a *laissez-faire* approach).

10.1 'New' Classical views: depression and stagflation

In the formation of present-day policies concerning important economic issues – e.g. unemployment, inflation – the Classical belief in price-adjustment mechanisms has become increasingly widespread once more; a so-called 'counter-revolution' to the Keynesian 'revolution'. This does not, however, mean that Interventionism is dead, and there are many vigorous 'neo-Keynesians' ready to continue debate. It is the purpose of this chapter to describe this debate, beginning at the point where we left the strict Classical model and introduced the ideas of Keynes; *viz*, the Great Depression of the 1930s.

Looking at this phenomenon now from a New Classical perspective (recall the main differences between this and the 'old' Classical school centre on: (1) the replacement of the concept of velocity as an institutional constant by the concept of its stability (predictability) in response to changes in economic variables, especially the rate of interest; and (2) the replacement of the implicit notion of 'perfect foresight' which Keynes attacked directly, by the notion of 'rational expectations'), we are immediately struck by the assumption that this might have been triggered by a fundamental shift in household consumption and savings patterns (and/or expectations regarding investment). This was a perfectly legitimate device with which to motivate our discussion of adjustment processes, but while it is also in keeping with the Keynesian view that Western industrial economies had reached a point of virtual exhaustion, it does not sit well with the new Classical view that markets change slowly and adapt quickly.

10.1.1 Monetary contraction

Of course the fact of the Depression's occurrence indicates that Western economies had suffered some kind of shock, but it did not emanate from any sudden shift in the behaviour of households or firms. Instead, it was government itself that was largely to blame; i.e. a 'self-administered shock'.

The signal event in this interpretation is the stock market crashes of 1929–30. For Keynes this merely exposed the inherent weakness of demand in twentieth-century post-industrial economies. However, there were other ramifications that his view tended to ignore. Chief among these was the fact that the quantity of money had contracted sharply (in fact, New Classical economists prefer the term 'Great Contraction'). Particularly in the United States, where there was – and is – a large number of small banks, a sizeable percentage of banks' loans had been made for stock market investment. The security, or 'collateral' for these loans was the shares themselves; hence, when they declined in value borrowers were asked to put up additional funds to cover. This they could only do through further sales, and so prices plummeted. Consequently, banks were forced to write off many of their loans as bad debts, and thus into bankruptcy. This of course meant that the aggregate level of deposits in the banking system fell.

New Classicals point out that this contraction could have been restrained, if not halted, by the central bank (the Federal Reserve), but was not. As a result the economy had to cope with the shock of a sudden decrease in its money supply (M_S).

In terms of our earlier *IS–LM* apparatus (Fig. 9.1c) this meant a leftward shift of the *LM* schedule. This immediate decline in income was interpreted by Keynes – wrongly, the Classicals would say – as a leftward shift in the *IS* schedule.

Going back to our earlier set of diagrams (Figs. 6.1–6.5) the initial shock to the economy was not the leftward and rightward shifts in the consumption goods demand and saving (as well as bond demand) schedules, respectively. Instead, it was a leftward shift in the M_S schedule of Fig. 6.1.

10.1.2 Recovery: money wage cuts *vs* monetary reflation

The appropriate response of the economy to this deflation is, in Classical analysis, obvious: if all money-related schedules shift downwards (in the case of Figs 6.2, 6.3a and 6.4a) or leftwards (in the case of Figs. 6.4b,c,d) by the same proportion that the quantity of money has decreased, there will be absolutely no change in any *real* quantity (e.g. Fig. 6.3b is unaffected). This is a vivid illustration of the Classical 'neutrality' of money: a doubling of M merely doubles P; a halving of M merely halves P; etc. In Quantity-theoretic terms, in which:

$$P \times Q = M \times V$$

this is consistent with the view that Q is determined by the real underlying forces of supply and demand, and with V also determined, changes in M manifest themselves as changes in P only.

During the 1930s money goods prices did actually decline, at least until the middle of the decade, but the persistence of unemployment was in this Classical view a consequence of the failure of money wages to decline sufficiently. Indeed, we observe that the real wage rate did rise during this period of depression!

Thus, we are back to the simple banana analogy. The stickiness of the money wage rate, due to supply factors, meant that the labour market was stuck at a point like U in Fig. 6.3a when all other relevant (money-related) schedules had at least partly adjusted to the contraction of the quantity of money. The result was unemployment, and the cure was for money wages to fall.

This is quite a contrast with the Keynesian view on the causes and remedies of the Depression. Moreover, although governments of the day were ostensibly undertaking fiscal expansion, often through the medium of public works projects, the Classical view is that this was in fact a surreptitious monetary expansion.

Because central banks act as bankers not only to commercial (private-sector) banks, but also as bankers to governments, they are in a position to make loans to the latter. In simplest terms, in exchange for a promissory note from the government – i.e. a promise to repay at some future date out of tax receipts or further borrowings – the central bank can create balances (deposits) that the government intends to spend. When it does, this money – in practice, cheques rather than cash (see below) – will be deposited in accounts at commercial banks, who will then go to the central bank and present the cheques for payment. Hence, the central bank debits the government's account (which it had created in the first place) and credits the commercial banks' accounts.

As we shall see, this constitutes an addition to the 'reserve base' of the banking system. For the moment, however, it is sufficient to observe that the central bank has literally 'printed money' to finance government's increased spending. (This is in fact why in both the US with its twelve regional Federal Reserve Banks (and a coordinating Federal Reserve Board), and in the UK the Bank of England are supposed to be 'autonomous' in their actions. On the other hand, it is occasionally difficult to maintain real independence.)

The alternative means of financing a deficit is for the government to borrow not from the central bank – i.e. not to 'print money' – but instead from the private sector. In this way the government is borrowing money already in existence; hence, conducting a 'pure' fiscal policy with no significant impact on the quantity of money. (The instruments of this borrowing are usually thought of as government bonds, which are longer-term in nature. In reality much borrowing is short-term, through the sale of 'Treasury Bills' (TBs).)

To return to our Classical *post mortem* on the experience of the 1930s, the explanation for the recovery which began to occur in the second half of the decade is attributable not to the fact that governments of the day spent more, but primarily to the fact that this was underwritten by an expansion of the money supply. This obviated the need for price reductions.

10.1.3 **Post-war events**

For 20–25 years following the Second World War, Western governments likewise convinced themselves that steady growth with very low recorded rates of unemployment (not much over 1–2% in Europe, nor 3–4% in the US) and low rates of inflation (rarely exceeding 2–3%) was the result of adherence to Keynesian policies; in particular, the fiscal stimulus of deficit spending. According to the Classical analysis, however, this merely reflected the ability of market economies to sustain full employment. Indeed, to the extent that deficits occurred, government borrowing was simply displacing private expenditure. Moreover, the 'creeping inflation' – which was worrying at the time – simply reflected the predictions of the Quantity Equation:

$$M \times V = P \times Q$$

With output (Q) at its full-employment level, and velocity (V) nearly constant, the price level (P) rises roughly in proportion to the growth in the quantity of money (M). Thus, it was government's predilection for monetary expansion that was responsible for inflation. (Why, if the predominant Keynesian thinking tends to dismiss the importance of money, did this happen? Firstly, the quantity of money only becomes irrelevant in the case of a liquidity trap. Otherwise, as when the economy is near full-employment, even Keynesians maintain that an expansionary policy can help to keep interest rates down and thus help to stimulate investment somewhat. Secondly, and more cynically, this easy monetary policy relieves the negative ('crowding out') effect of the higher level of government borrowing on investment, and of course directly reduces the future burden of debt payments as well.)

Unfortunately, this implicit balancing act got out of hand in the latter half of the 1960s and in the early 1970s. Governments attempted to massively increase spending (military and/or social welfare programmes) without any corresponding rise in taxation. Without the accommodating monetary expansion (rightward shift of the *LM* curve) this would have pushed interest rates to wholly unacceptable levels (rightward shift of *IS*). In Classical terms this represented a real increase in the share of output being commanded by the public sector, except that it was primarily a rise in the price level (P) rather than a rise in the interest rate (r) that served as the mechanism of this crowding out. Not only would-be borrowers, such as firms considering investment, but also would-be purchasers, like households considering buying goods, were thus displaced.

10.1.4 **The rate of interest: real and nominal**

Notice that we are focusing on the price-level effects of monetary expansion as per the Quantity Equation above. At the same time, we note that a rise in the rate of interest might occur, indicating a dominance of the *IS* shift over the *LM* shift. We ought to mention here that it is the real interest rate (r_R) which is our focus of attention insofar as economic decisions are concerned. This is related to the nominal interest rate (r_N) by the condition:

$$r_N = r_R + E\,(\dot{P}/P)$$

The term on the right is the *expected* ($E(-)$) rate of inflation. $\dot{P}$ is a symbol often used for the change in P (i.e. ΔP in our earlier notation) per unit of time. Therefore $\dot{P}/P$ is also read as $\Delta P/P$ per unit of time: the 'rate of inflation'.

Therefore, this equation only states that the observed, nominal rate is actually equal to some real rate of return plus an inflation 'premium' equal to the prevailing expected inflation rate. And yet it has an important implication; namely, monetary expansion can only reduce the observed (nominal) rate of interest for as long as markets fail to adjust their expectations concerning inflation. Under these circumstances, any fall in r_N appears to be a fall in r_R and could be stimulatory. Of course, as soon as the inflationary implications of the expansion are perceived, r_N will rise; and by even more than the expected increase in the rate of inflation, to the extent that the increased government spending competes with borrowers for finance.

This introduces the important element of the time period during which expectations are formed; i.e. we have again come around to the central role of expectations. The so-called 'Rational Expectations' school – an extreme Classical position – believes that the consequences of, for example, our monetary expansion, are almost instantly perceived and therefore almost instantly achieved. The main body of 'New Classical' opinion believes that there may be 'long and variable lags' in this process, though nothing of the order of Interventionist time scales. For instance, we might be looking at anything from 6 months to 2½ years before the increased quantity of money is transmitted into a higher price level.

10.1.5 **Unanticipated inflation**

In the meantime, as noted, it is possible for the government to 'fool' the markets through unanticipated actions (as for example the Great Contraction of the money supply in the 1930s). Thus, in an attempt to avoid the interest-rate consequences of increased spending, governments found themselves accelerating the rate of monetary expansion. At first, perhaps in the late 1960s, this was unforeseen. As we have remarked, it was therefore possible for a net stimulus to exist as real interest rates appeared to decline. In addition, and undoubtedly of even greater moment, money wage rates remained unadjusted for the imminent inflation. (This is not to say that wages declined in real terms at this stage, since productivity – real output per unit of labour – was still rising.) Hence, net product (Q) could actually be pushed beyond its full-employment level by making labour and (new) capital goods deceptively cheaper. It did not take long for inflation to be incorporated in nominal wage and interest rates, however. The early (1970s) response to this was to engage in even more expansive policies that served to raise the inflation rate above that which had become expected. Clearly this could not go on for long, short of hyperinflation (at which point confidence in holding money – its 'store of value' function – collapses and velocity rises without limit. If it persists long enough confidence in currency even as a means of payment disappears, and we are back to a 'barter' economy). Therefore in the second half of the 1970s governments began to try to exercise control over monetary growth. This threw the adjustment mechanism of the economy into reverse. Whereas there had been some previous rise in unemployment due to: (a) money wage increases out-stripping price increases, and (b) expected net revenues from investment becoming more risky from a subjective point of view, now the rate of inflation was supposed to decelerate. With nominal wage and interest rates still rising under expectations of acclerating inflation this produced the observed sharp rise in unemployment occurring at the end of the decade. In terms of the Quantity Equation what we had observed was initially, a rising M translating partly into a rising P and partly into a rising Q; later into a sharply rising P and slightly falling Q; and then into a more slowly rising P and a sharply falling Q. Fig. 10.1 shows this (stylized) process graphically in terms of the rate of inflation as related to the rate of unemployment. At first the economy moves north-west to higher inflation and lower unemployment. However, the higher inflation becomes anticipated and hence incorporated in wage rates, leading to a rise in unemployment back to its 'natural' rate. A second wave of expansion generates the same sequence of events, although now the inflation rate is still higher and unemployment is

Figure 10.1 The Phillips curve

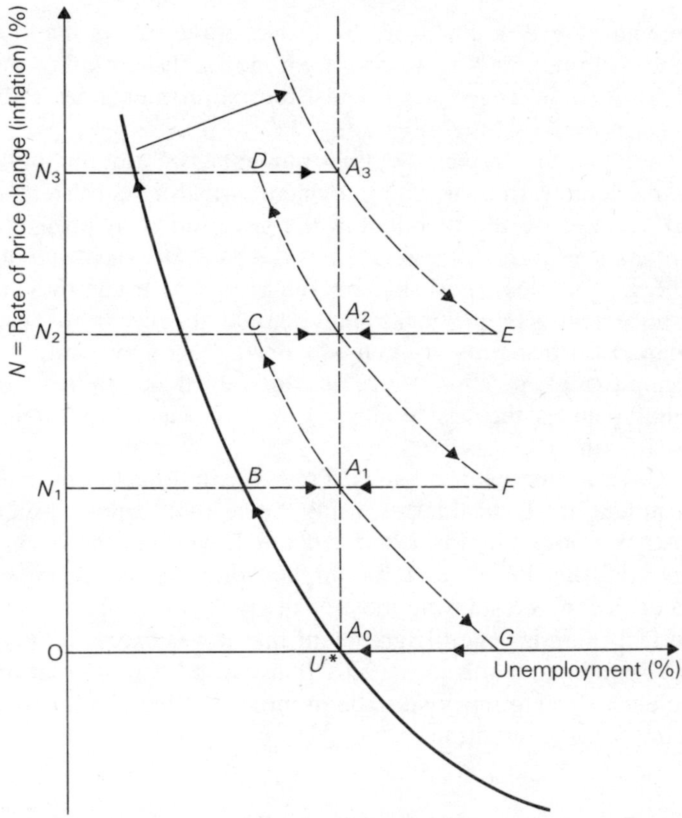

The curve through A_0 is the original 'Phillips' curve. In some Keynesian models unemployment can be maintained at any desired level by sufficient spending. The resulting 'demand-pull' inflation reduces the real wage rate to the desired extent! 'Cost-push' inflation has supposedly pushed this curve outwards (*NE*). In the Classical view the economy can move from A_0 to *B* when expected inflation is zero. After N_1 occurs, wage adjustments move us back to A_1, until a further unanticipated burst of monetary expansion pushes us to *C*. However, this leads eventually to A_2; etc. In reverse, deceleration of *M*-growth will raise unemployment until expectations are also reduced: e.g. A_3 to *E* to A_2; etc. The 'natural' or 'non-accelerating inflation' rate of unemployment (U*) measures frictional/structural unemployment, not due to deficient demand.

somewhat above its long-run level, due to the causes mentioned above. The monetary slowdown then moves the economy south-east since these wage- and interest-rate adjustments are initially operating in the wrong direction.

Eventually the predicted equilibrium must occur at the 'natural' market-clearing rate of unemployment, which is consistent with whatever steady rate of inflation the government is prepared to countenance (preferably, zero?) For the New Classicals the moral of the story is clear: governments ought to stop trying to achieve the impossible. In particular they should foreswear the use of monetary instruments to manoeuvre the economy into some imagined 'real' position, since it can only make things worse. 'Monetarism' is the best policy: i.e. stick to a steady monetary growth path.

What we have been doing so far is tracing out the process of adjustment in Classical terms, using the last half-century as a case study. We have already examined the Keynesian views on the events of the 1930s, and by implication, on the progress of Western economies during most of the post-war period.

In fact there is general agreement that it was excessive government spending in the late 1960s that caused our stagflationary problems of the following decade or more, but the way it occurred is a matter of contention.

10.2 Neo-Keynesianism: the Phillips curve

Going back to original Keynesian ideas, there is no doubt that when the economy is at or near full employment additional spending will merely serve to increase the price level. This is regardless of the quantity of money, since velocity is completely variable. In terms of the Quantity Equation, Q rises little if at all and P rises instead, while M stays constant and V increases. In fact, inflationary pressure is inherent in the simple 'multiplier' model as well. Although that model is developed on the assumption that the price level remains constant up to the point of full employment it is in reality likely that certain sectors of the economy will reach capacity – sharply rising marginal costs – before others. As production nears its limit, this will increasingly occur. Therefore, assuming that government applies continuous expansionary policies, we will observe the gradual rise shown in

Fig. 10.1 in the rate of inflation as unemployment declines, possibly starting from a deflationary situation with very low output. In this sense the rate of inflation is a gauge of 'demand-pull' pressures in the economy. (Note also that if money illusion – in the dynamic sense of wage increases lagging always behind price increases – prevails, then this trade-off need not stop at any 'natural' rate. In theory, workers could be made cheap enough to achieve zero measured unemployment; see below.)

The type of curve drawn in Fig. 10.1 showing an inflation–unemployment trade-off is called a 'Phillips curve' after its originator (though we have modified the original). Obviously it is not at the moment capable of explaining why we observed a rise in both inflation and unemployment during the 1970s. For this we need the concept of 'cost-push' inflation, which is formally very similar to the Classical interpretation, except that for Keynesians, wage increases can be an independent cause of inflation rather than merely a response. That is, once inflation had been ignited by excess spending, it became incorporated into wage demands – so far, as in the Classical analysis – but these increases could themselves fuel subsequent price increases in a wage–price inflationary spiral that required no accommodating monetary expansion. At first, wages were 'catching-up' with prices, then began to 'keep ahead', making labour more expensive in real terms. On top of this there were of course two sharp oil price rises, as well as a commodity price inflation worldwide, so demand for labour probably declined even more. Hence, in terms of Fig. 10.1 we observe a strong(er) increase in both inflation and unemployment in the second phase.

However, this unemployment was bound eventually to reduce wage demands, and so we began to observe a deceleration of inflation (also, no further oil or commodity price rises – quite the contrary in the first half of the 1980s). This did not lead to an immediate fall in unemployment, though, because in pursuing Monetarist policies governments also reined-in their deficits and therefore deflated demand. This leaves us with another moral: whereas it is still true that fiscal expansion is required to restore and maintain full employment in an economy with chronically weak demand, neither should deficits become excessive, nor should money wage rates be allowed to rise unconstrained. Unfortunately for economists of interventionist persuasion, the implied prospect of wage (and price) controls is uncomfortable, and many ingenious alternatives have been proposed which we shall not attempt to cover here.

So far we have been assuming on one hand that for Keynesians the quantity of money does not matter very much, and on the other hand that it can be controlled as an instrument of policy. There are in fact many economists who would perhaps describe themselves as 'eclectic' Keynesians, believing that money does matter – at least insofar as velocity is reasonably stable – but that it can be only very imperfectly controlled.

10.3 The banking system and monetary control

In order to develop this argument it is necessary to describe briefly the method(s) by which the quantity of money is increased. Although these differ among countries, the basic process is similar.

First, however, what is 'money'? (As with most concepts in economics, although we can usually discuss them as if they were commonly understood, when it comes to implementation we sometimes find that they have only a vague correspondence to reality.) Although later on we shall re-open this question, for present purposes we define money as any type of asset that is universally – at least, almost – acceptable as final settlement in exchange for goods and services. (This distinguishes money from 'credit' which, although frequently accepted in exchange for goods, is not final: i.e., a note of credit is a promise to pay money at some future date.)

Historically this medium-of-exchange function was performed by gold, or other precious metals, particularly if it were in a sense validated as genuine by government minting. In time it was discovered that governments could instead simply issue certificates that the metal was in their vaults; and eventually, simply issue certificates with no redemption value whatever. By this latest stage it did not matter: the public had become fully accustomed to transacting business by means of the official currency.

Meanwhile – although this is necessarily a rather stylized account – people had begun to deposit their gold coins with goldsmiths for safe keeping. However, it was realized that rather than withdraw coins physically to transfer to someone who would then redeposit them, the goldsmith-*cum*-banker could issue them with a book of *cheques* that could be drawn in lieu. Therefore it was only necessary to keep a record of who owned the currency, most of which never left the vault.

The final stage in this simple tale is obvious: if the bank (goldsmith) found that physical cash (coin) withdrawals never accounted for more than say, 10% of the total cash reserve held in the vaults, then it would be possible to support ten times the volume of transactions with the initial reserve! Hence, our banker would aggressively seek to make new loans – yielding interest – until a ratio of reserves to total deposit liabilities of one-tenth was reached.

In modern economies, cheques drawn on commercial banks are nearly as acceptable as cash. This means that, like these latter certificates issued by governments, people must have a high degree of implicit confidence in the bank and the individual drawing the cheque. (Indeed, there are everyday examples of limits to confidence. People will generally not accept 'foreign' currency, nor in the US cheques drawn on out-of-state banks, nor in most countries any cheques not backed by evidence of individual trustworthiness such as a 'guarantee' card.) Therefore, cash plus the amount held by the public in chequing accounts ('demand deposits') are commonly deemed to constitute the money supply (which is therefore a stock concept, being measured at a point in time). No other assets have anything like the acceptability of these two items (try paying for a hotel/restaurant bill with a stock certificate).

10.3.1 **Monetary control**

Now, although we will question this conclusion at a later stage, the problem of monetary control really boils down to one of control over the total volume of demand deposits held within the banking system. In turn, this can be separated into: (a) exercising control over the reserve base (i.e. cash); and (b) exercising control over the ratio of deposits to reserves.

With regard to the latter, central banks all set 'reserve requirements' that basically attempt to limit the expansion of bank lending. In some countries these are more flexible than in others, but in any case it is not something that is altered in the short run. In this context it is instead control over the reserve base that is of primary importance. Again, some central banks make it harder on themselves – as in the UK – by including a number of short-term assets as 'reserves' in addition to cash balances. In a comparatively pure system like the US control is easier, and takes two basic forms: (a) lending (or calling-in) reserves to (from) the banks; or (b) selling (or buying) reserves to (from) the banks. The former method – taking the case of reserve expansion – involves the loan of additional cash to enable the banks to increase their lending. In so doing the central bank charges a 'discount rate' generally slightly above the rate at which the government itself borrows. The size of this differential then becomes an indicator of central bank intentions. The security for these loans is usually previously issued government debt (hence, the interest charged is sometimes called the 're-discount' rate). In the second method of control the central bank simply buys these securities back from the banks. This is called an 'open-market' operation (in this case a purchase), since the central bank enters the (secondary) market in government – or indeed other-issuer – securities like any other participant. In particular, if it wishes to make sizeable purchases it will have to offer higher prices (and in so doing, the central bank will thus incur a lower rate of return than currently available in these markets). Banks are thereby persuaded to exchange their interest-bearing assets for cash reserves, which can generate an expansion of total deposits (see Appendix 10 for details of this process). When the central bank wishes to exert contractionary pressure on the banking system it sells on the 'open' market which (by persuading banks to exchange their cash reserves for interest-bearing securities through the offer of lower prices, hence higher rate of return to buyers) reduces their capacity to lend.

However, this has often been likened to 'pushing on a string' in the sense that when the commercial banks are loaned-up to the limits of their legal reserve ratios, changes in reserves affect the quantity of money fairly predictably (see Appendix 10); but when they are not at or near these limits the effects of these changes are unpredictable.

Specifically, consider the alternative possibility of an institution which sold at a gain, taking the proceeds and re-purchasing other interest-bearing financial assets. Suppose they went out and bought more government bonds. Initially, these carry a higher market rate of interest, but as their prices are bid up, through a series of transactions triggered by the original purchase, this market rate declines. However, this consequence has to be weighted against two alternatives: (1) on-lending as in the original example. Presumably, the expansion of 'loanable funds' in this way would also tend to reduce interest rates (and increase the riskiness of marginal borrowers); and (or 2) hold on to excess reserves.

In reality, monetary authorities have considerable difficulty in forecasting the effects of their open-market operations, which makes the steady-as-she-goes prescription very difficult to follow (as witness the enormous attention to weekly figures in Western financial markets).

Also, we should observe that the option of holding excess reserves was precisely the point of Keynes' elaboration of the speculative demand for money. In extreme form, perfectly elastic money demand thus reflects the willingness to accumulate unlimited excess reserves; while a perfectly inelastic demand reflects on-lending up to the limit of reserves.

10.3.2 **What is 'money'?**

This establishes an important point: the supply of money is not something separate from its demand (which is why speaking about the 'quantity of money' is more correct). Indeed, it is apparent that central banks actually try to exercise control through acting upon demand; e.g. as in raising the discount rate.

Following this line of reasoning we can again ask the question: what is 'money'? If we say that it is currency plus demand deposits (the so-called 'narrow' measure, M–1), then by definition we exclude, for example, time deposits. (These are included in the 'broad' measure M–2 in the US, £M3 in the UK). Or, what about certificates of deposit and other 'near-monies'? The point here – and one that governments recognize – is that with the existence of so many closely substitutable assets for money, their composition in the typical (institutional) portfolio might vary quite sharply. Small changes in interest rates might move huge funds between chequing accounts (counted as 'money') and some types of interest-bearing but readily-transferable accounts not counted as 'money'. In other words, when we are forced to designate a particular measure of money it appears that its velocity may be less stable than originally thought. Instead, a whole range of 'monetary aggregates' has come to be monitored, making interpretation and control even more difficult.

Finally, even if control could be exercised over the quantities of existing types of assets, there is the possibility that new media of exchange (e.g. coupons instead of cash) would be introduced as a way round. In short, this neo-Keynesian argument is that modern financially sophisticated economies are not really susceptible to 'monetary' control.

10.4 Structural problems: the emergence of microeconomic policy

As we move into the latter half of the 1980s there is a persistent concern about unemployment. To simply repeat the arguments of the 1930s – if you are Keynesian, the problem is deficient demand, if Classical it is excessive real wages – is generally perceived as fruitless. There are in truth few economists who would agree that the solution would be either massively increased government spending or substantial wage reductions. In that sense the problem is becoming perceived as structural: a loss of competitiveness – therefore, collapse of demand – in particular microeconomic sectors of the economy. As these sectors contract, the factors of production made redundant are ill-suited to alternative employment, and therefore could command incomes only a fraction of their previous levels.

This is 'structural unemployment' and it is evidenced by the increasingly long periods that people have been out of work. This is in contrast to 'frictional unemployment', which occurs when factors are moving between employments, and 'cyclical unemployment' which, as its name suggests, follows the inevitable ups and downs of economic activity (around a secular trend).

Undoubtedly this type of structural problem is currently worse in Europe than in either the US or Japan. This has led some economists to call for an end to the more generous subsidies given to both firms and households, who would then have more 'incentive' to be mobile. At the same time, tax rates ought to be significantly reduced to encourage new enterprise: the carrot and the stick. Loosely, these are termed 'supply-side' policies, and in a sense they are the microeconomic corollary of Classical economics. Analogously, the microeconomic, or structural counterpart to Keynesian macroeconomics is to subsidize not only the unemployed, but also firms in those sectors that are forecast as being future successes: i.e. a planning approach. In this author's opinion, if these structural problems of low growth and high unemployment remain with us for long, the controversies between believers in *laissez-faire* and interventionists will undoubtedly shift from their present macro-focus to a more intense – and technical – debate about microeconomic policies.

Summary

If deficient demand were not the shock that caused the Depression of the 1930s, in the Classical view it was the result of a (preventable) monetary contraction. With wages – and therefore prices – 'sticky downwards' this meant that the 'real' quantity of money, in terms of purchasing power, also decreased. Hence, real spending contracted, which Keynes mistook as a manifestation of inherent demand deficiency. Instead, the solution was to have a more rapid decline in money wage rates in proportion to the monetary contraction.

In contrast, by the late 1960s uncontrolled government spending was being financed not by borrowing, but by 'printing money'. This caused money prices to rise, and with some lag, money wage rates. The interim effect was to actually reduce unemployment below its 'natural' (market-clearing) rate, but not for long. In order to sustain the expansion, increasingly large injections of new money had to be made, causing inflation to accelerate. This was itself beginning to distort economic calculations, and with the eventual ability of workers to gain increases in excess of actual inflation, unemployment did in fact begin to rise instead of falling. The sharp rise at the end of the 1970s was thus the result of bringing monetary growth under control while inflationary expectations still persisted. When these are expunged, non-inflationary growth can resume.

In rebuttal, Keynesians claim that the connection between money and spending may not be so close (velocity is unstable), and that in any case adequate control of the money supply is not possible: it is endogenous rather than exogenous. Instead, the 'stagflation' of the 1970s was due to cost-push pressures, with the quantity of money merely serving to accommodate. The implication is thus that in order for demand management to work, some form of wage-and-price controls may ultimately be needed. This brings us to their argument for intervention on a micro-scale, which has as its antithesis the modern 'supply-side' approach which would instead seek to eliminate market distortions.

Appendix 10 Money creation via the fractional reserve banking system

When the central bank creates additional deposits in the banking system (e.g. buys bonds from the banks) this is 'high-powered' money in the sense that it allows a multiple expansion of total deposits through additional lending. The extent depends on the reserve ratio (say, 10%).

A 'new' £100 injected into the system enables the recipient bank to on-lend £90 (keeping £10 as the required reserve). This £90 is drawn by the borrower to pay for goods and services; the payee then deposits this amount in another bank. For this second bank, this is new money – it physically claims the £90 from the first bank through the clearing system – of which it can on-lend £81 and retain a reserve of £9. The process looks like the following:

Bank	*Deposits*	*Loans*	*Reserves*
1	£100	£90	£10
2	90	81	9
3	81	72.90	8.10
4	.	.	.
.	.	.	.
∞	£1000	£900	£100

This is formally similar to the Keynesian multiplier process. The end result is, theoretically, a ten-fold expansion of total deposits: £900 of lending based upon the £100 additional reserves, distributed amongst the commercial banks. This is of course a theoretical maximum, since banks might not make loans up to their full capacity, either by choice or due to lack of loan demand.

Index